Knitting for the Family

Knitting for the Family
Caroline Carr

Paul Hamlyn
Sydney·London·New York·Toronto

First published 1973
© Paul Hamlyn Pty Ltd 1973
Printed in Singapore
ISBN 0600 07121 9
Published by Paul Hamlyn Pty Ltd
176 South Creek Road, Dee Why West, NSW 2099

Designer: Catherine Higson
Editor: Judith Dine
Photographer: Reg Morrison

Page 1: *Raglan, stocking stitch sweater features contrast stripe along centre of sleeve, with contrast k.1, p.1 ribbed neckband (see page 129 for instructions).*

Page 2: *Girl's poncho is knitted entirely in stocking stitch with contrast fringing along the lower edge...features back zip opening and roll collar which is made separately and attached during make up (see page 94 for instructions).*

Contents

Introduction

The art of Knitting began over 1,500 years ago in North
Africa when the Nomadic Arabs, whilst guarding their sheep
and cattle, made socks to wear with their sandals from
wool spun by their wives. Since this time the craft has
gained international popularity, and today there are numerous,
interesting yarns and designs available for the home knitter.
In writing this book I have endeavoured to design a wide
selection of easy-to-make, classical garments, and have
worded the instructions as simply as possible. There are
separate sections for babies, children, teenagers, women and
men, and for accessories, toys and bazaar items.
If you are a beginner be sure to carefully read the technical
information given at the front of this book before you start
to knit your garment.
Wishing you many relaxed hours of knitting.

Caroline Carr

Villawool Yarns

Useful Facts and Figures

The Villawool yarns used throughout this book are as follows:

YARN	% DESCRIPTION
BOUCLE DOUBLE KNITTING	100% Pure Wool, equivalent to 6 ply, knits into a textured fabric.
NYLO TWEED	87½% Wool/12½% Nylon Rayon, an 8 ply, tough wearing, tweed yarn.
SUPER SLALOM	100% Pure Wool, a 12 ply sports yarn which is machine washable and water repellent.
SUPERKNIT DC8	100% Pure Wool, an 8 ply yarn which is sturdy and machine washable.
SUPERKNIT 5 PLY CREPE	100% Pure Wool, a finer yarn which is machine washable.
SUPERKNIT 12 PLY CREPE	100% Pure Wool, a bulky yarn which is machine washable.
SUPERKNIT 4 PLY CREPE	100% Pure Wool, a fine yarn which is machine washable.
DINKUM 8 PLY	100% Pure Wool, a natural Australian undyed, bulky yarn, suitable for Aran designs.
BAN-LON— PURPLE LABEL	100% Nylon yarn which is machine washable.
CASCADE NYLON 4 PLY CREPE	100% Nylon yarn, a fine Super Crimp Nylon yarn which is machine washable.
CASCADE NYLON 8 PLY CREPE	100% Nylon, a thicker Super Crimp Nylon yarn which is machine washable.
3 PLY BABY WOOL	100% Wool, a fine baby yarn which is machine washable.
3 PLY BABY NYLON	100% Nylon, a fine baby yarn which is machine washable.

MACHINE WASHING

NOTE: Villawool's machine washable qualities are guaranteed not to shrink, pill, rub or felt.

ALTERNATIVE YARNS

3 PLY BABY WOOL with 3 PLY BABY NYLON.
SUPERKNIT 4 PLY CREPE with CASCADE NYLON 4 PLY CREPE.
SUPERKNIT DC8 with CASCADE NYLON 8 PLY CREPE.
SUPERKNIT 5 PLY CREPE with CASCADE NYLON 5 PLY CREPE.

Both Imperial Standard and metric sizes, measurements and weights are given in the knitting instructions. The metric weight equivalent to ounces is grams and all yarn will soon be packed in grams. All Villawool yarns with the exception of Ban-Lon are sold in gram weights.

Imperial measurements are given first and the metric equivalent is in square brackets, e.g. Work measures 10½ (12) ins. [26.67 (30.48) cm].

A simple conversion chart is given below as a guide for converting to the appropriate metric equivalents. It is very useful to make a list of body measurements in centimetres and keep it for reference when checking a pattern.

WEIGHTS
1 oz = 28.36 grams
4 oz = 113.4 grams
8 oz = 226.8 grams
1 lb = 454 grams
2 lb 3 oz (approx.) = 1 kilogram
Note: buying knitting yarn, a 25-gram ball of yarn will very approximately equal a 1-oz ball. But as 1 oz equals slightly over 25 grams for larger quantities increase the number of gram balls, e.g. if 12 oz yarn is required, buy fourteen 25-gram balls, and if 20 oz is required, buy twenty-three 25-gram balls.

LINEAR MEASURES
⅛ inch = .3 centimetres
¼ inch = .6 centimetres
½ inch = 1.3 centimetres
¾ inch = 1.9 centimetres
1 inch = 2.54 centimetres
3 inches = 7.5 centimetres
6 inches = 15.2 centimetres
9 inches = 22.86 centimetres
10 inches = 25.40 centimetres
15 inches = 38.1 centimetres
1 foot (12 inches) = 30.48 centimetres
1 yard = 0.914 metre (just over 91 centimetres)
1 yard 4 ins. (approx.) = 1 metre

COMPARATIVE SIZES OF KNITTING NEEDLES

CONVERSION TABLE OUNCES TO GRAMS
1 oz. = 28.3495 Grams

British	Continental	American
14	2	0
13	—	—
12	2.50	1
11	3.00	2
10	3.25	3
—	3.50	4
9	4.00	5
8	4.50	6
7	4.75	7
6	5.00	8
5	5.50	9
4	6.00	10
3	7.00	10½
2	8.00	11
1	9.25	13

1 oz. BALLS	25 Gram BALLS*	2 oz. BALLS	50 Gram BALLS*
1	1	1	1
2	3	2	3
3	4	3	4
4	5	4	5
5	6	5	6
6	7	6	7
7	8	7	8
8	9	8	9
9	10	9	10
10	12	10	12
11	13	11	13
12	14	12	14
13	15	13	15
14	16	14	16
15	17	15	17
16	18	16	18
17	20	17	20
18	21	18	21
19	22	19	22
20	23	20	23
21	24	21	24
22	25	22	25
23	26	23	26
24	27	24	27
25	29	25	29
26	30	26	30
27	31	27	31
28	32	28	32
29	33	29	33
30	34	30	34
31	35	31	35
32	37	32	37

With the Compliments of the
Hand Knitting Yarn Manufacturers
of Australia

*Suggested use

1
All About Knitting

THE THREE IMPORTANT R'S
1. THE RIGHT YARN

The designs in this book have been knitted and tested in their respective Villawool qualities. To achieve perfect results use the yarn specified in the instructions (or an alternative yarn if given, see page 10) as substituting another manufacturer's yarn of the same ply could easily result in an ill-fitting garment.

2. THE RIGHT TENSION

The way in which one knits varies according to each individual. You must discover BEFORE beginning each new garment just how you knit—in other words, how many stitches you knit to the inch in the particular yarn which has been chosen. This is called TENSION and in each set of instructions the correct tension is given. The whole garment has been calculated on this stated number of stitches per inch.

3. THE RIGHT NEEDLES

The right needles are the ones whose size will give the correct tension when you knit. In every set of instructions the designer will recommend a certain size of needle but because tension may differ it may be necessary to change the size of needle in order to obtain the given tension.

To ensure your work is even use AERO brand knitting needles which are made from a light-weight alloy metal with perfectly tapered points. Make sure you choose the correct length of needles for your requirements—14 in. long needles are adequate for knitting an average size lady's or man's sweater or jacket.

ABBREVIATIONS

K., knit
P., purl
st(s)., stitch(es)
in(s)., inch(es)
cm., centimetres
cont., continue(uing)
sl., slip
p.s.s.o., pass sl. st. over
inc., increase(ing) by knitting into front and back of same st.
M.1., inc. by picking up horizontal loop lying before next st., placing st. on left hand needle and knitting into back of it.
dec., decrease by working 2 sts. tog.
tog., together
alt., alternate
foll., following

rep., repeat
patt., pattern
rem., remain(ing)
beg., beginning
st. st., stocking stitch
m.st., moss stitch
g.st., garter stitch
t.b.l., through back of loops
y.fwd., yarn forward
y.o.n., yarn over needle
y.r.n., yarn round needle
r.s.f., right side of work facing
m., main colour
c., contrast colour
no(s)., number(s)
approx., approximately
k.1 b., k. into back of st.
ch., chain
d.c., double crochet
oz, ounce
k.1 d., k. into st. BELOW next st.
m.b., make a bobble: (k.1, p.1, k.1, p.1, k.1) all into next st., pass 1st, 2nd, 3rd then 4th sts. over last st.
tw.2b., k. into back of 2nd st. on left-hand needle, then k. 1st st., slipping both sts. off needle tog.
tw.2f., k. into front of 2nd st. on left-hand needle, then k. 1st st., slipping both sts. off needle tog.
tw.3f., k. into front of 3rd st. on left-hand needle, then k. 2nd st., then 1st st., slipping 3 sts. off needle tog.
c.4b., sl. next 2 sts. on cable needle and hold at back of work, k.2, then k.2 sts. from cable needle.
c.4f., sl. next 2 sts. on cable needle and hold at front of work, k.2, then k.2 sts. from cable needle.
cr.2b., sl. next 2 sts. on cable needle and hold at back of work, k.2, then p.2 sts. from cable needle.
cr.2f., sl. next 2 sts. on cable needle and hold at front of work, p.2, then k.2 sts. from cable needle.
cr.2 over 1 b., sl. next st. on cable needle and hold at back of work, k. 2, then p.1 st. from cable needle.
cr.2 over 1 f., sl. next 2 sts. on cable needle and hold at front of work, p.1, then k.2 sts. from cable needle.

UNDERSTANDING YOUR INSTRUCTIONS

* Asterisk. If an asterisk appears it indicates that—
(a) certain pattern rows have to be repeated, i.e. Front. Work as given for Back to * ; or
(b) indicates that a section of work is to be repeated, i.e. repeat from * 3 times, or from ** to ** once.

() Brackets. These have two meanings—
(a) the instructions inside the brackets are repeated the number of times stated after the brackets, i.e. (k.2, p.2) twice; or
(b) the figures inside the brackets denote the instructions for the various sizes in which the instructions have been written, i.e. to fit 32 (34, 36, 38) in. bust, or k.12 (14, 16, 18) sts.

Cont. straight means to work in the same stitch as before without shaping.

When you are instructed to turn in your work, continue on these first stitches only, leaving remaining stitches on a spare needle or stitch holder.

Slipping a stitch or stitches means to transfer stitch(es) from one needle to another without knitting or purling stitch(es).

Row means the number of stitches on one needle—the first row being knitted on the cast-on stitches. This is the first of odd-numbered rows and is usually the right side of work, unless otherwise instructed.

KNITTING ACCESSORIES

Before beginning any design it is advisable to see that you have the exact materials given, such as zips, buttons, elastic, etc. In addition to these you will need a tape measure, a tapestry needle (large-eyed, blunt-pointed needle used for making up garments), pins and scissors. Other accessories include stitch holders, cable needles, row counters and a clean cloth to wrap work in when not in use.

KNITTING KNOW-HOW

The following is a list of golden rules to help you obtain a professional look to your finished garments:
1. Never rush your work—relax and enjoy it.
2. Always have smooth clean hands.
3. As dye-lots vary, always buy the full quantity of yarn required to complete the garment.
4. Check your tension from time to time during the making.
5. Keep your needles and yarn clean.
6. Join in new yarn only at the end of a row.
7. Do not leave your knitting in the middle of a row.
8. Never push your needles through the ball of yarn.
9. Correct and neat making up is just as important as good knitting.
10. Wash knitted garments frequently and carefully.
11. Always use the yarn specified in the instructions.
12. Never alter the size of your needles in an attempt to produce a larger or smaller garment.
13. If knitting has been left unworked for a time unpick a few rows before beginning again.
14. No two people knit alike—don't allow anyone to 'help you with a few rows'.
15. When instructions call for a marker to be attached to a stitch use a contrasting yarn.
16. Always measure knitting on the flat.
17. Make sure you cast off at the same tension as you have worked your garment.
18. Don't be too ambitious in your choice of intricate patterns until you have perfected simple fabrics. Progress slowly.
19. When knitting in rounds, mark beginning by tying a marker over the needles, then pass it from point to point as each round is finished.
20. If you have difficulty in understanding a pattern and have reached the point of exasperation, don't persevere. Lay the work aside and come back to it later on when you will no doubt see your error clearly.

LEARNING TO KNIT
CASTING ON
Casting on is the first step in knitting as it provides the first row of stitches on the needle.

There are various methods of casting on, but the following two methods are the most popular:

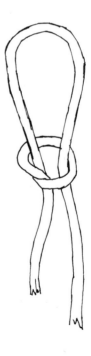

Diagram 1

1. **THE THUMB METHOD**—using one needle. Diagrams 1, 2 and 3.

(a) Make a slip loop (diagram 1) about one yard before the end of the yarn and place the loop on the right-hand needle. Draw the knot firmly round the needle.

(b) Working with the short length of yarn in the left hand, pass this round the left-hand thumb (diagram 2).

(e) Draw the stitch up firmly on the needle. Repeat the last four operations for the required length.

2. **THROUGH THE STITCH METHOD**—using two needles. Diagrams 4, 5, 6, 7.

(a) Make a slip loop (diagram 1) about 3 ins. [7.62 cm] before the end of the yarn and place it on the left-hand needle.

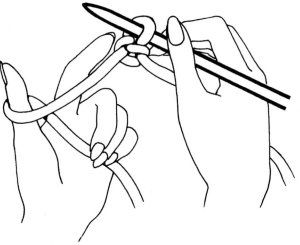

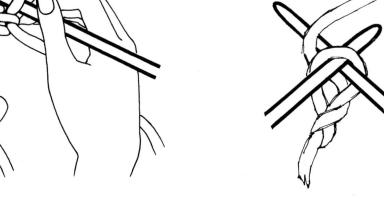

Diagram 4

(c) Insert the point of the needle beneath the loop on the thumb and draw the loop up firmly (diagram 3).

(b) Holding the yarn from the ball in your right hand, place the right-hand needle through the loop and pass the yarn round the point of the right-hand needle (diagram 4).

(c) Draw the yarn through the loop on the left-hand needle (diagram 5).

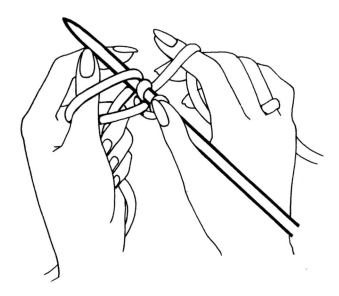

Diagram 3

Diagram 5

(d) Holding the yarn from the ball in the right hand, pass it round the point of the needle and draw it through the loop on the thumb.

(d) Place the new loop formed on the right-hand needle on to the left-hand needle (diagram 6). There are now two stitches on the left-hand needle.

15

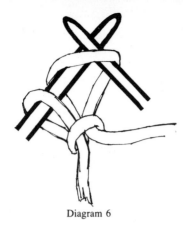

Diagram 6

(e) Insert the point of the right-hand needle between these two stitches and wrap the yarn round the end of the right-hand needle (diagram 7).

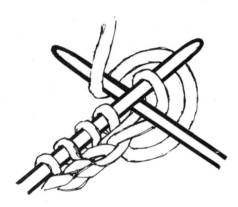

Diagram 7

(f) Draw this new loop between the last two stitches and place it on the left-hand needle.
Repeat the last two operations for the required length.

BASIC STITCHES

There are only two stitches used in knitting and these are called knit and purl (sometimes referred to as plain and purl).

Every knitted fabric, no matter how complicated, is a combination or variation on these two stitches.

Diagram 8

THE KNIT STITCH Diagrams 8, 9, 10 and 11.
(a) Insert the point of the right-hand needle in through the first stitch on the left-hand needle from front to back (diagram 8).

Diagram 9

(b) While holding the yarn in the right hand pass the yarn over the point of the right-hand needle (diagram 9).

Diagram 10

(c) Draw the loop through the stitch on the left-hand needle with the point of the right-hand needle (diagram 10).

Diagram 11

(d) Slip the stitch off the left-hand needle (diagram 11).

Diagram 12

THE PURL STITCH Diagrams 12, 13, 14 and 15.

(a) Insert the point of the right-hand needle in through the first stitch on the left-hand needle from back to front (diagram 12).

(b) Pass the yarn over the point of the right-hand needle (diagram 13).

(b) Place the point of the left-hand needle under the first stitch on the right-hand needle and lift it over the second stitch (diagram 16).

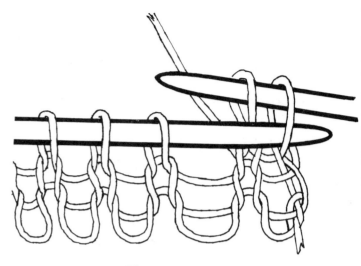

Diagram 16

Diagram 13

(c) Draw the loop through the stitch on the left-hand needle (diagram 14).

(c) Drop this stitch off the needle and then continue in the same way (diagram 17).

(d) When the required number of stitches have been cast off, cut yarn and draw the end through the last stitch.

Diagram 14

(d) slip the stitch off the left-hand needle (diagram 15).

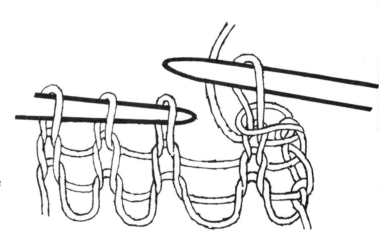

Diagram 17

IF A PATTERN SAYS...

Cast off ribwise—either knit or purl the stitch to be cast off, keeping continuity of the ribbing as set.

Cast off in pattern—either knit or purl the stitch to be cast off, as it would have been worked in the corresponding row of the pattern.

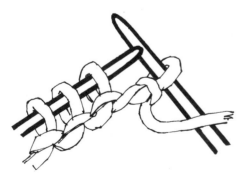

Diagram 15

CASTING OFF Diagrams 16 and 17.

(a) Knit the two stitches on the left-hand needle in the usual way.

TENSION Diagram 18

Before beginning any garment, work a small stitch sample about 4 ins. by 4 ins. in the main pattern and on the needles stated. Place the knitted sample on a flat surface and mark out 1 in. [2.54 cm] (or 2 ins. [5.08 cm] if stated) with pins (diagram

18). Count the number of stitches between the pins carefully and if your tension is correct then you may proceed with the garment. If you have fewer stitches to the inch than stated, your tension is too

STOCKING STITCH Diagram 20.
This fabric is formed by knitting one row and then purling one row alternately. The knit row is the right side of work.

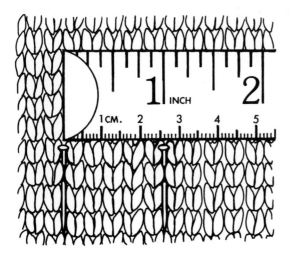

Diagram 18

Diagram 20

loose and you should work another sample using a size smaller needle. If you have more stitches to the inch, then your tension is too tight and you should work another sample using a size larger needle. Continue in this way, altering the size of your needles until you obtain the correct tension given. Do not proceed with your garment until you are satisfied that your tension is correct.

REVERSED STOCKING STITCH
Worked exactly the same as Stocking Stitch. The purl row is the right side of work.

MOSS STITCH Diagram 21.
Moss Stitch is normally worked over an uneven number of stitches thus:
Moss stitch row. K.1, (p.1, k.1) to end. This row is repeated throughout.

BASIC FABRICS

GARTER STITCH Diagram 19.
This fabric is formed by knitting every row.

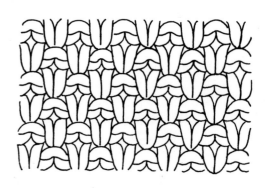

Diagram 21

Boucle mix and match wardrobe consists of trousers, skirt, pinafore dress and jacket (see page 86 for instructions). Trousers and skirt are knitted in stocking stitch with k.1, p.1 rib at lower edge and waistline—elastic is herringboned to inside waistband. A-line pinafore dress is knitted in stocking stitch with contrast bands as a feature; lower edge has a garter stitch edging, whilst neck and armbands are in k.1, p.1 rib. Jacket is knitted in stocking stitch with k.1, p.1 rib edgings, features raglan sleeves and patch pockets.

Diagram 19

Right: *All-in-one jumpsuit is knitted in an 8-row pattern, features raglan sleeves and k.1, p.1 rib edgings (see page 43 for instructions).*

Below: *Coat is worked in a Vandyke pattern with garter stitch yoke and borders (see page 46 for instructions).*

RIBBING Diagram 22.

The closest form of ribbing is k.1, p.1 rib, normally worked over an even number of stitches thus:

Rib row. (K.1, p.1) to end. This row is repeated throughout.

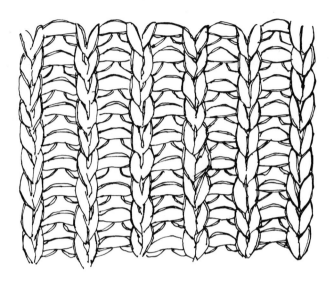

Diagram 22

There are many variations in ribbing built up from the basic k.1, p.1 rib, such as:

K.2, p.2 rib—cast on a multiple of 4 stitches.

Rib row. (K.2, p.2) to end. This row is repeated throughout; or

K.3, p.3 rib—cast on a multiple of 6 stitches.

Rib row. (K.3, p.3) to end. This row is repeated throughout.

Diagram 23

SHAPING

DECREASING ON A KNIT ROW Diagrams 23, 24, 25, 26.

1. To decrease one stitch put right-hand needle knitwise through the next 2 stitches and knit them together in the usual way. The abbreviation for this is "k.2 tog.". (23)

2. To decrease one stitch, slip the next stitch purlwise on to the right-hand needle, knit the next stitch, put the point of the left-hand needle purlwise into the slipped stitch and lift this over the knitted stitch and off the right-hand needle. The abbreviation for this is "sl.1, k.1, p.s.s.o.". (24)

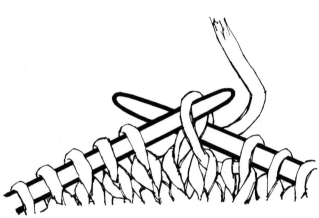

Diagram 24

3. To decrease 2 stitches, put the right-hand needle knitwise through the next 3 stitches and knit them together in the usual way. The abbreviation for this is "k.3 tog.". (25)

Diagram 25

4. To decrease 2 stitches, slip next stitch purlwise on to the right-hand needle, knit the next 2 stitches together, put the point of the left-hand needle purlwise into the slipped stitch and lift this over the 2 stitches knitted together and off the right-hand needle. The abbreviation for this is "sl.1, k.2 tog., p.s.s.o.". (26)

21

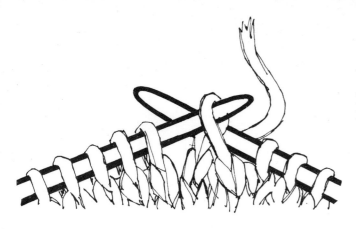

Diagram 26

DECREASING ON A PURL ROW Diagram 27.

To decrease one stitch, put the right-hand needle purlwise through the next 2 stitches and purl them together in the usual way. The abbreviation for this is "p.2 tog.". (27)

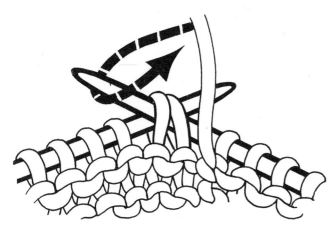

Diagram 27

DECREASING BY KNITTING THROUGH BACK OF LOOPS Diagram 28.

Knitting 2 stitches together through back of loops is a form of decreasing by 'twisting' the stitch:

Diagram 28

On a purl row—Purl 2 stitches together in the usual way to form one stitch, but work through the BACK loops instead of the front loops. The abbreviation for this is "p.2 tog. t.b.l.". (28)

On a knit row—Knit 2 stitches together in the usual way to form one stitch, but work through the BACK loops instead of the front loops. The abbreviation for this is "k.2 tog. t.b.l.".

INCREASING BY MEANS OF A STITCH
Diagrams 29 and 30.

1. To increase one stitch, put the point of the right-hand needle into the back of the stitch and knit or purl into the stitch again. Slip both these stitches on to the right-hand needle, thus making two stitches out of one. The abbreviation for this is "inc.". (29)

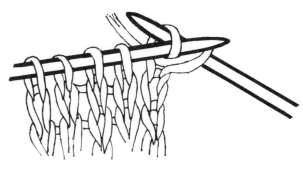

Diagram 29

2. To increase one stitch, pick up the horizontal loop lying between the two needles, place it on the left-hand needle and knit into the back of it. The abbreviation for this is "m.1". (30)

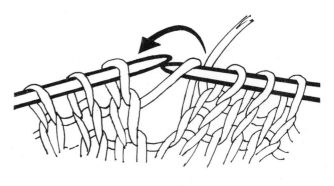

Diagram 30

INCREASING BY MEANS OF A LOOP
Diagrams 31, 32 and 33.

These operations are used in fancy patterns:

1. Make a stitch on a knit row by bringing the yarn forward between the needles, then knit the next stitch in the usual way, carrying the yarn over the right-hand needle. The abbreviation for this is "y.fwd.". (31)

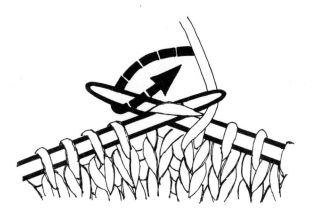

Diagram 31

2. Make a stitch on a purl row by bringing the yarn over and round the right-hand needle to the front, then purl the next stitch in the usual way. The abbreviation for this is "y.r.n.". (32)

Diagram 32

3. Make a stitch between a purl and a knit stitch by purling the stitch in the usual way, then take the yarn over the right-hand needle and knit the next stitch in the usual way. The abbreviation for this is "y.o.n.". (33)

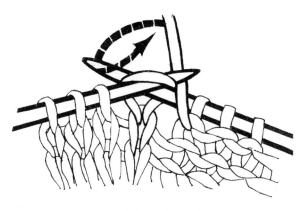

Diagram 33

JOINING IN NEW YARN

Always join in a new ball of yarn at the beginning of a row, leaving about 3 ins. [7.62 cm] hanging at the end to darn into the work when you are making-up.

PICKING UP DROPPED STITCHES Diagram 34.
Use a crochet hook to pick up the dropped stitch, drawing the released strands through the stitch row by row, replacing the stitch on the needle.

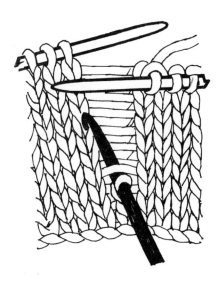

Diagram 34

KNITTING INTO ROW BELOW Diagram 35.
The abbreviation for this is "k.1 d". Knit through the loop below the next stitch, dropping the stitch above off the left-hand needle.

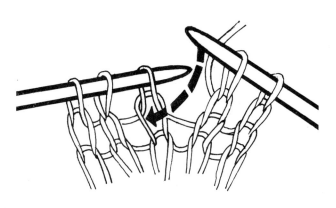

Diagram 35

KNITTING INTO BACK OF STITCH
The abbreviation for this is "k.1 b". Knit a stitch in the usual way but through the BACK loop.

THE CABLE STITCH Diagram 36.
The principle of cable knitting is to slip a given number of stitches on to a cable needle and leave them either at the front or back of work as directed. Work the given number of stitches from

23

the left-hand needle, then work the stitches from the cable needle which completes the cable operation.

The diagram shows a simple form of the cable stitch: slip 2 stitches on to cable needle and hold at front of work, knit the next 2 stitches, then knit the 2 stitches from the cable needle.

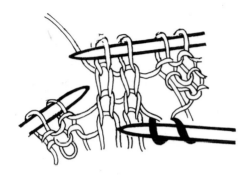

Diagram 36

TWO-COLOUR KNITTING Diagram 37.

If a large number of stitches are to be worked in different colours, either vertically or otherwise, use a separate ball of yarn for each colour and twist the yarn firmly on the wrong side of work when changing colours to avoid a hole.

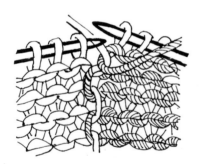

Diagram 37

FAIR ISLE KNITTING Diagrams 38, 39 and 40.

These patterns are always worked in stocking stitch, with groups of stitches knitted in different

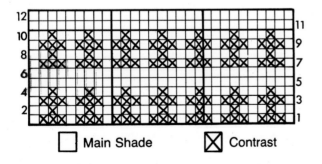

☐ Main Shade   ☒ Contrast

Diagram 38

colours to form a pattern. The Fair Isle design is usually given in the instructions in the form of a chart with each square representing one stitch and a different symbol representing each colour. When working from a chart the odd-numbered rows are the knit rows and the right side of work, and the purl rows are the even-numbered rows and the wrong side of work. The chart is read from right to left on the knit rows and from left to right of the purl rows. (38)

When changing colours horizontally the change can be made by either weaving or stranding:

WEAVING—this method gives a professional finish, especially if a colour is out of use across a large number of stitches. The principle is to weave the colour not in use under the colour being used. This is done by taking the colour in use under the out-of-work strand before working the next stitch. (39)

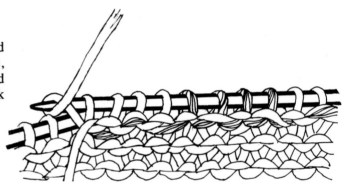

Diagram 39

STRANDING—the colour which is not in use is taken across the back of the work while the colour in use is being worked. It is important not to pull the yarn too tight or the work will 'pucker'. (40)

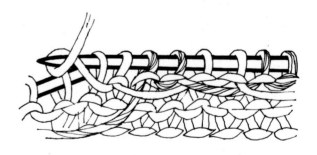

Diagram 40

MARKERS Diagram 41.

Sometimes it is necessary to mark a particular point in the work as a visual guide later. A short length of contrasting yarn is threaded through the stitch and tied in place so that it does not accidentally come out. Once it has served its purpose, simply pull it out.

Diagram 41

CIRCULAR KNITTING Diagram 42.

Working with four double-pointed needles or a circular needle creates a tubular type of seamless fabric suitable for neckbands, skirts, etc.—one round equals one row in flat knitting—with the right side of work facing all the time.

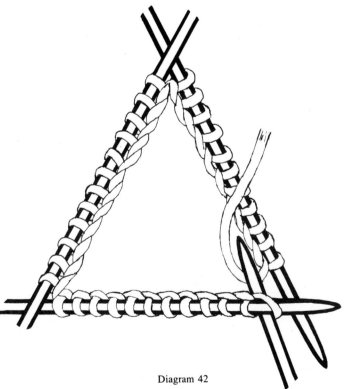

Diagram 42

Casting on with four needles: Cast on 45 sts. evenly divided on three of the needles (15 x 15 x 15),

forming a triangle. Using the fourth needle, knit across the stitches on the first needle, then work across the second and third needles, thus ending one round.

Using a circular needle: These are used on the same principle as above, except that you have only one needle. Aero circular needles are made in varying sizes and lengths...the minimum number of stitches to be knitted decides the maximum needle length required.

Circular Fair Isle Knitting: If you are working Fair Isle on four needles, or on a circular needle, then every row on your chart will be a knit row and each row will read from right to left.

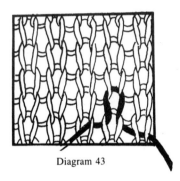

Diagram 43

KNITTING STITCH EMBROIDERY Diagram 43.

This type of embroidery is always worked over stocking stitch fabric. Using a tapestry needle and a contrasting yarn of the same thickness as the fabric, embroider over each individual stitch so that the finished pattern or motif has the appearance of being knitted in. This type of embroidery is often used in Fair Isle designs, in which case a graph is given in the instructions. Read the graph exactly as you would for a normal Fair Isle chart.

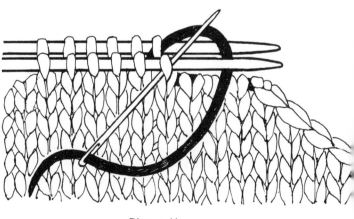

Diagram 44

GRAFTING Diagram 44.

This means the joining of two sets of stitches, horizontally and invisibly. Firstly, you must have

25

the same number of stitches on each of the needles facing each other (wrong sides of work together) then, with a tapestry needle and the same yarn as you have been working with proceed as follows:

* Insert sewing needle knitwise through the first stitch on the front needle, draw yarn through and slip stitch off knitting needle; insert sewing needle purlwise through next stitch on front needle, draw yarn through and leave stitch on knitting needle; insert sewing needle purlwise through first stitch on back needle; draw yarn through and slip stitch off knitting needle; insert sewing needle knitwise through next stitch on back needle, draw yarn through and leave on knitting needle; repeat from * until all stitches are worked off both needles.

PICKING UP STITCHES Diagram 45.
When you are instructed to pick up stitches around a neckline, armhole, etc., have yarn at back of work * put knitting needle through from front to back, pick up a loop of yarn and bring loop through to right side and leave on needle; repeat from * for required number of stitches, being careful to knit up in a smooth curve.

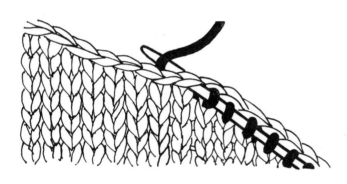

Diagram 45

LEFT-HAND KNITTING
Follow the instructions but change your copy to read left hand where it says 'right hand' and vice versa. Use a mirror to study diagrams and charts as this will reverse the image for you.

PULLING A THREAD
This is done to alter the length of knitteds.
To lengthen: Cut the thread at each edge of the work. Draw the cut thread out to the side and cut it to release the stitches on each side of the thread...a few stitches at a time. Use a smaller needle to pick up the released stitches, then with the right size needles work the required number of rows. Finally, graft the stitches together as shown in diagram 44.
To shorten: Unravel the required number of rows, then graft the stitches together as shown in diagram 44.

MEASURING Diagram 46.
Always lay knitting on a flat surface then, with a ruler or clearly marked tape, measure on the straight of the fabric. Never measure round curves or along a shaped edge.

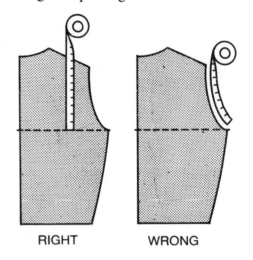

RIGHT   WRONG

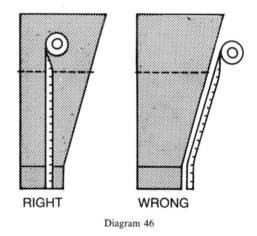

RIGHT   WRONG

Diagram 46

MAKING UP
Firstly, using a tapestry needle, darn in all ends.

PRESSING
Wool: Press lightly on the wrong side with a steam iron, or with a warm iron over a damp cloth.
Synthetics: Do not press unless instructed.
Mixtures of Wool and Synthetics: Press LIGHTLY on the wrong side, using a warm iron.
Embossed patterns: Heavy cables, Aran stitches, etc., should be steamed rather than pressed, using a very damp cloth and holding the iron over the surface, so as not to use any pressure which would "flatten" the knitting.

BLOCKING Diagram 47.
When pressing is directed, place each piece on a padded surface with wrong side of work facing you. without stretching any of the fabric, pin pieces to the padded surface as shown in diagram 47, then press. Wait until the fabric has cooled before taking out the pins. *Note:* Do not press ribbing.

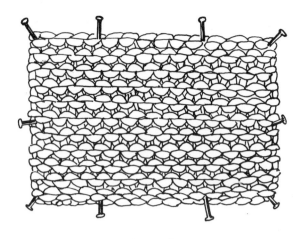

Diagram 47

SEAMING

Only two seams are used for joining knitted garments—a backstitch seam for the body of garment, and a flat seam for ribbed sections (unless otherwise instructed). Use a tapestry needle threaded with the same yarn you have used in making the original garment. If a chunky yarn has been used, stand the plys and use two of these strands together for seaming. If the yarn is not suitable for sewing, use a 3-ply yarn in the same shade.

THE BACKSTITCH SEAM Diagram 48.

Place the two pieces of fabric with right sides facing each other, so that the rows of knitting in each piece correspond. Pin the pieces together about ½ in. [1.27 cm] from edge. Now sew pieces together one stitch in from the edge, using a backstitch seam. Finally, remove pins and, using the point of an iron at the correct temperature for the fabric, press the seam open.

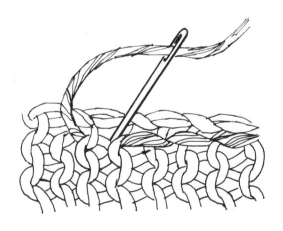

Diagram 48

THE FLAT SEAM Diagram 49.

Place the two pieces together edge to edge with right sides facing each other. With the forefinger of the left hand placed under the line of the seam, draw the two edges together with an overstitch so that they lie flat against each other, moving the finger along as the seaming proceeds.

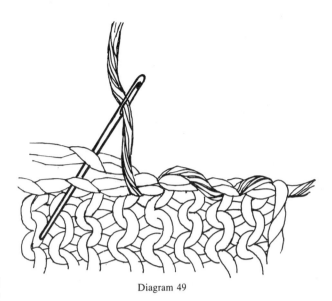

Diagram 49

THE SLIP STITCH Diagram 50.

Use a fine slip stitch for sewing hems, matching stitch for stitch.

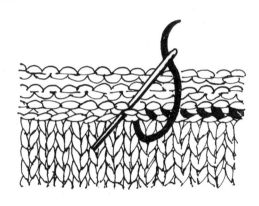

Diagram 50

SHOULDER SEAMS

Backstitch firmly, taking the stitching across the shaped steps in a straight line.

SET-IN SLEEVES

Mark centre top of sleeve and pin in position to shoulder seam, then pin cast off stitches of sleeve to cast off stitches at underarm of body of garment. Backstitch firmly around the curves as near to the edge as possible.

SIDE AND SLEEVE SEAMS

Join with a backstitch in one complete seam as near to the edge as possible.

SEWING ON COLLARS

Place right side of collar to wrong side of neck, matching centre backs and taking care not to stretch the neckline. Join with a flat seam.

SEWN-ON BANDS

Ribbed bands whether worked in one piece or two pieces are joined to the body of garment by a flat seam.

SEWN-ON POCKETS

Using matching yarn, slip stitch pocket in position, taking care to keep the line absolutely straight.

HERRINGBONE STITCH Diagram 51.

For encasing waist elastic use a herringbone stitch. Cut elastic to the size required and join into a

Diagram 51

circle. Pin elastic into position on the wrong side of work. Hold the knitting over the fingers of the left hand and with the elastic slightly stretched, work a herringbone stitch, catching the elastic above and below as you work.

INSERTING A ZIP Diagram 52.

Pin the zip into position, taking care not to stretch the knitting. Using a backstitch and working as near as possible to the zip edge, sew zip into position.

POCKET LININGS

Pin linings in place along each side and lower edge in a straight line, then slip stitch linings into position.

WASHING

Most of Villawool's yarns are machine washable. However, if you intend to hand wash your garment, the following points should be of interest to you:
1. Never allow the garment to get too dirty. Gentle washing does not damage any fabric, but when a knitted garment is very soiled, normal use of washing powders will not remove all the dirt without rubbing, and it is this rubbing action which causes damage to the fibres.
2. Choose a washing powder suitable for handknits.
3. Make sure the washing powder is thoroughly dissolved before putting the garment in the solution. Make sure also that there is enough

water to completely cover the garment.
4. Never boil your garment. The water temperature should be hand hot.
5. Do not bleach handknits.

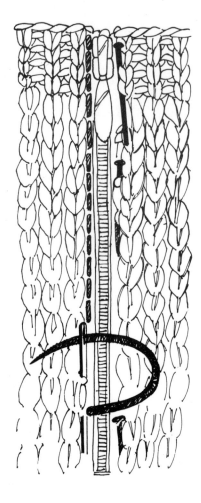

Diagram 52

6. Do not stretch the garment by lifting it in and out of the water.
7. Remove the garment from the water and gently squeeze out as much water as you can.
8. Rinse the garment several times until the rinsing water is absolutely clear.
9. Remove the garment from the water and gently squeeze (never wring), then roll garment in a clean, dry towel, thus absorbing the moisture.
10. Spread the garment out flat on the towel and ease it into the correct shape and size. Allow it to dry free from any direct sunlight or artificial heat. Never hang your garment to dry.

LOOKING AFTER YOUR HANDKNITS

Keep your handknits folded in individual polythene bags when not in use, with tissue paper in the folds to prevent creases forming, then lay them in a drawer or on a shelf.

Never leave your handknits on a hanger or hook, as the weight will cause them to drop.

PATTERNED FABRICS

CABLE (Above).
Cast on a multiple of 9 sts. plus 5.
1st row. Sl.1, * p.3, k.6; rep. from * to last 4 sts., p.3, k.1.
2nd row. Sl.1, * k.3, p.6; rep. from * to last 4 sts., k.4.
Rep. above 2 rows once more.
5th row. Sl.1, * p.3, sl. next 3 sts. on a cable needle and hold at back of work, k.3, then k.3 sts. from cable needle; rep. from * to last 4 sts., p.3, k.1.
6th row. As 2nd row.
Rep. 1st and 2nd rows 3 times.

13th row. Sl.1, * p.3, sl. next 3 sts. on a cable needle and hold at front of work, k.3, then k.3 sts. from cable needle; rep. from * to last 4 sts., p.3, k.1.
14th row. As 2nd row.
Rep. 1st and 2nd rows once more.
Rep. above 16 rows for length required.

FISHERMAN RIB (Below).
Cast on an even number of sts.
1st row. K.
2nd row. K.1, (k.1 d., p.1) to last st., k.1.
Rep. 2nd row for length required.
Note: See diagram 35 for k.1 d.

BASKET STITCH (Above).
Cast on a multiple of 6 sts.
1st row. (K.3, p.3) to end.
Rep. 1st row twice.
4th row. (P.3, k.3) to end.
Rep. 4th row twice.
Rep. above 6 rows for length required.

EASY LACE PATTERN (Below).
Cast on a multiple of 6 sts. plus 2.
1st row. K.1, * k.3, y.fwd., sl.1, k.2 tog., p.s.s.o., y.fwd.; rep. from * to last st., k.1.
2nd row. P.
3rd row. K.1, * y.fwd., sl.1, k.2 tog., p.s.s.o., y.fwd., k.3; rep. from * to last st., k.1.
4th row. P.
Rep. above 4 rows for length required.

BLACKBERRY STITCH (Above).
Cast on a multiple of 4 sts. plus 2.
1st row. K.1, * (k.1, p.1, k.1) all into next st.,
p.3 tog.; rep. from * to last st., k.1.
2nd row. P.
3rd row. K.1, * p.3 tog., (k.1, p.1, k.1) all into
next st.; rep. from * to last st., k.1.
4th row. P.
Rep. above 4 rows for length required.

DOUBLE MOSS STITCH (Below).
Cast on a multiple of 4 sts.
1st row. (K.2, p.2) to end.
2nd row. As first row.
3rd row. (P.2, k.2) to end.
4th row. As 3rd row.
Rep. above 4 rows for length required.

VANDYKE PATTERN (Above).
Cast on a multiple of 12 sts. plus 2.
1st row. K.1, * k.3, y.fwd., sl.1, k.1, p.s.s.o., k.2, k.2 tog., y.fwd., k.1, y.fwd., sl.1, k.1, p.s.s.o.; rep. from * to last st., k.1.
2nd row. P.
3rd row. K.1, * k.1, k.2 tog., y.fwd., k.1, y.fwd., sl.1, k.1, p.s.s.o., k.1, k.2 tog., y.fwd., k.1, y.fwd., sl.1, k.1, p.s.s.o.; rep. from * to last st., k.1.
4th row. P.
5th row. K.1, * k.2 tog., y.fwd., k.3, y.fwd., sl.1, k.1, p.s.s.o., k.2 tog., y.fwd., k.1, y.fwd., sl.1, k.1, p.s.s.o.; rep. from * to last st., k.1.

6th row. P.
Rep. above 6 rows for length required.

RIB VARIATION (Below).
Cast on a multiple of 5 sts. plus 3.
1st row. (P.3, k.2) to last 3 sts., p.3.
2nd row. (K.3, p.2) to last 3 sts., k.3.
3rd row. As 1st row.
4th row. As 2nd row.
5th row. (P.3, k. second st. on left-hand needle then first st.) to last 3 sts., p.3.
6th row. As 2nd row.
Rep. above 6 rows for length required.

PATTERNS

Seventy exclusive and easy-to-follow patterns using the
knitting stitches and techniques described in the previous pages.

2
Knitting for the New Arrival

Carrying cape is knitted in a 6-row pattern with garter stitch edging and features ribbon tie at neck edge (see page 36 for instructions).

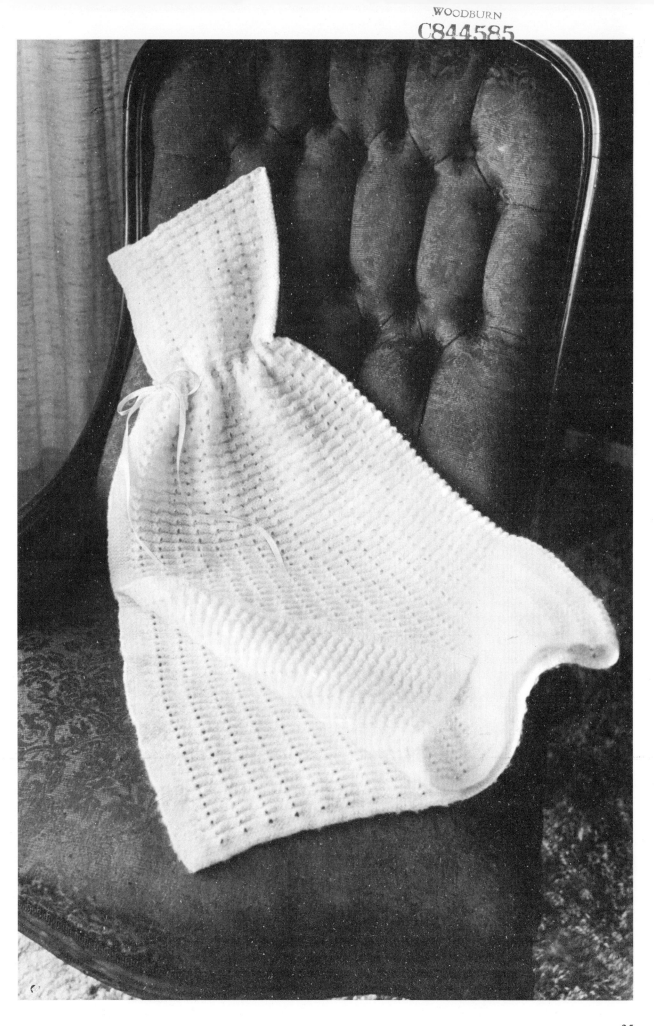

Carrying Cape

See photograph on page 35.

MATERIALS: 8 balls of Villawool 3 ply Baby Wool; a pair of long No. 10 needles; ribbon.

MEASUREMENTS: To fit from birth to approx. six months old. Length, 22¼ ins. [56.51 cm].

TENSION: 8 sts. to 1 inch [2.54 cm].

ABBREVIATIONS: See page 13.

TO MAKE:

MAIN PART (worked in one piece). With No. 10 needles cast on 251 sts. and k. 6 rows, then cont. in patt.:

1st row. K.5, (k.3, k.2 tog., y.fwd., k.1) to last 6 sts., k.6.

2nd row. K.6, p. to last 6 sts., k.6.

3rd row. K.

4th row. K.4, (k.4, k.2 tog., y.fwd.) to last 7 sts., k.7.

5th row. As 2nd row.

6th row. K.

Rep. above 6 rows until work measures 8 ins. [20.32 cm], ending on 5th row.

1st (dec.) row. K.11, (k.2 tog., k.18) to end. (239 sts.). Beg. 1st row, cont. in patt. until work measures 10 ins. [25.40 cm], ending on 5th row.

2nd (dec.) row. K.11, (k.2 tog., k.17) to end. (227 sts.).

Cont. in patt. until work measures 12 ins. [30.48 cm], ending on 5th row.

3rd (dec.) row. K.11, (k.2 tog., k.16) to end. (215 sts.).

Cont. in patt. until work measures 14 ins. [35.56 cm], ending on 5th row.

4th (dec.) row. K.11, (k.2 tog., k.15) to end. (203 sts.).

Cont. in patt. until work measures 16 ins. [40.64 cm], ending on 5th row.

5th (dec.) row. K.11, (k.2 tog., k.14) to end. (191 sts.).

Cont. in patt. until work measures 18 ins. [45.72 cm], ending on 5th row.

6th (dec.) row. K.11, (k.2 tog., k.13) to end. (179 sts.).

Cont. in patt. until work measures 20 ins. [50.80 cm], ending on 5th row.

7th (dec.) row. K.11, (k.2 tog., k.12) to end. (167 sts.).

Cont. in patt. until work measures 22 ins. [55.88 cm], ending on 5th row.

8th (dec.) row. K.14, (k.2 tog., k.1) 46 times, k. to end. (121 sts.).

Next (ribbonhole) row. K.1, (y.fwd., k.2 tog., k.1) to end.

K.2 rows, then cast off.

HOOD. With No. 10 needles cast on 53 sts. and k. 2 rows, then cont. in 6-row patt., as given for main part, until work measures 13½ ins. [34.29 cm], ending on 5th row. Cast off.

TO MAKE UP. Using a small backstitch join side of piece tog. to form 'hood'. Using a flat seam attach hood to main part, placing hood seam at centre of main part and leaving approx. 1 in. [2.54 cm] free at each outer edge. Thread ribbon through ribbonholes and tie at front.

Layette

See photograph on page 40.

MATERIALS:

Dress—4 balls of Villawool 3 ply Baby Wool; a pair of Nos. 10 and 11 needles; 3 buttons.

Jacket—3 balls of Villawool 3 ply Baby Wool; a pair of Nos. 10 and 11 needles; ribbon.

Bonnet, bootees and mitts—1 ball of Villawool 3 ply Baby Wool; a pair of No. 10 needles for bonnet and No. 11 needles for bootees and mitts; ribbon.

Shawl—13 balls of Villawool 3 ply Baby Wool; a pair of long No. 10 needles.

MEASUREMENTS:

Dress: To fit 16 (18) in. [40.64 (45.72) cm] chest. Length, 13 (14) ins. [33.02 (35.56) cm]. Sleeve, 1 in. [2.54 cm].

Jacket: To fit 16 (18) in. [40.64 (45.72) cm] chest. Length, 9 (10) ins. [22.86 (25.40) cm]. Sleeve, 5 ins. [12.70 cm].

Bootees: Leg seam, 2½ ins. [6.35 cm]. Foot, 3¼ ins. [8.25 cm].

Four-piece pram set is made up of Leggings, Angel Top, Cap and Mitts and is knitted in a combination of garter and stocking stitch (see page 48 for instructions).

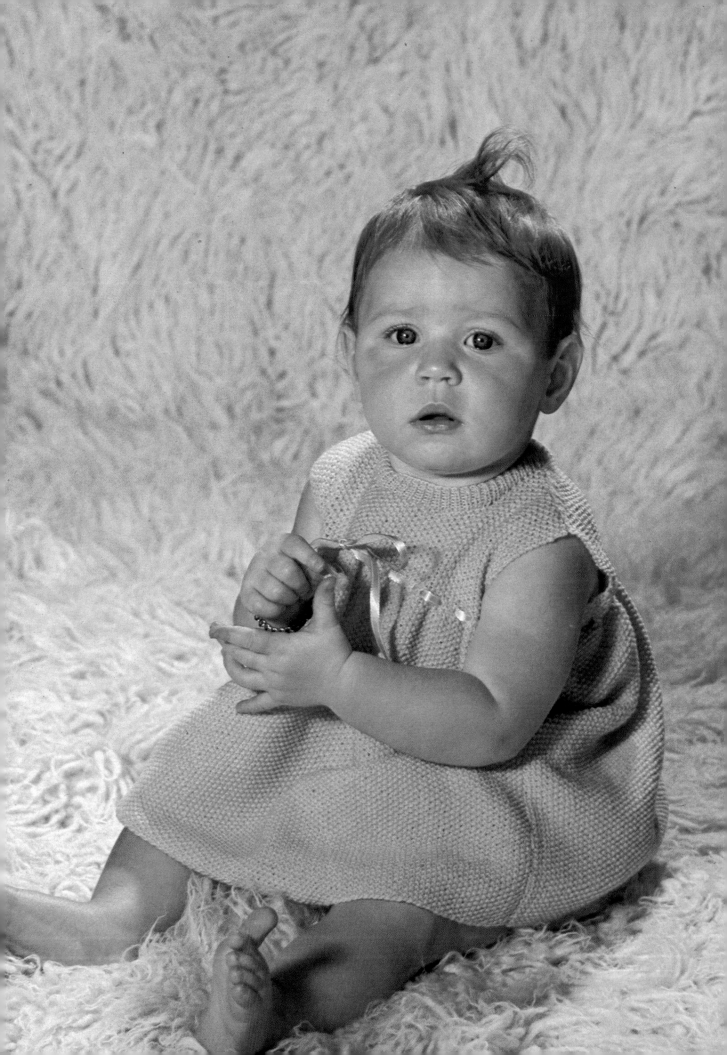

Bonnet: Around face edge, 12 ins. [30.48 cm].
Mitts: 3½ ins. [8.89 cm].
Shawl: Approx. 37 in. square [93.98 cm].
TENSION: 8 sts. to 1 inch [2.54 cm].
ABBREVIATIONS: See page 13.

TO MAKE:

DRESS

BACK. With No. 11 needles cast on 114 (121) sts. and k. 7 rows. Change to No. 10 needles and cont. in patt.:

1st row. K.1, (k.2, k.2 tog., y.fwd., k.3) to last st., k.1.

2nd row. P.1, (p.1, p.2 tog. t.b.l., y.r.n., p.1, y.r.n., p.2 tog., p.1) to last st., p.1.

3rd row. K.1, (k.2 tog., y.fwd., k.3, y.fwd., sl.1, k.1, p.s.s.o.) to last st., k.1.

4th row. P.

5th row. K.1, (y.fwd., sl.1, k.1, p.s.s.o., k.5) to last st., k.1.

6th row. K.1, (y.r.n., p.2 tog., p.2, p.2 tog. t.b.l., y.r.n., p.1) to last st., k.1.

7th row. K.1, (k.2, y.fwd., sl.1, k.1, p.s.s.o., k.2 tog., y.fwd., k.1) to last st., k.1.

8th row. P.

Rep. above 8 rows 8 times.

Next (dec.) row. K.17 (20), (k.2 tog.) 40 (41) times, k. to end. (74, 80 sts.).

Beg. p. row, cont. in st. st. until work measures 10 (10½) ins. [25.40 (26.67) cm], ending on p. row. **

Shape raglan. Cast off 4 sts. at beg. of next 2 rows. (66, 72 sts.).

Divide for back opening. 1st row. (Sl.1, k.1, p.s.s.o.) twice, y.fwd., k. until there are 35 (38) sts. on needle, turn and cont. on these sts. only.

2nd row. K.5, p. to last 5 sts., p.2 tog. t.b.l., p.3.

3rd (buttonhole) row. (Sl.1, k.1, p.s.s.o.) twice, y.fwd., k. to last 3 sts., y.fwd., k.2 tog., k.1.

4th row. As 2nd row.

5th row. (Sl.1, k.1, p.s.s.o.) twice, y.fwd., k. to end.

Rep. above 2 rows twice, then 4th row again.

Next row. (Sl.1, k.1, p.s.s.o.) twice, y.fwd., k. to end.

Next row. K.5, p. to end.

Rep. above 2 rows until 17 (18) sts. rem., making another buttonhole as before at 1 in. [2.54 cm] from previous buttonhole. Leave sts. on holder.

Return to rem. sts. Rejoin yarn to inner end of rem. sts. and cast on 6 sts.

1st row. K. to last 4 sts., y.fwd., (k.2 tog.) twice.

2nd row. P.3, p.2 tog., p. to last 5 sts., k.5.

Rep. above 2 rows 4 times.

Next row. K. to last 4 sts., y.fwd., (k.2 tog.) twice.

Next row. P. to last 5 sts., k.5.

Rep. above 2 rows until 17 (18) sts. rem. Leave sts. on holder.

FRONT. Work as given for Back to **.

Shape raglan. Cast off 4 sts. at beg. of next 2 rows.

3rd row. (Sl.1, k.1, p.s.s.o.) twice, y.fwd., k. to last 4 sts., y.fwd., (k.2 tog.) twice.

4th row. P.3, p.2 tog., p. to last 5 sts., p.2 tog. t.b.l., p.3.

Rep. above 2 rows 4 times.

Next row. As 3rd row.

Next row. P.

Rep. above 2 rows until 36 (38) sts. rem., ending on p. row.

Shape neck. Next row. (Sl.1, k.1, p.s.s.o.) twice, y.fwd., k.6, turn. Cont. on these sts. only and dec. 1 st. at neck edge on next row and on every foll. alt. row, at the same time, keeping raglan as set, until 2 sts. rem. K.2 tog. and fasten off. Return to rem. sts. Sl. centre 16 (18) sts. on a holder; rejoin yarn to inner end of rem. sts. and work to correspond with other side.

SLEEVES. With No. 11 needles cast on 48 (52) sts. and k. 7 rows.

Change to No. 10 needles and cont. in st. st. for 8 rows, inc. 1 st. each end of the 1st and 5th of these rows. (52, 56 sts.).

Cast off 4 sts. at beg. of next 2 rows.

3rd row. (Sl.1, k.1, p.s.s.o.) twice, y.fwd., k. to last 4 sts., y.fwd., (k.2 tog.) twice.

4th row. P.3, p.2 tog., p. to last 5 sts., p.2 tog. t.b.l., p.3.

Rep. above 2 rows 4 times.

Next row. As 3rd row.

Next row. P.

Rep. above 2 rows until 8 sts. rem.

Next row. (Sl.1, k.1, p.s.s.o.) twice, y.fwd., (k.2 tog.) twice. Leave rem. 5 sts. on holder.

NECKBAND. Firstly, using a flat seam, join raglans. With No. 11 needles and r.s.f., k. across 17 (18) sts. of Left Back, 5 sts. of one sleeve, pick up and k. 8 sts. down Left Front, k. across 16 (18) sts. of Centre Front, pick up and k. 8 sts. up Right Front, k. across 5 sts. of second sleeve and, finally, k. across 17 (18) sts. of Right Back (76, 80 sts.).

K. 1 row.

Next (dec.) row. K.0 (5), (k.5, k.2 tog.) 10 times, k.6 (5). (66, 70 sts.).

K.4 rows, making final buttonhole as before, then cast off.

TO MAKE UP. Press work on the wrong side. Using a small backstitch join side and sleeve seams. Sew on buttons.

Sleeveless dress is worked in moss stitch with k.1, p.1 ribbed neckband, features back neck opening and ribbon ties at front (see page 42 for instructions).

JACKET

BACK. With No. 11 needles cast on 92 (98) sts. and k. 7 rows.

Change to No. 10 needles and, beg. k. row, cont. in st. st., dec. 1 st. each end of every foll. 7th row until 82 (88) sts. rem.

Cont. straight until work measures 5½ (6) ins. [13.97 (15.24) cm], ending on p. row

Shape raglan. Cast off 4 sts. at beg. of next 2 rows.

3rd row. (Sl.1, k.1, p.s.s.o.) twice, y.fwd., k. to last 4 sts., y.fwd., (k.2 tog.) twice.

4th row. P.3, p.2 tog., p. to last 5 sts., p.2 tog. t.b.l., p.3.

Rep. above 2 rows 4 times.

Next row. As 3rd row.

Next row. P.

Rep. above 2 rows until 30 (32) sts. rem., ending on p. row.

Leave sts. on holder.

LEFT FRONT. With No. 11 needles cast on 49 (52) sts. and k. 7 rows.

Change to No. 10 needles and cont. in patt.:

1st row. K.27 (30), (k.2, k.2 tog., y.fwd., k.3) twice, k.8.

2nd row. K.6, p.2, (p.1, p.2 tog. t.b.l., y.r.n., p.1, y.r.n., p.2 tog., p.1) twice, p. to end.

3rd row. K.27 (30), (k.2 tog., y.fwd., k.3, y.fwd., sl.1, k.1, p.s.s.o.) twice, k.8.

4th row. K.6, p. to end.

5th row. K.27 (30), (y.fwd., sl.1, k.1, p.s.s.o., k.5) twice, k.8.

6th row. K.6, p.2, (y.r.n., p.2 tog., p.2, p.2 tog. t.b.l., y.r.n., p.1) twice, p. to end.

7th row. K.2 tog., k.25 (28), (k.2, y.fwd., sl.1, k.1, p.s.s.o., k.2 tog., y.fwd., k.1) twice, k.8.

8th row. K.6, p. to end.

Rep. above 8 rows, dec. 1 st. at side edge on every foll. 7th row as set until 44 (47) sts. rem. Cont. straight until work measures same as Back to raglan shaping, ending at side edge.

Shape raglan. Cont. in patt. and cast off 4 sts. at beg. of next row.

Patt. 1 row.

Next row. (Sl.1, k.1, p.s.s.o.) twice, y.fwd., patt. to end.

Next row. K.6, patt. to last 5 sts., p.2 tog. t.b.l., p.3.

Rep. above 2 rows 4 times.

Next row. (Sl.1, k.1, p.s.s.o.) twice, y.fwd., patt. to end.

Next row. K.6, patt. to end.

Rep. above 2 rows until 23 (24) sts. rem., ending at front edge.

Shape neck. Patt. 11 (12) sts. and leave sts. on a holder, patt. to end.

Six-piece layette consists of shawl, raglan style dress and jacket, bonnet, bootees and mitts, and is knitted in a combination of a fancy trellis stitch and stocking stitch (see page 36 for instructions).

Dec. 1 st. at neck edge on next and every foll. alt. row, at the same time, cont. to dec. at raglan edge as set until 2 sts. rem. K.2 tog. and fasten off.

RIGHT FRONT. Work as given for Left Front, reversing position of pattern panel, i.e. 1st row will read: k.8, (k.2, k.2 tog., y.fwd., k.3) twice, k. to end.

SLEEVES. With No. 11 needles cast on 43 (45) sts. and k. 7 rows.

Change to No. 10 needles and, beg. k. row, cont. in st. st., inc. 1 st. each end of every foll. 4th row to 57 (61) sts. Cont. straight until work measures 5 ins. [12.70 cm] (or length required), ending on p. row.

Cast off 4 sts. at beg. of next 2 rows.

3rd row. (Sl.1, k.1, p.s.s.o.) twice, y.fwd., k. to last 4 sts., y.fwd., (k.2 tog.) twice.

4th row. P.3, p.2 tog., p. to last 5 sts., p.2 tog. t.b.l., p.3.

Rep. above 2 rows 4 times.

Next row. As 3rd row.

Next row. P.

Rep. above 2 rows until 5 sts. rem. Leave sts. on holder.

NECKBAND. Firstly, using a flat seam, join raglan seams. With No. 11 needles and r.s.f., k. across 11 (12) sts. of Right Front, pick up and k. 6 sts. up Right Front, k. across 5 sts. of one sleeve and 30 (32) sts. of Back Neck, k. across 5 sts. of second sleeve, pick up and k. 6 sts. down left front neck, then k. across 11 (12) sts. of Left Front. (74, 78 sts.).

K. 2 rows.

Next (ribbonhole) row. K.5 (7), (y.fwd., k.2 tog.) to last 5 (7) sts., k.5 (7).

K. 4 more rows, then cast off.

TO MAKE UP. Press work on the wrong side. Using a small backstitch join side and sleeve seams. Thread ribbon through ribbonholes and tie at front.

BONNET

With No. 10 needles cast on 100 sts. and k. 7 rows. Now cont. in 8-row patt., as given for Back of Dress, until work measures 4¾ ins. [12.06 cm], ending on p. row.

Shape crown. 1st row. K.1, (k.2 tog., k.10) 7 times, k.2 tog., k.13.

2nd row. P.

3rd row. K.1, (k.2 tog., k.9) 7 times, k.2 tog., k. to end.

Cont. to dec. in this way, working 1 st. less between decs. on every alt. row until 21 sts. rem., ending on p. row.

Next row. K.1, (k.2 tog.) to end.

Break yarn; thread through rem. sts.; draw up and fasten off.

TO MAKE UP. Press work on the wrong side. Join seam, leaving 2 ins. [5.08 cm] open at outer edge. Thread ribbon through first row of holes of patt.

BOOTEES

With No. 11 needles cast on 40 sts. and k. 7 rows, then cont. in st. st. until work measures 1¼ ins. [3.17 cm], ending on p. row.

Next (ribbonhole) row. K.2, (y.fwd., k.2 tog., k.1) to last 2 sts., y.fwd., k.2 tog.

P.1 row.

Next row. K.27, turn.

Next row. P.12, turn and work 20 rows in st. st. on these sts. for instep. Break yarn.

R.s.f. Pick up and k. 14 sts. on side of instep, k. across 12 instep sts., pick up and k. 14 sts. on other side of instep, then k. rem. sts. (68 sts.). Beg. p. row, work in st. st. for 9 rows.

Shape toe. Next row. K.1, k.2 tog., k.29, (k.2 tog.) twice, k.29, k.2 tog., k.1.

Next row. P.30, (p.2 tog.) twice, p.30.

Next row. K.1, (k.2 tog., k.26, (k.2 tog.) twice, k.26, k.2 tog., k.1.

Next row. P.27, (p.2 tog.) twice, p.27.

Next row. K.26, (k.2 tog.) twice, k.26.

Cast off.

TO MAKE UP. Join leg and foot seams. Thread ribbon through ribbonholes and tie at front.

MITTS

With No. 11 needles cast on 34 sts. and k. 9 rows. Beg. k. row work 6 rows in st. st.

Next (ribbonhole) row. K.1, (k.2 tog., y.fwd., k.2) to last st., k.1.

P.1 row.

Next row. Inc., k.17, inc., k. to end, inc. (37 sts.). Beg. p. row, work in st. st. for 2 ins. [5.08 cm], ending p. row.

Shape top. 1st row. K.1, (k.2 tog., k.4) to end.

2nd row. P.

3rd row. K.1, (k.2 tog., k.3) to end.

Cont. to dec. in this way, working 1 st. less between decs. until 7 sts. rem.

Next row. K.1, (k.2 tog.) 3 times.

Break yarn; thread through rem. sts.; draw up and fasten off.

TO MAKE UP. Join seam. Thread ribbon through ribbonholes and tie at front.

SHAWL

With No. 10 needles cast on 291 sts. and k. 9 rows. Placing 8 sts. at beg. and end of next row on a safety pin, cont. on rem. 275 sts. and rep. the 8-row patt., as given for Back of Dress until work measures 36¾ ins. [93.34 cm]. Leave aside.

Return to sts. on safety pin and work on these 8 sts. in garter st. until border measures length of main part. Leave aside.

Work other border in same way.

Now work 9 rows in garter st. across 291 sts., then cast off.

TO MAKE UP. Press main part lightly on the wrong side. Flat seam borders to main part.

Summer Dress

See photograph on page 38.

MATERIALS: 4 balls of Villawool 3 ply Baby Wool; a pair of Nos. 11 and 12 needles; 3 buttons; length of narrow ribbon.

MEASUREMENTS: To fit 18/19 in. [45.72/48.26 cm] chest. Length, 14¼ ins. [36.83 cm].

TENSION: 8½ sts. to 1 inch [2.54 cm].

ABBREVIATIONS: See page 13.

TO MAKE:

BACK. With No. 11 needles cast on 141 sts.

Next (m.st.) row. K.1, (p.1, k.1) to end.

Rep. above row until work measures 10¼ ins. [26.03 cm].

Next (dec.) row. K.13, (k.2 tog.) 58 times, k. to end. (83 sts.).

Next (ribbonhole) row. (K.1, y.fwd., k.2 tog.) to end, k.2. Work 3 rows.

Shape armholes. Cast off 4 sts. at beg. of next 2 rows, then dec. 1 st. each end of next row and every foll. alt. row until 67 sts. rem. Cont. until armholes measure 1¼ ins. [3.17 cm].

Divide for back opening. Work 36 sts., turn. Cont. on these sts. only.

Work 1 row.

Next (buttonhole) row. Work to last 3 sts., y.fwd., k.2 tog., k.1.

Cont. in m.st., making another buttonhole as before when armhole measures 2½ ins. [6.35 cm].

Cont. straight until armhole measures 3¼ ins. [8.25 cm], ending at side edge.

Shape shoulder. Cast off 7 sts. at beg. of next row and foll. alt. row, then 6 sts. at beg. of foll. alt. row. Work 1 row, then leave rem. sts. on a holder.

Return to rem. sts. Rejoin yarn to inner end of sts.; cast on 5 sts., then cont. to correspond with other side, omitting buttonholes.

FRONT. Work as given for Back until armholes measure 1½ ins. [3.81 cm].

Shape neck. Next row. Work 27 sts., turn. Cont. on these sts. only. Dec. 1 st. at neck edge of foll. 7 rows, then cont. straight until armhole measures same as back armhole, ending at side edge.

Shape shoulder. Cast off 7 sts. at beg. of next row and foll. alt. row. Work 1 row, then cast off rem. sts.

Return to rem. sts. Place centre 13 sts. on a holder. Rejoin yarn to inner end of rem. sts., then cont. to correspond with other side.

NECKBAND. Firstly, join shoulder seams. With No. 12 needles and r.s.f., k. across 16 sts. of back neck, pick up and k. 26 sts. down left side of neck, k. across 13 sts. at centre front, pick up and k. 26 sts. up right side of neck, then k. across sts. at back neck (97 sts.). Work in k.1, p.1 rib for 6 rows, making final buttonhole on 4th row, then cast off ribwise.

TO MAKE UP. Join side seams. Sew on buttons. Thread ribbon through ribbonholes and tie at front.

Jumpsuit

See photograph on page 20.

MATERIALS: 5 (5) balls of Villawool 3 ply Baby Wool; a pair of Nos. 10 and 12 needles; 4 in. [10.16 cm] zip; 3 press studs; ribbon.
MEASUREMENTS: To fit 18 (19) in. [45.72 (48.26) cm] chest. Length, 14 (16) ins. [35.56 (40.64) cm]. sleeve, 5½ (6½) ins. [13.97 (16.51) cm].
TENSION: 8 sts. to 1 inch [2.54 cm].
ABBREVIATIONS: See page 13.

TO MAKE:
BACK. With No. 10 needles cast on 22 sts. and work 4 rows in garter st., then cont. in patt.:
1st row. K.2, (p.2, k.2) to end.
2nd row. P.2, (k.2, p.2) to end.
3rd row. K.
4th row. P.
5th row. P.2, (k.2, p.2) to end.
6th row. K.2, (p.2, k.2) to end.
7th row. K.
8th row. P.
Rep. above 8 rows, at the same time, cast on 2 sts. at beg. of every row to 78 (86) sts. Cont. in patt. until work measures 6½ ins. [16.51 cm], ending on 2nd or 6th row.
Next (ribbonhole) row. K.3 (1), (y.fwd., k.2 tog., k.4) to last 3 (1) st(s)., k.3 (1).
Cont. in patt. until work measures 10½ (12) ins. [26.67 (30.48) cm], ending on 4th or 8th patt. row.
Shape raglan. Cont. in patt. and cast off 3 (4) sts. at beg. of next 2 rows, then dec. 1 st. each end of next row and every foll. alt. row until 46 (48) sts. rem. ** Dec. 1 st. each end of every foll. row until 26 (28) sts. rem. Leave sts. on a holder.
FRONT. Work as given for Back to **. (46, 48 sts.).
Shape neck. Next row. K.2 tog., patt. 13 sts., turn and cont. on these sts. only. Dec. 1 st. at neck edge of next 4 (3) rows, at the same time,

cont. to dec. at raglan edge as set on every foll. row until 2 sts. rem. K.2 tog. and fasten off.
Return to rem. sts. Sl. centre 16 (18) sts. on a holder. Rejoin yarn to inner end of rem. sts. and work to correspond with other side.

SLEEVES. With No. 12 needles cast on 38 (42) sts. and work in k.1, p.1 rib for 10 rows. Change to No. 10 needles and cont. in patt. as given for Back, inc. 1 st. each end of every foll. 5th row to 50 (56) sts. Cont. straight until work measures 5½ (6½) ins. [13.97 (16.51) cm], ending on 4th or 8th patt. row.
Cast off 3 (4) sts. at beg. of next 2 rows, then dec. 1 st. each end of next row and every foll. alt. row until 8 sts. rem. Leave sts. on holder.

NECKBAND. Firstly, join two front and right back raglan seams. R.s.f. and with No. 12 needles k. across 8 sts. of left sleeve, pick up and k. 8 sts. down left side of neck, k. across centre sts., pick up and k. 8 sts. up right side of neck, k. across 8 sts. of other sleeve, then k. across sts. at back neck. (74, 78 sts.). Work in k.1, p.1 rib for 6 rows, then cast off ribwise.

LEG BANDS. Firstly, join rem. raglan seam, leaving 4 ins. open at neck edge for zip. Join side and sleeve seams. R.s.f. and with No. 12 needles, pick up and k. 78 (84) sts. along each leg edge. Work in k.1, p.1 rib for 6 rows, then cast off ribwise.

TO MAKE UP. Insert zip at neck edge. Attach press studs to crutch opening. Thread ribbon through ribbonholes and tie at front.

Vest and Matching Pants

MATERIALS:
Vest—3 balls of Villawool 3 ply Baby Wool; a pair of No. 10 needles; a No. 2.50 crochet hook.
Pants—3 balls of Villawool 3 ply Baby Wool; a pair of No. 10 needles; 2 buttons; ribbon.
MEASUREMENTS:
Vest: To fit 18 in. [47.72 cm] chest. Length, 10¼ ins. [26.03 cm].
Pants: Width around widest part, 19¾ ins. [50.16 cm].
TENSION: 8 sts. to 1 inch [2.54 cm].
ABBREVIATIONS: See page 13.

TO MAKE:

VEST
BACK AND FRONT ALIKE. With No. 10 needles cast on 77 sts. and work in garter st. until work measures 7½ ins. [19.05 cm].
Shape armholes. Cont. in garter st. and cast off 5 sts. at beg. of next 2 rows (67 sts.).
Cont. straight until work measures 9 ins. [22.86 cm].
Shape neck. Next row. K.18, turn and cont. on these sts. only.
Cont. until work measures 10¼ ins. [26.03 cm], then cast off.
Return to sts. on needle. Rejoin yarn to inner end of rem. sts. and cast off centre 31 sts., then cont. to correspond with other side.
TO MAKE UP. Join shoulder and side seams. Press seams. R.s.f. and with crochet hook, work 1 row of d.c. around neck edge.

PANTS
FRONT. With No. 10 needles cast on 83 sts. and work in k.1, p.1 rib for 6 rows.
Next (ribbonhole) row. K.1, (y.fwd., k.2 tog., rib 2) to last 2 sts., y.fwd., k.2.
Work 7 more rows in k.1, p.1 rib, then cont. in garter st. until work measures 6¼ ins. [15.87 cm].
Cont. in garter st., dec. 1 st. each end of every foll. row until 25 sts. rem. K. 3 rows, then fasten off.
BACK. Work as given for Front until ribbing is completed.
Shape back. 1st Row. K. to last 10 sts., turn.
2nd row. As 1st row.
3rd row. K. to last 20 sts., turn.
4th row. As 3rd row.

5th row. K. to last 30 sts., turn.
6th row. As 5th row.
7th row. K. to end.
Cont. in garter st. until work measures 6¼ ins. [15.87 cm]. Cont. in garter st., dec. 1 st. each end of every foll. row until 25 sts. rem., then cont. straight for 7 rows.
Next (buttonhole) row. K.6, cast off 3 sts., k.7, cast off 3 sts., k.6.
Next row. K. and cast on 3 sts. over those cast off in previous row.
K. 3 rows, then cast off.
TO MAKE UP. Join side seams. Press seams. Sew buttons to Front to correspond with buttonholes at Back. Thread ribbon through holes at waist and tie at front.

Poncho

See photograph on page 47.

MATERIALS: 6 balls of Villawool Cascade Nylon 8 ply Crepe; a pair of No. 9 needles; crochet hook.
MEASUREMENTS: To fit 20/22 in. [50.80/55.88 cm] chest. Approx. length from V of neck to front point, 12 ins. [30.48 cm].
TENSION: 6 sts. to 1 inch [2.54 cm] over patt.
ABBREVIATIONS: See page 13.

TO MAKE:
MAKE TWO PIECES.
With No. 9 needles cast on 48 sts. and work in patt. as follows:
1st row. ((K.1, y.r.n. and k.1) into 1st st., p.3) to end.
2nd row. (P.3 tog., k.3) to end.
3rd row. (P.3, (k.1, y.r.n. and k.1) into next st.) to end.
4th row. (K.3, p.3 tog.) to end.
Rep. above 4 rows until work measures 16 ins. [40.64 cm], ending on 4th row. Cast off.
TO MAKE UP. Using a flat seam join one narrow end of each strip to the long side of other strip.
FRINGE. Cut four 8 in. [20.32 cm] lengths of yarn for each tassel and proceed as follows: With

Vest and matching pants are knitted entirely in garter stitch with k.1, p.1 rib at waistband of pants.

the wrong side of the edge to be fringed facing you, insert a crochet hook as near as possible to the edge, fold strands in half to form a loop, put loop on hook, pull through edge of work, place hook behind all strands of yarn and draw through loop. Cont. along outer edge of poncho, at regular intervals.

Finally, trim ends of fringing to neaten.

Carrying Coat

See photograph on page 20.

MATERIALS: 6 balls of Villawool 3 ply Baby Wool; a pair of No. 11 needles and a pair of long No. 11 needles for yoke; ribbon.

MEASUREMENTS: To fit 18/19 in. [45.72/48.26 cm] chest. Length, 15½ ins. [39.37 cm]. Sleeve, 6 ins. [15.24 cm].

TENSION: 8½ sts. to 1 inch [2.54 cm] over patt.

ABBREVIATIONS: See page 13.

TO MAKE:

BACK. With No. 11 needles cast on 141 sts. and work in g.st. for 8 rows, then cont. in patt.:

1st row. K.1, (y.fwd., k.2 tog. k.5, k.2 tog., y.fwd., k.1) to end.

2nd row. P.

3rd row. K.2, (y.fwd., k.2 tog., k.3, k.2 tog., y.fwd., k.3) to last 9 sts., y.fwd., k.2 tog., k.3, k.2 tog., y.fwd., k.2.

4th row. P.

5th row. K.3, (y.fwd., k.2 tog., k.1, k.2 tog., y.fwd., k.5) to last 8 sts., y.fwd., k.2 tog., k.1, k.2 tog., y.fwd., k.3.

6th row. P.

7th row. K.4, (y.fwd., sl.1, k.2 tog., p.s.s.o., y.fwd., k.7) to last 7 sts., y.fwd., sl.1, k.2 tog., p.s.s.o., y.fwd., k.4

8th row. P.

Rep. above 8 rows until work measures 11½ ins. [29.21 cm], ending on 8th patt. row.

Shape armholes. Cont. in patt. and dec. 1 st. each end of the next 8 rows. Leave rem. 125 sts. on a holder.

LEFT FRONT. With No. 11 needles cast on 78 sts. and work in g.st. for 8 rows, then cont. in patt.:

1st row. K.1, (y.fwd., k.2 tog., k.5, k.2 tog., y.fwd., k.1) to last 7 sts., k.7.

2nd row. K.7, p. to end.

3rd row. K.2, (y.fwd., k.2 tog., k.3, k.2 tog., y.fwd., k.3) to last 16 sts., y.fwd., k.2 tog., k.3,

k.2 tog., y.fwd., k. to end.

4th row. K.7, p. to end.

5th row. K.3, (y.fwd., k.2 tog., k.1, k.2 tog., y.fwd., k.5) to last 15 sts., y.fwd., k.2 tog., k.1, k.2 tog., y.fwd., k. to end.

6th row. K.7, p. to end.

7th row. K.4, (y.fwd., sl.1, k.2 tog., p.s.s.o., y.fwd., k.7) to last 14 sts., y.fwd., sl.1, k.2 tog., p.s.s.o., y.fwd., k. to end.

8th row. K.7, p. to end.

Rep. above 8 rows until work measures same as Back to beg. of armhole shaping, ending on 8th patt. row.

Shape armhole. Cont. in patt. and dec. 1 st. at the armhole edge of next 8 rows. Leave rem. 70 sts. on a holder.

RIGHT FRONT. Work as given for Left Front, reversing position of g.st. border thus:

1st patt. row. K.8, (y.fwd., k.2 tog., k.5, k.2 tog., y.fwd., k.1) to end.

SLEEVES. With No. 11 needles cast on 34 sts. and work in g.st. for 11 rows.

Next (inc.) row. (K.1, inc.) to end. (51 sts.)

Cont. in 8-row patt. as given for Back until work measures 6 ins. [15.24 cm], ending on 8th patt. row. Cont. in patt. and dec. 1 st. each end of next 8 rows, then leave rem. 35 sts. on a holder.

YOKE. R.s.f. and with long No. 11 needles, join pieces as follows:

K. across 70 sts. of Right Front, 35 sts. of one sleeve, 125 sts. of Back, 35 sts. of second sleeve and, finally, 70 sts. of Left Front (335 sts.).

Next (dec.) row. K.7, (k.2 tog.) 32 times, k.40, (k.2 tog.) 56 times, k.41, (k.2 tog.) 32 times, k. to end (215 sts.).

Work in g.st. for 26 rows.

Next (dec.) row. K.10, (k.3 tog., k.7) to last 5 sts., k.5 (175 sts.).

Work in g.st. for 7 rows.

Next (dec.) row. K.7, (k.3 tog., k.3) to last 6 sts., k.6 (121 sts.).

Work in g.st. for 5 rows.

Next (dec.) row. K.16, (k.3 tog., k.3) to last 15 sts., k. to end. (91 sts.).

K.1 row, then cast off.

TO MAKE UP: Join side and sleeve seams, then armhole seams. Sew ribbon to either side of neck and tie at front.

Poncho is knitted in blackberry stitch in two pieces . . . the joining forms the shaping of the garment. Outer edges are fringed (see page 44 for instructions).

Pram Set

See photograph on page 37

MATERIALS:

Leggings—7 balls of Villawool Cascade Nylon 4 ply Crepe; a pair of Nos. 10 and 12 needles; ribbon.

Angel Top—5 balls of Villawool Cascade Nylon 4 ply Crepe; a pair of Nos. 10 and 12 needles; ribbon.

Cap and Mitts—2 balls of Villawool Cascade Nylon 4 ply Crepe; a pair of No. 10 needles.

MEASUREMENTS:

Leggings: Cast-on edge to crutch, 8½ ins. [21.59 cm]. Foot, 4½ ins. [11.43 cm].

Angel Top: To fit 20 in. [50.80 cm] chest. Length, 10½ ins. [26.67 cm]. Sleeve, 6 ins. [15.24 cm].

TENSION: 15 sts. to 2 inches [5.08 cm].

ABBREVIATIONS: See page 13.

TO MAKE:

LEGGINGS

RIGHT LEG. Beg. at waist—with No. 12 needles cast on 82 sts. and work in k.1, p.1 rib for 6 rows.

Next (ribbonhole) row. K.1, (k.2 tog., y.fwd., rib 2) to last st., k.1.

Rib 7 more rows.

Change to No. 10 needles.

Shape back. 1st row. K.12, turn.

2nd row. P. to end.

3rd row. K.24, turn.

4th row. P. to end.

5th row. K.36, turn.

6th row. P. to end.

7th row. K.48, turn.

8th row. P. to end.

9th row. K.60, turn.

10th row. P. to end.

11th row. K.72, turn.

12th row. P. to end.

Cont. in st. st., inc. 1 st. at beg. of 3rd row and at beg. of every foll. 8th row to 90 sts. Cont. straight until work measures 8½ ins. [21.59 cm], ending on p. row. Place a marker each end of last row.

Shape leg. Dec. 1 st. each end of next row and every foll. alt. row until 42 sts. rem. Cont. straight until work measures 7½ ins. [19.05 cm]. from markers, ending on p. row.

Next (ribbonhole) row. K.1, (y.fwd., k.2 tog.) to last st., k.1. P. 1 row.

Shape foot. Next row. K.33, turn.

Next row. K.12, turn.

Cont. in garter st. on these sts. and work 24 rows for instep, then break yarn.

Rejoin yarn at beg. of instep and pick up and k. 13 sts. on side of instep, k. across 12 instep sts., pick up and k. 13 sts. on other side of instep, then k. rem. sts. (68 sts.). Cont. in garter st. for 15 rows.

Next row. K.3, k.2 tog., k.2, k.2 tog., k.25, k.2 tog., k.8, k.2 tog., k.22.

Next row. K.

Next row. K.3, (k.2 tog.) twice, k.25, k.2 tog., k.6, k.2 tog., k.22.

Next row. K.

Cast off.

LEFT LEG. Work as given for Right Leg until waist ribbing is completed. Change to No. 10 needles and k. 1 row.

Shape back. 1st row. P.12, turn.

2nd row. K. to end.

3rd row. P.24, turn.

4th row. K. to end.

5th row. P.36, turn.

6th row. K. to end.

7th row. P.48, turn.

8th row. K. to end.

9th row. P.60, turn.

10th row. K. to end.

11th row. P.72, turn.

12th row. K. to end.

Cont. in st. st., inc. 1 st. at the end of the next row and at the end of every foll. 8th row to 90 sts. Cont. straight until work measures 8½ ins. [21.59 cm], ending on p. row. Place marker each end of last row.

Shape leg. Work as given for Right Leg, including ribbonhole row. P. 1 row.

Shape foot. Next row. K.21, turn.

Next row. K.12, turn.

Cont. in garter st. on these sts. and work 24 rows for instep, then break yarn.

Rejoin yarn at beg. of instep and pick up and k. 13 sts. on side of instep, k. across 12 instep sts., pick up and k. 13 sts. on other side of instep, then k. rem. sts. (68 sts.). Cont. in garter st. for 15 rows.

Next K.22, k.2 tog., k.8, k.2 tog., k.25, k.2 tog., k.2, k.2 tog., k.3.

Next row. K.

Next row. K.22, k.2 tog., k.6, k.2 tog., k.25, (k.2 tog.) twice, k.3.

Next row. K.

Cast off.

TO MAKE UP. Join front and back seams to markers. Join leg and foot seams. Thread ribbon through ribbonholes at waist and foot and tie in front.

ANGEL TOP

BACK. With No. 10 needles cast on 106 sts. and work in garter st. for 10 rows. Beg. k. row, cont. in st. st., dec. 1 st. each end of every 5th row until 92 sts. rem. Cont. straight until work measures 7 ins. [17.78 cm], ending on p. row.

Shape raglan. Cast off 4 sts. at beg. of next 2 rows.
Next row. K.1, sl.1, k.1, p.s.s.o., k. to last 3 sts., k.2 tog., k.1.
Next row. P.1, sl.1, p.1, p.s.s.o., p. to last 3 sts., p.2 tog. t.b.l., p.l.
Rep. above 2 rows once.
Next row. K.1, sl.1, k.1, p.s.s.o., k. to last 3 sts., k.2 tog., k.1.
Next row. P.
Rep. above 2 rows until 60 sts. rem., ending on p. row.
Divide for back opening. Next row. K.1, sl.1, k.1, p.s.s.o., k.27, turn and cont. on these sts. only.
Next row. K.3, p. to end.
Next row. K.1, sl.1, k.1, p.s.s.o., k. to end.
Rep. above 2 rows until 21 sts. rem., ending on p. row. Leave sts. on holder.
Return to sts. on needle. Rejoin yarn to inner end of rem. sts.
Next row. K. to last 3 sts., k.2 tog., k.1.
Next row. P. to last 3 sts., k.3.
Rep. above 2 rows until 21 sts. rem., ending on p. row. Leave sts. on a holder.
FRONT. With No. 10 needles cast on 106 sts. and work in garter st. for 10 rows.
Next row. K.
Next row. P.38, k.30, p.38.
Rep. above 2 rows, at the same time dec. 1 st. each end of 3rd row and every foll. 5th row until 92 sts. rem. Cont. straight until work measures 7 ins. [17.78 cm], ending on wrong side of work.
Shape raglan. Cont. in patt. and cast off 4 sts. at beg. of next 2 rows.
Next row. K.1, sl.1, k.1, p.s.s.o., work to last 3 sts., k.2 tog., k.1.
Next row. P.1, sl.1, p.1, p.s.s.o., work to last 3 sts., p.2 tog. t.b.l., p.l.
Rep. above 2 rows once.
Next row. K.1, sl.1, k.1, p.s.s.o., work to last 3 sts., k.2 tog., k.1.
Next row. P.
Rep. above 2 rows until 56 sts. rem., ending on wrong side of work.
Shape neck. Next row. K.1, sl.1, k.1, p.s.s.o., k.17, turn and cont. on these sts. only. Work 1 row. Cont. to shape reglan as set, at the same time, dec. 1 st. at neck edge of foll. 11 rows, then p.2 tog. and fasten off.
Return to sts. on needle. Sl. centre 16 sts. on a holder. Rejoin yarn to inner end of rem. sts.
Next row. K. to last 3 sts., k.2 tog., k.1.
Now cont. to correspond with other side.
SLEEVES. With No. 12 needles cast on 37 sts. and work in garter st. for 10 rows. Change to No. 10 needles and, beg. k. row, cont. in st. st., inc. 1 st. each end of every foll. 4th row to 55 sts. Cont. straight until work measures 6 ins. [15.24 cm], ending on p. row.
Cast off 4 sts. at beg. of next 2 rows.
Next row. K.1, sl.1, k.1, p.s.s.o., k. to last 3 sts., k.2 tog., k.1.

Next row. P.1, sl.1, p.1, p.s.s.o., p. to last 3 sts., p.2 tog. t.b.l., p.1.
Rep. above 2 rows twice.
Next row. K.1, sl.1, k.1, p.s.s.o., k. to last 3 sts., k.2 tog., k.1.
Next row. P.
Rep. above 2 rows until 5 sts. rem., ending on p. row.
Next row. K.1, sl.1, k.2 tog., p.s.s.o., k.1.
Next row. P.3 tog. and fasten off.
NECKBAND. Firstly, join raglan seams. R.s.f. and with No. 12 needles, k. across 21 sts. of left back, pick up and k. 24 sts. down left side of neck, k. across 16 sts. of front thus: k.2, (k.2 tog.) to last 2 sts., k.2, pick up and k. 24 sts. up right side of neck and k. across 21 sts. of right back (100 sts.). Keeping garter st. edgings as set at back opening, work in k.1, p.1 rib for 6 rows, then cast off ribwise.
TO MAKE UP. Join side and sleeve seams. Sew a ribbon tie to each side of back opening at neck edge.

CAP

With No. 10 needles cast on 93 sts. and work in garter st. until work measures 6¼ ins. [15.87 cm].
Shape crown. Next row. K.1, (k.2 tog., k.9) 7 times, k.2 tog., k. to end. K. 1 row.
Next row. K.1, (k.2 tog., k.8) 7 times, k.2 tog., k. to end.
Cont. to dec. in this way, working 1 st. less between decs. on every alt. row until 21 sts. rem. K. 1 row.
Next row. K.1, (k.2 tog.) 10 times. Break yarn and thread through rem. sts.; draw up and fasten off.
TO MAKE UP. With a flat seam, join seam. Turn back 1¾ ins. [4.44 cm] at lower edge to outside as pictured. Make a pom-pom and sew to top of cap: Cut two circles of cardboard the size you require the finished pom-pom to be, then cut out a circular hole in the centre of each. Wind yarn evenly around the two pieces of cardboard and through the centre hole, until the hole is filled. Cut yarn through at outer edge of cardboard only, then tie a piece of yarn between the two circles of cardboard in the middle and, when strands are secure, cut away the cardboard and leave end of yarn for sewing to cap. Shake well and trim ends.

MITTS

With No. 10 needles cast on 36 sts. and work in k.1, p.1 rib for 14 rows. Cont. in garter st. until work measures 4 ins. [10.16 cm].
Shape top. Next row. (K.2, k.2 tog.) to end.
Next row. K.
Next row. (K.1, k.2 tog.) to end.
Next row. K.
Next row. (K.2 tog.) to end.
Break yarn; thread through rem. sts.; draw up and fasten off.
TO MAKE UP. With a flat seam, join seam.

Garter Stitch Bootees

Patterned Bootees

MATERIALS: 1 ball of Villawool 3 ply Baby Wool; a pair of No. 10 needles; ribbon.
MEASUREMENTS: Leg seam, 3 ins. [7.62 cm]. Foot, 3½ ins. [8.89 cm].
TENSION: 8 sts. to 1 inch [2.54 cm].
ABBREVIATIONS: See page 13.

TO MAKE: With No. 10 needles cast on 40 sts. and work in garter st. for 24 rows.
Next (ribbonhole) row. K.1, (y.fwd., k.2 tog., k.1) to end. K. 1 row.
Next row. K.26, turn.
Next row. K.12, turn and work 20 rows in garter st. on these sts. for instep. Break yarn.
R.s.f., pick up and k. 14 sts. on side of instep, k. across 12 instep sts., pick up and k. 14 sts. on other side of instep, then k. rem. sts. (68 sts.). K. 9 rows.
Shape toe. Next row. K.1, k.2 tog., k.29, (k.2 tog.) twice, k.29, k.2 tog., k.1.
Next row. K.30, (k.2 tog.) twice, k.30.
Next row. K.1, k.2 tog., k.26, (k.2 tog.) twice, k.26, k.2 tog., k.1.
Next row. K.27, (k.2 tog.) twice, k.27.
Next row. K.26, (k.2 tog.) twice, k.26.
Cast off.
TO MAKE UP. Join leg and foot seams. Thread ribbon through ribbonholes and tie at front.

PATTERNED BOOTEES
MATERIALS: 1 ball of Villawool 3 ply Baby Wool; a pair of No. 10 needles; ribbon.
MEASUREMENTS: Leg seam, 3 ins. [7.62 cm]. Foot, 3½ ins. [8.89 cm].
TENSION: 8 sts. to 1 inch [2.54 cm] over st. st.
ABBREVIATIONS: See page 13.
TO MAKE: With No. 10 needles cast on 42 sts. and k. 2 rows, then cont. in blackberry stitch patt.:
1st row. K.1, * (k.1, p.1, k.1) into next st., p.3 tog.; rep. from * to last st., k.1.
2nd row. P.
3rd row. K.1, * p.3 tog., (k.1, p.1, k.1) into next st.; rep. from * to last st., k.1.
4th row. P.
Rep. above 4 rows 3 times, then p. 1 row.
Next (ribbonhole) row. K.2, (y.fwd., k.2 tog., k.2) to end. P. 1 row.
Next row. K.27, turn.
Next row. P.12, turn and work 20 rows in st. st. on these sts. for instep. Break yarn.
R.s.f., pick up and k. 13 sts. on side of instep, k. across 12 instep sts., pick up and k. 13 sts. on other side of instep, then k. rem. sts. (68 sts.).
Beg. p. row, work in st. st. for 9 rows.
Shape toe. Next row. K.1, k.2 tog., k.29, (k.2 tog.) twice, k.29, k.2 tog., k.1.
Next row. P.30, (p.2 tog.) twice, p.30.
Next row. K.1, k.2 tog., k.26, (k.2 tog.) twice, k.26, k.2 tog., k.1.
Next row. P.27, (p.2 tog.) twice, p.27.
Next row. K.26, (k.2 tog.) twice, k.26.
Cast off.
TO MAKE UP. Join leg and foot seams. Thread ribbon through ribbonholes and tie at front.

Above: *Bootees are knitted in a combination of stocking and blackberry stitch.*

Below: *Bootees are knitted entirely in garter stitch.*

Shawl

MATERIALS: 14 balls of Villawool Cascade Nylon 4 ply Crepe; a pair of Nos. 8 and 10 needles.
MEASUREMENT: Approx. 34 ins. square [86.36 cm].
TENSION: 7 sts. to 1 inch [2.54 cm] over patt.
ABBREVIATIONS: See page 13.

TO MAKE: With No. 10 needles cast on 182 sts. and work in patt. as follows:
1st row. (K.1, p.1) to end.
2nd row. As 1st row.
3rd row. (P.1, k.1) to end.
4th row. As 3rd row.
Rep. above 4 rows until work measures 26 ins. [66.04 cm], then cast off.
BORDER. With No. 8 needles cast on 26 sts. and work in patt. as follows:
1st row. K.1, p.1, (y.o.n., k.1, p.1) to end.
2nd row. (K.1, p.2 tog., y.o.n.) to last 2 sts., k.1, p.1.
3rd row. K.1, p.1, (y.o.n., k.2 tog., p.1) to end.
Rep. above 2 rows 3 times more.
10th row. As 2nd row.
11th row. K.1, p.1, (sl.1 k.wise, k.1, p.s.s.o., y.r.n., p.1) to end.
12th row. (K.1, y.r.n., p.2 tog.) to last 2 sts., k.1, p.1.
Rep. above 2 rows 4 times more.
21st row. K.1, p.1, (y.o.n., sl.1, k.1, p.s.s.o., p.1) to end.
Rep. from 2nd to 21st row inclusive until border is long enough to fit around edge of main part, ending on completion of a patt.
Cast off by k.1, p.2 tog., pass k. st. over method.
TO MAKE UP. Sew border to edge of shawl, forming corners by joining the pointed edges of 2 patts. tog. Join cast-on and cast-off edges tog.

Raglan Cardigan

See photograph on page 54.

MATERIALS: 4 (4) balls of Villawool 3 ply Baby Wool in main colour (m) and 1 ball of contrast colour (c); a pair of Nos. 10 and 12 needles; 5 buttons.
MEASUREMENTS: To fit 18 (20) in. [45.72 (50.80) cm] chest. Length, 10 (11) ins. [25.40 (27.94) cm]. Sleeve, 6 (6¾) ins. [15.24 (17.14) cm].
TENSION: 8 sts. to 1 inch [2.54 cm].
ABBREVIATIONS: See page 13.

TO MAKE:
BACK. With No. 12 needles and m. cast on 82 (90) sts. and work in k.1, p.1 rib for 1 in. [2.54 cm], inc. 1 st. at end of last row. (83, 91 sts.). Change to No. 10 needles and, beg. k. row, work 4 rows in st. st.
Join in c. and work in two-colour patt.:
1st row. With c., k.1, (sl.1, k.3) to last 2 sts., sl.1, k.1.
2nd row. With c., p.1, (sl.1, p.3) to last 2 sts., sl.1, p.1.
3rd row. With c., k.
4th row. With c., p.
5th row. With m., k.3, (sl.1, k.3) to last 4 sts., sl.1, k.3.
6th row. With m., p.3, (sl.1, p.3) to last 4 sts., sl.1, p.3.
7th row. With m., k.
8th row. With m., p.
Rep. above 8 rows once. Break off c. and cont. with m. only.
Cont. in st. st. until work measures 5 (5½) ins. [12.70 (13.97) cm], ending on p. row.
Shape raglan. Cast off 4 sts. at beg. of next 2 rows.
Next row. K.1, p.3 tog., k. to last 4 sts., p.3 tog., k.1.
Next row. P.
Rep. above 2 rows until 55 (59) sts. rem., ending on p. row.
Next row. K.1, p.2 tog., k. to last 3 sts., p.2 tog., k.1.
Next row. P.
Rep. above 2 rows until 29 (31) sts. rem., then cast off.
RIGHT FRONT. With No. 12 needles and m. cast on 42 (46) sts. and work in k.1, p.1 rib for 1 in. [2.54 cm], inc. 1 st. at end of last row (43, 47 sts.). Change to No. 10 needles and, beg. k. row, work 4 rows in st. st. Join in c. and rep. the

Shawl is worked in two sections—centre part in double moss stitch and edging in an easy lacy design which forms picot edging.

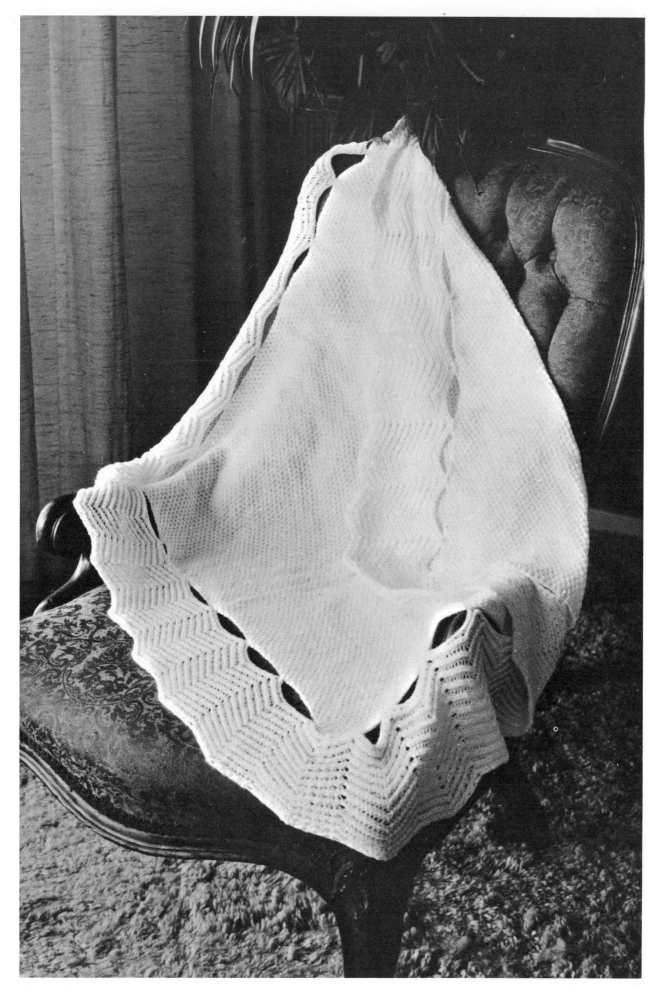

V-neck raglan cardigan is knitted in stocking stitch with contrast patterning and k.1, p.1 rib edgings (see page 52 for instructions).

Mix and match outfit consists of jumper, tunic top, shorts and trousers. Jumper and tunic top are knitted in stocking stitch with a blackberry stitch centre panel, whilst pants and trousers are knitted in stocking stitch (see page 64 for instructions).

Above: *Raglan cardigan is knitted in stocking stitch in a button-up style. Optional Soldier Boy motif in Knitting Stitch is given on Left Front (see page 66 for instructions).*

Left: *Striped boucle dress is knitted in stocking stitch with k.1, p.1 rib trim. Dress is fastened on shoulder (see page 67 for instructions).*

Page 56: *Dress is knitted in stocking stitch in a contrast diagonal design. Lower edge is hemmed, and neck and armbands are worked in k.1, p.1 rib. Back is opened and fastened with press studs (see page 65 for instructions).*

Page 57: *Boy's cardigan suit is knitted in stocking stitch with k.1, p.1 rib edgings. If required, cardigan can be knitted separately with the buttonhole band reversed for a girl (see page 61 for instructions).*

8 patt. rows as given for Back, twice. Break off c. and cont. with m. only until work measures same as Back to beg. of armhole shaping, ending at side edge.

Shape raglan and V neck. Next row. Cast off 4 sts., work to last 2 sts., dec. **.

Next row. K. to last 4 sts., p.3 tog., k.1.

Cont. to dec. at raglan edge on every alt. row as above, at the same time, dec. 1 st. at front edge on every foll. 3rd row 14 times altog., at the same time, when 5 (7) raglan decs. have been made, cont. to dec. 1 st. only at raglan edge thus:

Next row. K. to last 3 sts., p.2 tog., k.1.

When 2 sts. rem. in raglan shaping k.2 tog. and fasten off.

LEFT FRONT. Work as given for Right Front to **. Work 1 row.

Next row. K.1, p.3 tog., k. to end.

Now cont. to correspond with Right Front and when 5 (6) raglan decs. have been made, cont. to dec. 1 st. only at raglan edge thus:

Next row. K.1, p.2 tog., k. to end.

SLEEVES. With No. 12 needles and m. cast on 50 (54) sts. and work in k.1, p.1 rib for 1 in. [2.54 cm], inc. 1 st. at end of last row. (51, 55 sts.). Change to No. 10 needles and, beg. k. row, work 4 rows in st. st. Join in c. and rep. the 8 patt. rows, as given for Back, twice. Break off c. and cont. with m. only, inc. 1 st. each end of next row and every foll. 8th row to 61 (67) sts.

Cont. straight until work measures 6 (6¾) ins. [15.24 (17.14) cm], ending on p. row.

Cast off 4 sts. at beg. of next 2 rows.

Next row. K.1, p.3 tog., k. to last 4 sts., p.3 tog., k.1.

Next row. P.

Rep. above 2 rows until 33 (35) sts. rem., ending on p. row.

Next row. K.1, p.2 tog., k. to last 3 sts., p.2 tog., k.1.

Next row. P.

Rep. above 2 rows until 7 sts. rem., then cast off.

TO MAKE UP. Press work on the wrong side. Join raglan, side and sleeve seams. Press seams.

FRONT BAND (worked in one piece). With No. 12 needles and m. cast on 8 sts. and work in k.1, p.1 rib until band fits left front edge to beg. of V shaping. Mark positions for five buttonholes on this band—the first at ¼ in. [.63 cm] from beg. and the fifth at beg. of V, evenly spacing the others in between. Cont. in rib until band fits around entire front edge, making buttonholes on other side to correspond with markers thus:

Buttonhole row. Rib 3, y.fwd., k.2 tog., rib to end.

When band is completed, cast off ribwise.

TO FINISH OFF. Attach band to garment. Sew on buttons.

3
Knitting for Toddlers

Boy's Suit

See photograph on page 57.

MATERIALS:

Pants—4 (4) balls of Villawool Superknit DC8; a pair of Nos. 8 and 10 needles; a narrow length of elastic.

Cardigan—6 (7) balls of Villawool Superknit DC8; a pair of Nos. 8 and 10 needles; 4 buttons.

MEASUREMENTS:

Pants—Length at centre front, 8 (8½) ins. [20.32 (21.59) cm]

Cardigan—To fit 22 (24) in. [55.88 (60.96) cm] chest. Length, 12 (13½) ins. [30.48 (34.29) cm]. Sleeve, 8 (9) ins. [20.32 (22.86) cm].

TENSION: 23 sts. to 4 inches [10.16 cm].

ABBREVIATIONS: See page 13.

TO MAKE:

PANTS

RIGHT LEG. With No. 10 needles cast on 64 (68) sts. and work in k.1, p.1 rib for 6 rows.

Change to No. 8 needles and cont. in st. st., inc. 1 st. each end of 3rd row, then every foll. row to 72 (76) sts.

Work 4 rows straight, ending on p. row. Place a marker at end of last row to denote front edge (**Note:** When working Left Leg, place marker at beg. of row). Dec. 1 st. each end of next and every foll. 4th row until 64 (70) sts. rem., then dec. 1 st. at back edge only on every 4th row until 60 (64) sts. rem.

Cont. straight until front edge measures 6½ (7) ins. [16.51 (17.78) cm] from marker, ending on k. row. (**Note:** When working Left Leg end on p. row).

Shape back. Next 2 rows. Work 30 (32), turn and work to end.

Next 2 rows. Work 24 (26), turn and work to end.

Next 2 rows. Work 18 (20), turn and work to end.

Next 2 rows. Work 12 (14), turn and work to end.

Next 2 rows. Work 6 (8), turn and work to end.

Change to No. 10 needles and work in k.1, p.1 rib for 3 rows.

Next (elastic hole) row. (K.1, p.1, y.o.n., k.2 tog.) to end. Work 5 more rows in k.1, p.1 rib, then cast off ribwise.

LEFT LEG. Work as given for Right Leg.

TO MAKE UP. Press work on the wrong side. Join inner leg seams, then join two legs tog. from front to back waist. Press seams. Thread elastic through holes at waist.

CARDIGAN

BACK. With No. 10 needles cast on 66 (72) sts. and work in k.1, p.1 rib for 1½ ins. [3.81 cm]. change to No. 8 needles and st. st. and cont. until work measures 8 (8½) ins. [20.32 (21.59) cm], ending on p. row.

Shape raglan. Cast off 6 sts. at beg. of next 2 rows, then dec. 1 st. each end of next row and every foll. alt. row until 20 (22) sts. rem. Cast off.

RIGHT FRONT. With No. 10 needles cast on 30 (36) sts. and work in k.1, p.1 rib for 1½ ins. [3.81 cm]. Change to No. 8 needles and st. st. and cont. until work measures same as Back to armhole, ending at side edge.

Shape raglan and V Front. Cast off 6 sts. at beg. of next row. Dec. 1 st. at raglan edge on alt. rows to correspond with Back, at the same time, dec. 1 st. at front edge on next and every foll. 3rd row until 10 (6) sts. rem. Cont. to dec. at raglan edge only until 2 sts. rem. K.2 tog. and fasten off.

LEFT FRONT. Work as given for Right Front.

SLEEVES. With No. 10 needles cast on 30 sts. and work in k.1, p.1 rib for 1½ ins. [3.81 cm]. Change to No. 8 needles and st. st. and cont., inc. 1 st. each end of every 4th row to 52 (56) sts., then cont. straight until work measures 8 (9) ins. [20.32 (22.86) cm] (or length required), ending on p. row.

Cast off 6 sts. at beg. of next 2 rows, then dec. 1 st. each end of next row and every foll. alt. row until 6 sts. rem. Cast off.

POCKET (2). With No. 8 needles cast on 18 sts. and work in st. st. for 2 ins. [5.08 cm]. Change to No. 10 needles and work in k.1, p.1 rib for 1 in. [2.54 cm], then cast off ribwise.

TO MAKE UP. Press work on the wrong side. Join raglan, side and sleeve seams. Press seams. Attach a pocket to each front, above ribbing, as pictured.

FRONT BAND (worked in one piece). With No. 10 needles cast on 8 sts. and work in k.1, p.1 rib for ½ in. [1.27 cm].

Next (buttonhole) row. Rib 3, cast off 2, rib 3.

Next row. Rib and cast on 2 sts. over those cast off in previous row.

Cont. in rib and rep. buttonhole row at 2½ in. [6.35 cm] intervals until 4 buttonholes have been worked, then cont. straight until band fits around entire front edge, slightly stretched. Cast off ribwise.

TO FINISH OFF. Placing buttonhole section to Left Front, attach band to garment. Sew on buttons.

Jumper

MATERIALS: Villawool Boucle Double Knitting—
V neck sleeveless style—5 (6, 7) balls.
V neck style with short sleeves—6 (7, 8) balls.
V neck style with long sleeves—7 (8, 9) balls.
Crew neck style with short sleeves—6 (7, 8) balls.
Crew neck style with long sleeves—7 (8, 9) balls.
Polo neck style with long sleeves—7 (8, 9) balls.
A pair of Nos. 8 and 10 needles.
MEASUREMENTS: To fit 20 (22, 24) in. [50.80 (55.88, 60.96) cm] chest. Length, 10 (11½, 13) ins. [25.40 (29.21, 33.02) cm]. Short sleeve, 1½ (2, 2½) ins. [3.81 (5.08, 6.35) cm]. Long sleeve, 7½ (9, 10½) ins. [19.05 (22.86, 26.67) cm] (or length required).
TENSION: 6 sts. to 1 inch [2.54 cm].
ABBREVIATIONS: See page 13.

TO MAKE:
BACK (All Styles). With No. 10 needles cast on 66 (72, 78) sts. and work in k.1, p.1 rib for 1 (1, 1½) ins. [2.54 (2.54, 3.81) cm]. Change to No. 8 needles and cont. in st. st. until work measures 6 (7, 8) ins. [15.24 (17.78, 20.32) cm], ending on p. row.
Shape armholes. Cast off 3 sts. at beg. of next 2 rows **, then dec. 1 st. each end of next row and every foll. alt. row until 48 (52, 56) sts. rem., then cont. straight until work measures 4 (4½, 5) ins. [10.16 (11.43, 12.70) cm] from beg. of armhole shaping, ending on p. row.
Shape shoulders. Cast off 7 (7, 8) sts. at beg. of next 2 rows, then 7 (8, 8) sts. at beg. of foll. 2 rows. Leave rem. 20 (22, 24) sts. on a holder.
FRONT—CREW OR POLO NECK STYLE. Work as given for Back until armholes measure 2½ (3, 3½) ins. [6.35 (7.62, 8.89) cm], ending p. row.
Shape neck. Next row. K. 18 (19, 20) sts., turn and cont. on these sts. only. Dec. 1 st. at neck edge of next and foll. alt. rows until 14 (15, 16) sts. rem., then cont. straight until armhole measures same as back armhole, ending at side edge.
Shape shoulder. Cast off 7 (7, 8) sts. at beg. of next row. Work 1 row, then cast off rem. sts.
Return to rem. sts. Sl. centre 12 (14, 16) sts. on a holder.
Rejoin yarn to inner end of rem. sts. and cont. to correspond with other side.
FRONT—V NECK STYLE. Work as given for Back to **
Shape neck. Next row. K.2 tog., k. 28 (31, 34) sts., turn and cont. on these sts. only. Dec. 1 st. at armhole edge of alt. rows 6 (7, 8) times more, at the same time, dec. 1 st. at neck edge of next and every foll. 3rd row until 14 (15, 16) sts.

rem., then cont. straight until armhole measures same as back armhole, ending at side edge.
Shape shoulder. Cast off 7 (7, 8) sts. at beg. of next row. Work 1 row, then cast off rem. sts.
Return to rem. sts. Rejoin yarn to inner end and cont. to correspond with other side.

SHORT SLEEVES. With No. 10 needles cast on 48 (48, 54) sts. and work in k.1, p.1 rib for 1 in. [2.54 cm]. Change to No. 8 needles and cont. in st. st. until work measures 1½ (2, 2½) ins. [3.81 (5.08, 6.35) cm], ending p. row.
*Cast off 3 sts. at beg. of next 2 rows. Dec. 1 st. each end of every foll. row until 32 (36, 40) sts. rem., then dec. 1 st. at beg. of every foll. row until 14 sts. rem. Cast off. *

LONG SLEEVES. With No. 10 needles cast on 30 (30, 36) sts. and work in k.1, p.1 rib for 1½ ins. [3.81 cm]. Change to No. 8 needles and cont. in st. st., inc. 1 st. each end of every foll. 4th row to 48 (48, 54) sts., then cont. straight until work measures 7½ (9, 10½) ins. [19.05 (22.86, 26.67) cm] (or length required), ending p. row. Now work from * to * as given for Short Sleeves.

CREW NECKBAND. Firstly, join right shoulder seam. R.s.f. and with No. 10 needles, pick up and k. 16 sts. down left side of neck, k. across centre sts., pick up and k. 16 sts. up right side of neck, then k. across back sts. (64, 68, 72 sts.). Work in k.1, p.1 rib for 1 in., then cast off ribwise.

POLO COLLAR. Work as given for Crew Neckband, working a further 2 (2, 2½) ins. [5.08 (5.08, 6.35) cm] in k.1, p.1 rib, then cast off ribwise.

V NECKBAND. Firstly, join right shoulder seam. R.s.f. and with No. 10 needles, pick up and k. 34 (38, 42) sts. down left side of neck, 1 centre st., pick up and k.33 (37, 41) up right side of neck, then k. across back sts. (88, 98, 108 sts.). Work in k.1, p.1 rib for 1 in. [2.54 cm], dec. 1 st. either side of centre V st. on every row thus: k.2 tog. t.b.l., work centre st., k.2 tog. Cast off ribwise.

ARMBANDS—SLEEVELESS STYLE. Join left shoulder seam, then neckband seam. R.s.f. with No. 10 needles pick up and k. 68 (74, 80) sts. evenly around entire armhole. Work in k.1, p.1 rib for 1 in. [2.54 cm], then cast off ribwise.

TO MAKE UP. Press work on the wrong side. For all styles except sleeveless sweater, join rem. shoulder seam and neckband. Join side and sleeve seams. Set in sleeves. For sleeveless style, join side and armband seams. Press all seams.

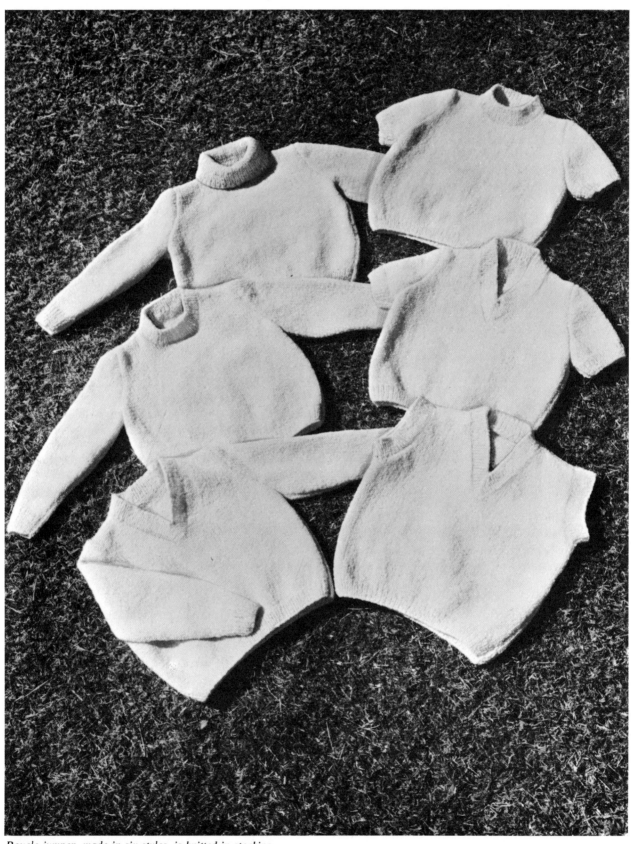

Boucle jumper, made in six styles, is knitted in stocking stitch with k.1, p.1 rib edgings.

Mix and Match Outfit

See photograph on page 55.

MATERIALS:

Jumper—5 (6) balls of Villawool Superknit 5 ply Crepe; a pair of Nos. 10 and 12 needles; a No. 3.00 crochet hook; 2 buttons.

Tunic—6 (7) balls of Villawool Superknit 5 ply Crepe; a pair of Nos. 10 and 11 needles; a No. 3.00 crochet hook; 2 buttons.

Shorts—3 (4) balls of Villawool Superknit 5 ply Crepe; a pair of Nos. 10 and 12 needles; a waist length of 1 inch [2.54 cm] wide elastic.

Trousers—8 (9) balls of Villawool Superknit 5 ply Crepe; a pair of Nos. 10 and 12 needles; a waist length of 1 inch [2.54 cm] wide elastic.

MEASUREMENTS:

Jumper—To fit 22 (24) in. [55.88 (60.96) cm] chest. Length, 12½ (14) ins. [31.75 (35.56) cm]. Sleeve, 2 (2½) ins. [5.08 (6.35) cm].

Tunic—To fit 22 (24) in. [55.88 (60.96) cm] chest. Length, 15½ (17) ins. [39.37 (43.18) cm]. Sleeve, 2 (2½) ins. [5.08 (6.35) cm].

Shorts—Length, 8½ (9½) ins. [21.59 (24.13) cm].

Trousers—Length, 19 (21) ins. [48.26 (53.34) cm].

TENSION: 7 sts. to 1 inch [2.54 cm] over st. st.

ABBREVIATIONS: See page 13.

TO MAKE:

JUMPER

BACK. With No. 12 needles cast on 82 (90) sts. and work in k.1, p.1 rib for 1 in. [2.54 cm], inc. 1 st. at end of last row (83, 91 sts.). Change to No. 10 needles and cont. in st. st. with blackberry st. centre panel:

1st row. K.27 (31), p.29, k. to end.

2nd row. P.27 (31), * (k.1, p.1, k.1) into next st., p.3 tog.; rep. from * 6 times, (k.1, p.1, k.1) into next st., p. to end.

3rd row. K.27 (31), p.31, k. to end.

4th row. P.27 (31), * p.3 tog., (k.1, p.1, k.1) into next st.; rep. from * 6 times, p.3 tog., p. to end.

Rep. above 4 rows until work measures 8 (9) ins. [20.32 (22.86) cm], ending on wrong side.

Shape armholes. Cont. in patt. and cast off 3 (4) sts. at beg. of next 2 rows, then dec. 1 st. each end of next row and foll. alt. rows until 65 (71) sts. rem. Cont. straight until armholes measure 4½ (5) ins. [11.43 (12.70) cm], ending on wrong side.

Shape shoulders. Cast off 7 sts. at beg. of next 2 rows, then 7 (8) sts. at beg. of foll. 4 rows. Leave rem. 23 (25) sts. on a holder.

FRONT. Work as given for Back until armholes measure 3 (3½) ins. [7.62 (8.89) cm], ending on wrong side.

Shape neck. Next row. Patt. 25 (27) sts., turn and cont. on these sts. only. Dec. 1 st. at neck edge of every foll. alt. row until 21 (23) sts. rem., then cont. straight until armhole measures same as back armhole, ending at side edge.

Shape shoulder. Cast off 7 sts. at beg. of next row, then 7 (8) sts. at beg. of foll. 2 alt. rows.

Return to rem. sts. Sl. centre 15 (17) sts. on a holder. Rejoin yarn to inner end of rem. sts. and cont. to correspond with other side.

SLEEVES. With No. 12 needles cast on 46 (52) sts. and work in k.1, p.1 for 6 rows. Change to No. 10 needles and st. st., inc. 1 st. each end of next row and every foll. 4th row to 54 (60) sts., then cont. straight until work measures 2 (2½) ins. [5.08 (6.35) cm], ending on p. row.

Cast off 3 (4) sts. at beg. of next 2 rows, Dec. 1 st. each end of every foll. row until 38 (42) sts. rem., then dec. 1 st. at beg. only of every foll. row until 20 (24) sts. rem. Cast off.

NECKBAND. Firstly, join right shoulder seam. R.s.f. with No. 12 needles, pick up and k. 18 sts. down left side of neck, k. across centre front sts., pick up and k. 18 sts. up right side of neck, then k. across sts. at back neck (74, 78 sts.). Work in k.1, p.1 rib for ½ inch [1.27 cm], then cast off ribwise.

TO MAKE UP. Press work on the wrong side. Join rem. shoulder seam ½ inch [1.27 cm] from armhole edge. Join side and sleeve seams. Set in sleeves. Press seams.

Crochet edging—R.s.f. and with No. 3.00 crochet hook, work 2 rows of d.c. along left back shoulder and 1 row of d.c. along left front shoulder, turn and work 2nd row, making 2 button loops along row. Fasten off. Sew on buttons.

TUNIC

BACK. With No. 11 needles cast on 83 (91) sts., and, beg. k. row, work 5 rows in st. st.

Next (picot) row. (K.2 tog., y.fwd.) to last st., k.1. Change to No. 10 needles and, beg. p. row, cont. in st. st. until work measures 2 ins. [5.08 cm] from picot row, ending on p. row. Now cont. in 4-row patt. as given for back of Jumper until work measures 11 (12) ins. [27.94 (30.48) cm] from picot row, ending on wrong side.

Shape armholes. Work as given for this section of Jumper to end.

FRONT. Work as given for Back until work measures same as Back to beg. of armhole shaping, ending on wrong side.

Shape armholes. Work as given for this section of Jumper to end.

SLEEVES. With No. 11 needles cast on 47 (53) sts. and, beg. k. row, work 5 rows in st. st., then rep. picot row as given for Back.

Change to No. 10 needles and, beg. p. row, cont. in st. st., inc. 1 st. each end of next row and every foll. 4th row to 55 (61) sts., then cont. straight until work measures 2 (2½) ins. [5.08 (6.35) cm] from picot row, ending p. row.

Cast off 3 (4) sts. at beg. of next 2 rows. Dec. 1 st. each end of every foll. row until 39 (43) sts. rem., then dec. 1 st. at beg. only of every foll. row until 21 (25) sts. rem. Cast off.

Cast off 3 (4) sts. at beg. of next 2 rows, then cast off 3 sts. at beg. of every row until 7 (11) sts. rem. Work 1 row, then cast off rem. sts.

NECKBAND. Work as given for this section of Jumper.

TO MAKE UP. Press work on the wrong side. Join rem. shoulder seam ½ in. from armhole edge. Join side and sleeve seams. Set in sleeves. Turn hems at lower and sleeve edges to inside and st. into position. Press seams and hems.

Crochet edging. Work as given for this section of Jumper.

SHORTS

RIGHT LEG. With No. 12 needles cast on 94 (98) sts. and work in k.1, p.1 rib for 4 rows. Change to No. 10 needles.

Next row. K.23 (24), sl.1 p.wise, k.46 (48), sl.1 p.wise, k. to end.

2nd row. P.

Rep. above 2 rows until work measures 1½ (2) ins. [3.81 (5.08) cm], ending on k. row.

Shape crutch. Keeping "crease" as set, cast off 2 sts. at beg. of next 2 rows, then dec. 1 st. each end of every foll. 4th row until 70 (74) sts. rem., then cont. straight until work measures 7 (7½) ins. [17.78 (19.05) cm] from beg. of crutch shaping, ending on k. row and inc. 1 st. at beg. of last row. (71, 75 sts.).

Shape back. Next row. P.40 (42), turn.

Next row. Sl.1, k. to end.

Next row. P.32 (34), turn.

Next row. Sl.1, k. to end.

Next row. P.24 (26), turn.

Next row. Sl.1, k. to end.

Next row. P.16 (18), turn.

Next row. Sl.1, k. to end.

Next row. P. across all sts.

Change to No. 12 needles and work in k.1, p.1 rib for 1 in. [2.54 cm], then cast off ribwise.

LEFT LEG. Work as given for Right Leg, reversing shapings.

TO MAKE UP. Press work on the wrong side. Join centre back and front seams, then join leg seams. Press seams. Encase elastic to inside waist ribbing with a herringbone stitch.

TROUSERS

RIGHT LEG. With No. 12 needles cast on 85 (89) sts. and, beg. p. row, work 9 rows in st. st.

Next (picot) row. (K.2 tog., y.fwd.) to last st., k.1.

Change to No. 10 needles and, beg. p. row, work 10 rows in st. st., inc. 1 st. at end of last row (86, 90 sts.). Cont. in st. st. and inc. 1 st. each end of 2nd row and every foll. 10th (12th) row to 94 (98) sts., then cont. straight until work measures 12 (13½) ins. [30.48 (34.29) cm] from picot row, ending on k. row.

Shape crutch. Omitting "crease" work as given for this section of Shorts to end.

LEFT LEG. Work as given for Right Leg, reversing shapings.

TO MAKE UP. Press work on the wrong side. Join centre back and front seams, then join leg seams. Turn hems at lower edges to inside and st. into position. Press seams and hems. Encase elastic to inside waist ribbing with a herringbone stitch.

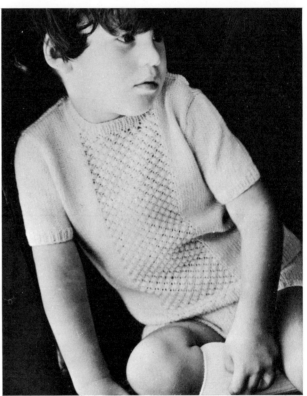

Boy's version of shorts and jumper.

Dress in Diagonal Stripe Design

See photograph on page 56.

MATERIALS: 3 (3, 4) balls of Villawool Super-knit 4 ply Crepe in main colour (m) and 4 (4, 5) balls of contrast colour (c); a pair of Nos. 10 and 12 needles; 4 press studs.

MEASUREMENTS: To fit 20 (22, 24) in. [50.80 (55.88, 60.96) cm] chest. Length, 15 (16¼, 17¾) ins. [38.10 (41.27, 45.08) cm].

TENSION: 15 sts. to 2 inches [5.08 cm].

ABBREVIATIONS: See page 13.

NOTE: When changing colours, twist yarns around each other to avoid a gap.

TO MAKE:

BACK. With No. 10 needles and c. cast on 94 (102, 110) sts. and, beg. k. row, work 9 rows in st. st. K. next row to form hemline.

Beg. k. row, work 6 (8, 10) rows in st. st., then cont. in diagonal stripe patt. as follows: **

1st row. K. to last st., join in m. and k.1 m.

2nd row. With m. p.1, then with c., p. to end.

Now cont. in st. st., working 1 st. less in c. and 1 st. more in m. on every k. row until 14 rows have been worked from hemline, then dec. 1 st. each end of next row and every foll. 12th row until 80 (88, 96) sts. rem. Cont. straight until work measures 10½ (11½, 12½) ins. [26.67 (29.21, 31.75) cm] from hemline, ending on p. row.

Shape armholes. Keeping diagonal patt. as set, cast off 4 (5, 6) sts. at beg. of next 2 rows, then dec. 1 st. each end of next row and every foll. alt. row until 64 (70, 76) sts. rem., ending p. row.

Divide for back opening. Next row. Work 34 (37, 40) sts., turn and cont. on these sts. only. Cont., keeping centre back 4 sts. in garter st. throughout, until armhole measures 4½ (4¾, 5¼) ins. [11.43 (12.06, 13.33) cm], ending at side edge.

Shape shoulder. Cast off 8 (9, 10) sts. at beg. of next row and foll. alt. row. Leave rem. 18 (19, 20) sts. on a holder.

Return to rem. sts. Join m. to inner end and cast on 4 sts.

Cont. to correspond with other side, keeping centre back 4 sts. in garter st. throughout.

FRONT. Work as given for Back to **. Join in m.

1st row. With m. k.1, then with c., k. to end.

2nd row. With c. p. to last st., with m. p.1.

Now cont. in st. st. as given for Back, keeping diagonal stripe patt. which is reversed in order, until armholes measure 3 (3¼, 3¾) ins. [7.62 (8.25, 9.52) cm], ending on a p. row.

Shape neck. Next row. K. 27 (29, 31) sts., turn and cont. on these sts. only. Dec. 1 st. at neck edge of every foll. row until 16 (18, 20) sts. rem., then cont. straight until armhole measures same as back armhole, ending at side edge.

Shape shoulder. Cast off 8 (9, 10) sts. at beg. of next row and foll. alt. row. Fasten off.

Return to rem. sts. Sl. centre 10 (12, 14) sts. on a holder.

Rejoin yarn to inner end of rem. sts. and cont. to correspond with other side.

POCKET (make two—one in each colour). With No. 10 needles cast on 23 sts. and work in st. st. for 3 ins. [7.62 cm], ending on k. row. K. next row to form hemline. Beg. k. row, work 4 more rows in st. st., then cast off.

NECKBAND. Firstly, join shoulder seams. R.s.f. and with No. 12 needles and m., k. across sts. on holder at left side of back neck, pick up and k. 18 sts. down left side of front neck, k. across centre front sts., pick up and k. 18 sts. up right side of neck, then k. across sts. at back neck (82, 86, 90 sts.).

Keeping centre back garter st. borders as set, work in k.1, p.1 rib for 8 rows, then cast off ribwise.

ARMBANDS. R.s.f., with No. 12 needles and m., pick up and k. 74 (80, 86) sts. evenly around left armhole edge. Work 9 rows in k.1, p.1 rib, then cast off ribwise.

With c., work right armhole in the same way.

TO MAKE UP. Press work on the wrong side. Join side seams and armbands. Turn hems at lower edge and pocket edges to inside and stitch into position. Making a 1-st. hem around raw edges of pockets, sew pockets to garment, placing c. pocket on m. part of garment, and m. pocket on c. part of garment as pictured. Sew press studs to back opening, securing flap at beg. of opening. Press seams and hems.

Raglan Cardigan with Embroidery Trim

See photograph on page 58.

MATERIALS: 10 balls of Villawool Superknit DC8 for the cardigan.

Soldier Boy embroidery: 1 ball each of the same yarn in black, white, red, gold and a length of blue for the eyes.

A pair of Nos. 8 and 10 needles; 5 buttons, a tapestry needle.

MEASUREMENTS: To fit 20/21 in. [50.80/53.34 cm] chest. Length, 10½ ins. [26.67 cm]. Sleeve, 8 ins. [20.32 cm] (or length required).

TENSION: 23 sts. to 4 inches [10.16 cm].

ABBREVIATIONS: See page 13.

TO MAKE:

BACK. With No. 10 needles cast on 66 sts. and work in k.1, p.1 rib for 1½ ins. [3.81 cm]. Change to No. 8 needles and st. st. and cont. until work measures 6 ins. [15.24 cm], ending p. row.

Shape raglan. Cast off 6 sts. at beg. of next 2 rows, then dec. 1 st. each end of next and every foll. alt. row until 20 sts. rem. Leave sts. on holder.

RIGHT FRONT. With No. 10 needles cast on 30 sts. and work in k.1, p.1 rib for 1½ ins. [3.81 cm]. Change to No. 8 needles and st. st. and cont. until work measures same as Back to raglan shaping, ending at side edge.

Shape raglan. Cast off 6 sts. at beg. of next row, then dec. 1 st. at same edge of every foll. alt. row until 12 sts. rem., ending at neck edge.

Shape neck. Dec. 1 st. at beg. of next and every foll. alt. row, at the same time, cont. to dec. at raglan edge as set, until 2 sts. rem. K.2 tog. and fasten off.

LEFT FRONT. Work as given for Right Front.

SLEEVES. With No. 10 needles cast on 30 sts. and work in k.1, p.1 rib for 1½ ins. [3.81 cm]. Change to No. 8 needles and st. st., inc. 1 st. each end of every foll. 4th row to 52 sts. Cont. straight until work measures 8 ins. [20.32 cm] (or length required), ending p. row.

Cast off 6 sts. at beg. of next 2 rows, then dec. 1 st. each end of next row and every foll. alt. row until 6 sts. rem. Leave sts. on holder.

NECKBAND. Firstly, join raglan seams. R.s.f. and with No. 10 needles pick up and k. 12 sts. up right side of neck, k. across 6 sts. of one sleeve, 20 sts. of back and 6 sts. of second sleeve, then pick up and k. 12 sts. down left side of neck (56 sts.).

Work in k.1, p.1 rib for 1 in. [2.54 cm], then cast off ribwise.

TO MAKE UP. Press work on the wrong side. Join side and sleeve seams. Press seams.

BUTTON BAND. With No. 10 needles cast on 8 sts. and work in k.1, p.1 rib until band fits along front edge, slightly stretched, then cast off ribwise.

Mark positions for five buttons on this band— the first ½ in. [1.27 cm] from beg. and the fifth at neck edge, evenly spacing the others in between.

BUTTONHOLE BAND. Work as given for Button Band, making buttonholes to correspond with markers as follows:

Buttonhole row. Rib 3, cast off 2, rib 3.

Next row. In rib, casting on 2 sts. over those cast off in previous row.

TO FINISH OFF. Attach bands to their respective fronts (buttonhole section to Right Front for a girl or Left Front for a boy). Sew on buttons.

EMBROIDERY: With tapestry needle and using a Knitting Stitch (see page 25), embroider design from chart on Left Front as pictured.

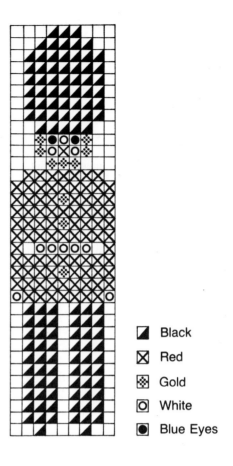

- ◹ Black
- ⊠ Red
- ▦ Gold
- ◯ White
- ◉ Blue Eyes

Striped Dress

See photograph on page 58.

MATERIALS: 5 (6) balls of Villawool Boucle Double Knitting in main colour (m); 4 (4) balls of 1st contrast colour (1st c.) and 2 (3) balls of 2nd contrast colour (2nd c.); a pair of Nos. 8, 9 and 10 needles; 3 buttons.

MEASUREMENTS: To fit 22 (24) in. [55.88 (60.96) cm] chest. Length, 17 (18½) ins. [43.18 (46.99) cm]. Sleeve, 9 (10½) ins. [22.86 (26.67) cm]. chest. Length, 9¾ ins. [24.76 cm]. Sleeve, 6 ins. [15.24 cm].

TENSION: 6 sts. to 1 inch [2.54 cm].

ABBREVIATIONS: See page 13.

TO MAKE:

BACK. With No. 9 needles and m. cast on 90 (96) sts. and k. 10 rows.

Change to No. 8 needles and cont. in st. st., dec. 1 st. each end of next and every foll. 10th row until 80 (86) sts. rem. Cont. straight until work measures 6 (6½) ins. [15.24 (16.51) cm], ending p. row. Now work in k.1, p.1 rib for 8 rows. Break off m. and cont. in st. st. with

1st. c. and 2nd c., working in stripe sequence of 4 rows 1st c. then 2 rows 2nd c. until work measures 12½ (13½) ins. [31.75 (34.29) cm], ending on p. row.

Shape armholes. Cont. in stripe patt. and cast off 4 sts. at beg. of next 2 rows, then dec. 1 st. each end of next and every foll. alt. row until 50 (54) sts. rem. Cont. straight until armholes measure 4½ (5) ins. [11.43 (12.70) cm], ending on p. row.

Shape shoulders. Cast off 8 sts. at beg. of next 2 rows, then 7 (8) sts. at beg. of foll. 2 rows. Leave rem. sts. on holder

FRONT. Work as given for Back until armholes measure 2½ (2¾) ins. [6.35 (6.98) cm], ending on p. row.

Shape neck. Next row. K.20 (21) sts., turn and cont. on these sts. only. Dec. 1 st. at neck edge of next and every foll. alt. row until 15 (16) sts. rem., then cont. straight until armhole measures same as back armhole, ending at side edge.

Shape shoulder. Cast off 8 sts. at beg. of next row. Work 1 row, then cast off rem. sts.

Return to rem. sts. Sl. centre 10 (12) sts. on a holder. Rejoin yarn to inner end of rem. sts. and cont. to correspond with other side.

SLEEVES. With No. 10 needles and m. cast on 40 (42) sts. and work in k.1, p.1 rib for 12 rows. Change to No. 8 needles. Break off m. and join in 1st c. and 2nd c. and cont. in stripe patt. as given for Back, inc. 1 st. each end of every foll. 6th row to 56 (60) sts.

Cont. straight until work measures 9 (10½) ins. [22.86 (26.67) cm] (or length required), ending on p. row.

Cast off 4 sts. at beg. of next 2 rows, then dec. 1 st. each end of next and every foll. alt. row until 30 (32) sts. rem., then dec. 1 st. each end of every row until 14 (16) sts. rem. Cast off.

NECKBAND. Firstly, join right shoulder seam. R.s.f., with No. 10 needles and m. pick up and k. 18 (20) sts. down left side of neck, k. across 10 (12) sts. at centre front, pick up and k. 18 (20) sts. up right side of neck and, finally, k. across sts. at back neck. (66, 74 sts.). Work in k.1, p.1 rib for 6 rows, then cast off ribwise.

TO MAKE UP. With No. 10 needles and m., pick up and k. 20 (21) sts. along front left shoulder and work 2 rows in k.1, p.2 rib.

Next (buttonhole) row. Rib 2, (cast off 2 sts., rib 4) 3 times, rib to end.

Next row. In rib, casting on 2 sts. over those cast off in previous row.

Rib 1 more row, then cast off ribwise.

With No. 10 needles and m., pick up and k. 20 (22) sts. along back shoulder and work 2 rows in k.1, p.1 rib, then cast off ribwise.

Join armhole end of shoulder, overlapping front shoulder on back.

Join side and sleeve seams. Set in sleeves. Sew on buttons. Press seams.

Patterned Cardigan

MATERIALS: 4 balls of Villawool Purple Label Ban-Lon; a pair of No. 7 needles; 4 buttons.
MEASUREMENTS: To fit 20 in. [50.80 cm] chest. Length, 9¾ ins. [24.76 cm]. Sleeve, 6 ins. [15.24 cm] (or length required).
TENSION: 6 sts. to 1 inch [2.54 cm] over patt.
ABBREVIATIONS: See page 13.

TO MAKE:
BACK. With No. 7 needles cast on 65 sts. and k. 6 rows, then cont. in patt. as follows:
1st row. K.
2nd row. K.
3rd row. K.
4th row. K.4, (k.1d., k.7) to last 5 sts., k.1d., k.4.
5th row. K.3, (p.3, k.5) to last 6 sts., p.3, k.3.
6th row. P.2, (k.2 tog., y.fwd., k.1d., y.fwd., sl.1, k.1, p.s.s.o., p.3) to last 7 sts., k.2 tog., y.fwd., k.1d., y.fwd., sl.1, k.1, p.s.s.o., p.2.
7th row. K.2, (p.5, k.3) to last 7 sts., p.5, k.2.
8th row. P.1, (k.2 tog., k.1, y.fwd., k.1d., y.fwd., k.1, sl.1, k.1, p.s.s.o., p.1) to end.
9th row. K.1, (p.7, k.1) to end.
10th row. K.2 tog., (k.2, y.fwd., k.1d., y.fwd., k.2, sl.1, k.2 tog., p.s.s.o.) to last 7 sts., k.2, y.fwd., k.1d, y.fwd., k.2, k.2 tog.
Rep. above 10 rows 4 times more.
Shape armholes. Cont. in patt. and cast off 7 sts. at beg. of next 2 rows, then dec. 1 st. each end of next row (49 sts.). Cont. straight until armholes measure 4 ins. [10.16 cm], ending on wrong side.
Shape shoulders. Cont. in garter st. and cast off 8 sts. at beg. of next 2 rows, then 7 sts. at beg. of foll. 2 rows. Cast off rem. 19 sts.
RIGHT FRONT. With No. 7 needles cast on 40 sts. and k. 6 rows, then cont. in patt. as follows:
1st row. K.
2nd row. K.
3rd row. K.
4th row. K.11, (k.1d., k.7) to last 5 sts., k.1d., k.4.
5th row. K.3, (p.3, k.5) to last 13 sts., p.3, k.10.
6th row. K.7, p.2, (k.2 tog., y.fwd., k.1d., y.fwd., sl.1, k.1, p.s.s.o., p.3) to last 7 sts., k.2 tog., y.fwd., k.1d., y.fwd., sl.1, k.1, p.s.s.o., p.2.
7th row. K.2, (p.5, k.3) to last 14 sts., p.5, k.9.
8th row. K.7, p.1, (k.2 tog., k.1, y.fwd., k.1d., y.fwd., k.1, sl.1, k.1, p.s.s.o., p.1) to end.

Ban-Lon cardigan is knitted in a textured 10-row pattern with collar and edgings in garter stitch.

9th row. K.1, (p.7, k.1) to last 15 sts., p.7, k.8.

10th row. K.7, k.2 tog., (k.2, y.fwd., k.1d., y.fwd., k.2, sl.1, k.2 tog., p.s.s.o.) to last 7 sts., k.2, y.fwd., k.1d., y.fwd., k.2, k.2 tog.

Rep. above 10 rows 3 times more, then first row again.

Next (buttonhole) row. K.3, y.fwd., k.2 tog., k. to end.

Cont. in patt. until work measures same as Back to beg. of armhole shaping, ending at side edge.

Shape armhole. Cont. in patt. and cast off 7 sts. at beg. of next row, then dec. 1 st. at same edge on foll. row (32 sts.). Cont. straight, making another 2 buttonholes at 1¼ in. [3.17 cm] intervals. Cont. straight until armhole measures 3 ins. [7.62 cm], ending at neck edge.

Shape neck. Next row. Cast off 11 sts., k. to end. Cont. in garter st. and cast off 2 sts. at neck edge on alt. rows until 15 sts. rem., then cont. straight until armhole measures same as back armhole, ending at side edge.

Shape shoulder. Cast off 8 sts. at beg. of next row. Work 1 row, then cast off rem. sts.

LEFT FRONT. With No. 7 needles cast on 40 sts. and k. 6 rows, then cont. in patt. as follows:

1st row. K.

2nd row. K.

3rd row. K.

4th row. K.4, (k.1d., k.7) to last 12 sts., k.1d., k.11.

5th row. K.10, (p.3, k.5) to last 6 sts., p.3, k.3.

6th row. P.2, (k.2 tog., y.fwd., k.1d., y.fwd., sl.1, k.1, p.s.s.o., p.3) to last 14 sts., k.2 tog., y.fwd., k.1d., y.fwd., sl.1, k.1, p.s.s.o., p.2, k.7.

7th row. K.9, (p.5, k.3) to last 7 sts., p.5, k.2.

8th row. P.1, (k.2 tog., k.1, y.fwd., k.1d., y.fwd., k.1, sl.1, k.1, p.s.s.o., p.1) to last 15 sts., k.2 tog., k.1, y.fwd., k.1d., y.fwd., k.1, sl.1, k.1, p.s.s.o., p.1, k.7

9th row. K.8, (p.7, k.1) to end.

10th row. K.2 tog., (k.2, y.fwd., k.1d., y.fwd., k.2, sl.1, k.2 tog., p.s.s.o.) to last 14 sts., k.2, y.fwd., k.1d., y.fwd., k.2, k.2 tog., k.7.

Now cont. to correspond with right Front, omitting buttonholes.

SLEEVES. With No. 7 needles cast on 41 sts. and k. 6 rows, then cont. in 10-row patt. as given Back, until work measures 6 ins. [15.24 cm], ending on wrong side.

Cont. in patt. and cast off 7 sts. at beg. of next 2 rows, then dec. 1 st. each end of every foll. row until 16 sts. rem. Cast off 2 sts. at beg. of next 2 rows, then cast off rem. sts.

COLLAR. With No. 7 needles cast on 58 sts. and work in garter st. for 26 rows, then cast off.

TO MAKE UP. Join shoulder, side and sleeve seams. Set in sleeves. Attach cast-off edge of collar to garment, leaving approx. 4 sts. at each outer edge free. Lightly press seams. Sew on buttons.

4
Knitting for Boys and Girls

School Sweater

MATERIALS: 11 (11, 12, 12, 13, 13) balls of Villawool Superknit 5 ply Crepe; a pair of Nos. 10 and 12 needles; a set of 4 double-pointed No. 12 needles.

MEASUREMENTS: To fit 26 (28, 30, 32, 34, 36) in. [66.04 (71.12, 76.20, 81.28, 86.36, 91.44) cm] chest. Length, 16½ (17½, 18½, 19½, 20½, 21½) ins. [41.91 (44.45, 46.99, 49.53, 52.07, 54.61) cm]. Sleeve, 12½ (13½, 14½, 15½, 16½, 17½) ins. [31.75 (34.29, 36.83, 39.37, 41.91, 44.45) cm] (or length required).

TENSION: 7 sts. to 1 inch [2.54 cm].

ABBREVIATIONS: See page 13.

TO MAKE:

BACK. With No. 12 needles cast on 94 (102, 110, 118, 126, 134) sts. and work in k.1, p.1 rib for 2 (2, 2, 3, 3, 3) ins. [5.08 (5.08, 5.08, 7.62, 7.62, 7.62) cm]. Change to No. 10 needles and cont. in st. st. until work measures 10 (10½, 11, 11½, 12, 12½) ins. [25.40 (26.67, 27.94, 29.21, 30.48, 31.75) cm], ending on p. row.

Shape raglan. Cast off 3 (4, 5, 6, 7, 8) sts. at beg. of next 2 rows. **

Next row. K.2, k.2 tog., k. to last 4 sts., k.2 tog. t.b.l., k.2.

Next row. K.2, p. to last 2 sts., k.2.

Rep. above 2 rows until 28 (30, 32, 34, 36, 38) sts. rem. Leave sts. on a holder.

FRONT. Work as given for Back to **.

Shape neck. Next row. K.2, k.2 tog., k.40 (43, 46, 49, 52, 55), turn and cont. on these sts. only. Work as follows:

1st row. P.2 tog., p. to last 2 sts., k.2.

2nd row. K.2, k.2 tog., k. to end.

3rd row. P. to last 2 sts., k.2.

4th row. K.2, k.2 tog., k. to end.

Rep. above 4 rows until 13 (14, 15, 16, 17, 18) decs. at neck edge altog. have been worked, then cont. to dec. at raglan edge only as set until 2 sts. rem. K.2 tog. and fasten off.

Return to sts. on needle.

Rejoin yarn to inner end of rem. sts. and work as follows:

1st row. K. to last 4 sts., k.2 tog. t.b.l., k.2.

2nd row. K.2, p. to last 2 sts., p.2 tog.

3rd row. K. to last 4 sts., k.2 tog. t.b.l., k.2.

4th row. K.2, p. to end.

Now cont. to correspond with other side.

SLEEVES. With No. 12 needles cast on 46 (48, 50, 52, 54, 56) sts. and work in k.1, p.1 rib for 3 ins. [7.62 cm].

Next (inc.) row. Rib 5 (1, 2, 3, 4, 5), (inc., rib 3 (4, 4, 4, 4, 4)) 9 times, inc., rib to end. (56, 58, 60, 62, 64, 66 sts.).

Change to No. 10 needles and cont. in st. st., inc. 1 st. each end of 3rd row, then every foll. 10th (9th, 8th, 7th, 7th, 7th) row to 72 (78, 84, 90, 96, 102) sts.

Cont. straight until work measures 12½ (13½, 14½, 15½, 16½, 17½) ins. [31.75 (34.29, 36.83, 39.37, 41.91, 44.45) cm] (or length required), ending on p. row.

Cast off 3 (4, 5, 6, 7, 8) sts. at beg. of next 2 rows.

Next row. K.2, k.2 tog., k. to last 4 sts., k.2 tog. t.b.l., k.2.

Next row. K.2, p. to last 2 sts., k.2.

Rep. above 2 rows until 6 sts. rem. Leave sts. on holder.

NECKBAND. Firstly, join raglan seams. R.s.f., with set of No. 12 needles, pick up and k. 58 (60, 62, 64, 66, 68) sts. down left side of neck, 1 centre st., pick up and k. 58 (60, 62, 64, 66, 68) sts. up right side of neck, k. across 6 sts. on holder, then sts. at back of neck and, finally, 6 sts. of second sleeve. (157, 163, 169, 175, 181, 187 sts.). Work 6 (6, 8, 8, 10, 10) rounds in k.1, p.1 rib, dec. 1 st. either side of centre V st. on every row thus: k.2 tog. t.b.l., work centre st., k.2 tog. Cast off ribwise.

TO MAKE UP. Press work on the wrong side. Join side and sleeve seams. Press seams.

Basic raglan school sweater is knitted in stocking stitch with k.1, p.1 rib edgings. This sweater can easily be adapted to any specific school stripe colourings.

Fair Isle Sweater

See photograph at right.

MATERIALS: 7 (8, 9, 10) balls of Villawool Superknit DC8 in main colour (m) and 5 (6, 7, 8) balls of contrast colour (c); a pair of Nos. 8 and 10 needles.

MEASUREMENTS: To fit 24 (26, 28, 30) in. [60.96 (66.04, 71.12, 76.20) cm] chest. Length, 15½ (16½, 17½, 18) ins. [39.37 (41.91, 44.45, 45.72) cm]. Sleeve, 11 (12, 13, 14½) ins. [27.94 (30.48, 33.02, 36.83) cm].

TENSION: 6 sts. to 1 inch [2.54 cm].

ABBREVIATIONS: See page 13.

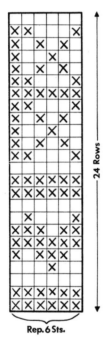

Rep. 6 Sts.

TO MAKE:

BACK. With No. 10 needles and m. cast on 78 (84, 90, 96) sts. and work in k.1, p.1 rib for 2 ins. [5.08 cm]. Change to No. 8 needles and st. st. and work from graph, rep. the 6 sts. and 24 rows inclusive. Cont. straight until work measures 9 (10, 11, 12) ins. [22.86 (25.40, 27.94, 30.48) cm] (or length required), ending on a p. row.

Shape raglans. Keeping Fair Isle patt. in order, cast off 3 sts. at beg. of the next 2 rows, then dec. 1 st. each end of next and foll. alt. rows until 28 (30, 32, 34) sts. rem. Work 1 row, then leave sts. on a holder.

FRONT. Work as given for Back until 48 (50, 52, 54) sts. rem. in raglan shaping, ending on a p. row.

Shape neck. Next row. K.2 tog., work until 17 sts. on needle, turn and cont. on these sts. only. Dec. 1 st. at neck edge on every alt. row 6 times altog., at the same time, cont. shaping raglan until 2 sts. rem. K.2 tog. and fasten off.

Return to sts. on needle. Sl. centre 12 (14, 16, 18) sts. on a holder. Rejoin yarn to inner end of rem. sts. and work to correspond.

SLEEVES. With No. 10 needles and m. cast on 46 (46, 46, 52) sts. and work in k.1, p.1 rib for 4 ins. [10.16 cm]. Change to No. 8 needles and st. st. and work from graph, at the same time, inc. 1 st. each end of the next row, then every 6th (6th, 6th, 8th) row to 58 (62, 66, 70) sts., taking the extra sts. into the patt. where possible.

Cont. straight until work measures 11 (12, 13, 14½) ins. [27.94 (30.48, 33.02, 36.83) cm] (or length required), ending on same patt. row as Back.

Cast off 3 sts. at beg. of next 2 rows, then dec. 1 st. each end of next and foll. alt. rows until 8 sts. rem. Work 1 row, then leave sts. on a holder.

CREW NECK BAND OR POLO COLLAR. Firstly, join 2 front and right back raglan seams. R.s.f., with No. 10 needles and m., k. across sts. at back neck and sleeve, pick up and k.14 (16, 18, 20) sts. down left side of neck, k. across centre sts., pick up and k. 14 (16, 18, 20) sts. up right side of neck, then k. across other sleeve sts. (84, 92, 100, 108 sts.). Work in k.1, p.1 rib for 2 ins. [5.08 cm] (crew neck) or 4½ ins. [11.43 cm] (polo neck), then cast off ribwise.

TO MAKE UP. Press work on the wrong side. Join rem. raglan and neck band seams. Join side and sleeve seams. Fold crew neck band in half to inside and slip st. down. Press seams.

Two-colour Fair Isle sweater is knitted in a 24-row design, features raglan sleeves and k.1, p.1 rib polo collar cuffs and basque.

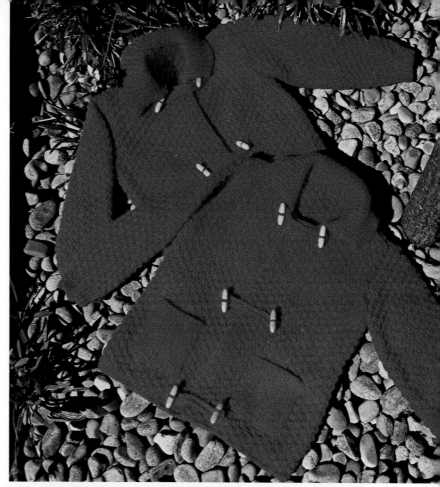

Left: *Sleeveless oversweater is knitted in a 4-row Houndstooth pattern with k.1, p.1 rib edgings (see page 80 for instructions).*

Right: *Duffle coat is knitted in a 4-row pattern with k.1, p.1 ribbed collar, cuffs and pockets. Front is fastened with toggles (see page 79 for instructions).*

Below: *Red, white and blue stripe design sweater is knitted in stocking stitch with k.1, p.1 ribbed basque, cuffs and neckband (see page 81 for instructions).*

His and Hers Duffle Coats

See photograph on page 77.

MATERIALS: 13 (14, 15) balls of Villawool Super Slalom; a pair of Nos. 5 and 7 needles; a No. 5.00 crochet hook; 6 toggles; a press stud.

MEASUREMENTS: To fit 26 (28, 30) in. [66.04 (71.12, 76.20) cm] chest. Length, 18 (19¾, 20½) ins. [45.72 (50.16, 52.07) cm]. Sleeve, 12 (14, 16) ins. [30.48 (35.56, 40.64) cm].

TENSION: 9 sts. to 2 inches [5.08 cm].

ABBREVIATIONS: See page 13.

TO MAKE:

BACK. With No. 5 needles cast on 64 (68, 72) sts. and work in patt.:

1st row. (K.2, p.2) to end.

2nd row. As 1st row.

3rd row. (P.2, k.2) to end.

4th row. As 3rd row.

Rep. above 4 rows until work measures 12½ (13½, 14½) ins. [31.75 (34.29, 36.83) cm].

Shape armholes. Cont. in patt. and cast off 3 sts. at beg. of next 2 rows, then dec. 1 st. each end of next and every foll. alt. row until 50 (52, 54) sts. rem. Cont. straight until armholes measure 5½ (6¼, 7) ins. [13.97 (15.87, 17.78) cm].

Shape shoulders. Cast off 7 sts. at beg. of 2 rows, then 7 (8, 8) sts. at beg. of foll. 2 rows. Cast off rem. 22 (22, 24) sts.

RIGHT FRONT. With No. 5 needles cast on 40 (42, 44) sts. and work in 4-row patt. as given for Back (noting extra 2 patt. sts. on 2nd size) until work measures same as Back to beg. of armhole shaping, ending at side edge.

Shape armhole. Cast off 3 sts. at beg. of next row, then dec. 1 st. at same edge of every foll. alt. row until 33 (34, 35) sts. rem.

Cont. straight until armhole measures 3½ (4¼, 4½) ins. [8.89 (10.79, 11.43) cm], ending at neck edge.

Shape neck. Cast off 10 sts. at beg. of next row, then dec. 1 st. at neck edge of next 6 rows, then at same edge of alt. rows until 14 (15, 15) sts. rem. Cont. straight until armhole measures same as back armhole, ending at side edge.

Shape shoulder. Cast off 7 sts. at beg. of next row. Work 1 row, then cast off rem. sts.

LEFT FRONT. Work as given for right Front.

SLEEVES. With No. 7 needles cast on 36 (40, 40) sts. and work in k.1, p.1 rib for 1½ (2, 2) ins. [3.81 (5.08, 5.08) cm]. Change to No. 5 needles and cont. in patt. as given for Back, inc. 1 st. each end of next row and every foll. 5th row to 54 (58, 62) sts. and including the extra sts. into the patt. as they occur. Cont. straight until work measures 12 (14, 16) ins. [30.48 (35.56, 40.64) cm] (or length required).

Cast off 3 sts. at beg. of next 2 rows, then dec. 1 st. each end of every alt. row until 38 (40, 42) sts. rem., then each end of every row until 18 (20, 22) sts. rem. Cast off 4 sts. at beg. of next 2 rows, then cast off rem. sts.

COLLAR. With No. 7 needles cast on 70 (72, 76) sts. and work in k.1, p.1 rib for 1 in. [2.54 cm]. Change to No. 5 needles and cont. in rib until work measures 3½ (3½, 4) ins. [8.89 (8.89, 10.16) cm], then cast off ribwise.

POCKET (2). With No. 5 needles cast on 24 (26, 28) sts. and work in k.1, p.1 rib for 4 (4½, 4½) ins. [10.16 (11.43, 11.43) cm], then cast off ribwise.

TO MAKE UP. Press patt. lightly on the wrong side. Join shoulder, side and sleeve seams. Set in sleeves. Press seams.

Sew cast-on edge of collar to neck edge, leaving 10 cast-off sts. at each end of neck free. Sew a pocket to each front. With crochet hook and r.s.f. work 1 row of d.c. around front and lower edges of garment.

TOGGLE LOOPS (3). Make 6 ch., join with a sl. st. to form ring, make 20 ch., turn.

Next row. 1 d.c. in 6th ch. from hook, 1 d.c. in each ch. to ring, 6 d.c. into ring and work in d.c. along other side of commencing ch., 6 d.c. into 2nd ring. Fasten off.

TO FINISH OFF. Sew toggles with loop fastenings as pictured to garment, placing Right Front over Left Front for a girl and vice versa for a boy. Sew press stud to neck edge.

Boy's raglan, stocking stitch sweater features contrast stripe design along centre of sleeve and contrast neckband. Sweater can be made with crew neck (as pictured) or polo neck alternative (see page 80 for instructions).

Raglan Sweater with Contrast Trim

See photograph on page 78.

MATERIALS: 12 (13) balls of Villawool Super-knit 5 ply Crepe in main colour (m.) and 1 (1) ball of contrast colour (c.); a pair of Nos. 10 and 12 needles; a set of 4 double-pointed No. 12 needles.

MEASUREMENTS: To fit 28 (30) in. [71.12 (76.20) cm] chest. Length, 18 (19½) ins. [45.72 (49.53) cm]. Sleeve, 14 (16) ins. [35.56 (40.64) cm] (or length required).

TENSION: 7 sts. to 1 inch [2.54 cm].

ABBREVIATIONS: See page 13.

TO MAKE:

BACK. With No. 12 needles and m. cast on 106 (114) sts. and work in k.1, p.1 rib for 2 ins. [5.08 cm]. Change to No. 10 needles and cont. in st. st. until work measures 11½ (12½) ins. [29.21 (31.75) cm], ending p. row.

Shape raglan. Cast off 6 sts. at beg. of next 2 rows.

Next row. K.1, sl.1, k.1, p.s.s.o., k. to last 3 sts., k.2 tog., k.1.

Next row. P.

Rep. above 2 rows until 32 (34) sts. rem., ending p. row. Leave sts. on holder.

FRONT. Work as given for Back until 52 (54) sts. rem. in raglan shaping, ending on p. row.

Shape neck. Next row. K.1, sl.1, k.1, p.s.s.o., k.17 (17) sts., turn and cont. on these sts. only.

Next row. P.

Next row. K.1, sl.1, k.1, p.s.s.o., k. to last 3 sts., sl.1, k.1, p.s.s.o., k.1.

Rep. above 2 rows 6 times more (5 sts.). P. 1 row.

Next row. K.1, sl.1, k.2 tog., p.s.s.o., k.1.

Next row. P.3.

Next row. K.1, sl.1, k.1, p.s.s.o.

Next row. P.2 tog. and fasten off.

Return to rem. sts. Sl. centre 12 (14) sts. on a holder. Rejoin yarn to inner end of rem. sts. and k. to last 3 sts., k.2 tog., k.1.

Next row. P.

Next row. K.1, k.2 tog., k. to last 3 sts., k.2 tog., k.1.

Now cont. to correspond with other side.

SLEEVES. With No. 12 needles and m. cast on 52 (54) sts. and work in k.1, p.1 rib for 2½ ins. [6.35 cm], inc. 1 st. at end of last row (53, 55 sts.).

Change to No. 10 needles. Join in c. in next row.

Next row. K.23 (24) m., k. 7 c., with m. k. to end.

Next row. P.23 (24) m., p. 7 c., with m. p. to end.

Cont. in st. st. with centre c. stripe, twisting colours around each other to avoid a gap, inc. 1 st. each end of every foll. 6th row to 81 (87) sts. Cont. straight until work measures 14 (16) ins. [35.56 (40.64) cm] (or length required), ending p. row.

Cast off 6 sts. at beg. of next 2 rows.

Next row. K.1, sl.1, k.1, p.s.s.o., k. to last 3 sts., k.2 tog., k.1.

Next row. P.

Rep. above 2 rows until 7 sts. rem., ending p. row. Leave sts. on holder.

NECKBAND (Crew or Polo Neck). Firstly, join raglan seams. R.s.f., with set of No. 12 needles and c., k. across sts. of right sleeve, back neck and left sleeve, pick up and k. 18 sts. down left side of neck, k. across sts. at centre front, then pick up and k. 18 sts. up right side of neck. (94, 98 sts.). Work in rounds of k.1, p.1 rib for 2 ins. [5.08 cm] for Crew Neck or 6 ins. [15.24 cm] for Polo Neck, then cast off ribwise.

TO MAKE UP. Press work on the wrong side. Join side and sleeve seams. Fold Crew Neckband in half to inside and sl. st. down. Press seams.

Houndstooth Overpull

See photograph on page 76.

MATERIALS: 4 (4, 5) balls of Villawool Super Slalom in main colour (m.) and 3 (3, 4) balls of contrast colour (c.); a pair of Nos. 5 and 7 needles; a set of 4 double-pointed No. 7 needles.

MEASUREMENTS: To fit 24 (26, 28) in. [60.96 (66.04, 71.12) cm] chest. Length, 13¾ (15¼, 16¾) ins. [34.92 (38.73, 42.54) cm].
TENSION: 9 sts. to 2 inches [5.08 cm].
ABBREVIATIONS: See page 13.

TO MAKE:

BACK. With No. 7 needles and m. cast on 60 (64, 68) sts. and work in k.1, p.1 rib for 1 (1¼, 1½) ins. [2.54 (3.17, 3.81) cm]. Change to No. 5 needles, join in c. and cont. in patt.:
1st row. K.2 c., (1 m., 3 c.) to last 2 sts., 1 m., 1 c.
2nd row. (P.1 c., 3 m.) to end.
3rd row. (K.1 c., 3 m.) to end.
4th row. P.2 c., (1 m., 3 c.,) to last 2 sts., 1 m., 1 c. Rep. above 4 rows until work measures 8¼ (9¼, 10) ins. [20.95 (23.49, 25.40) cm], ending on wrong side of work.
Shape armholes. Cont. in patt. and cast off 4 (5, 6) sts. at beg. of next 2 rows, then dec. 1 st. each end of next and every foll. alt. row until 44 (46, 48) sts. rem. ** cont. straight until armholes measure 5 (5½, 6¼) ins. [12.70 (13.97, 15.87) cm], ending on wrong side of work.
Shape neck. Next row. Patt. 9 (10, 11), turn and cont. on these sts. only. Dec. 1 st. at neck edge of next row and foll. alt. row (7, 8, 9 sts.).
Shape shoulder. Cast off 4 sts. at beg. of next row. Work 1 row, then cast off rem. sts.
Return to sts. on needle. Sl. centre 26 sts. on a holder. Rejoin yarn to inner end of rem. sts. and work to correspond with other side.
FRONT. Work as given for Back to **. Patt. 1 row.
Shape neck. Next row. Patt. 15 (16, 17), turn and cont. on these sts. only. Cast off 2 sts. at beg. of next row, then dec. 1 st. at same edge on every foll. alt. row until 7 (8, 9) sts. rem.
Cont. straight until armhole measures same as back armhole, ending at side edge.
Shape shoulder. Cast off 4 sts. at beg. of next row. Work 1 row, then cast off rem. sts.
Return to sts. on needle. Sl. centre 14 sts. on a holder. Rejoin yarn to inner end of rem. sts. and work to correspond with other side.
NECKBAND. Firstly, join shoulder seams. R.s.f., with set of No. 7 needles and m. pick up and k.28 (30, 36) sts. down left side of front neck, k. across centre front sts., pick up and k. 28 (30, 36) sts. up right side of front neck, 7 sts. down first side of back neck, k. across centre back sts., then pick up and k. 7 sts. up other side of back neck (110, 114, 126 sts.). Work in k.1, p.1 rib for 4 rounds, then cast off ribwise.
ARMBANDS. R.s.f., with No. 7 needles and m., pick up and k. 74 (78, 88) sts. around entire armhole. Work in k.1, p.1 rib for 4 rows, then cast off ribwise.
TO MAKE UP. Press work on the wrong side. Join side seam and armbands tog. Press seams.

Crew Neck Sweater in Stripe Design

See photograph on page 77.

MATERIALS: 3 (3, 4, 4, 5) balls of Villawool Superknit DC8 in main colour (m.); 2 (2, 2, 2, 3) balls of 1st contrast (1st c.) and 5 (5, 6, 6, 7) balls of 2nd contrast (2nd c.); a pair of Nos. 8 and 10 needles.
MEASUREMENTS: To fit 22 (24, 26, 28, 30) in. [55.88 (60.96, 66.04, 71.12, 76.20) cm] chest. Length, 11½ (14, 15½, 19, 19½) ins. [29.21 (35.56, 39.37, 48.26, 49.53) cm]. Sleeve, 9 (10½, 12, 14, 16) ins. [22.86 (26.67, 30.48, 35.56, 40.64) cm] (or length required).
TENSION: 23 sts. to 4 inches [10.16 cm].
ABBREVIATIONS: See page 13.

TO MAKE:

BACK. With No. 10 needles and m. cast on 66 (74, 80, 86, 92) sts. and work in k.1, p.1 rib for 1 (2, 2, 3, 3) in(s). [2.54 (5.08, 5.08, 7.62, 7.62) cm], then change to No. 8 needles and join in 1st c. Beg. k. row, work in st. st. stripe sequence of 1 in. [2.54 cm] in 1st c., then 1 in. [2.54 cm] in m. until work measures 7 (8, 10, 11, 13) ins. [17.78 (20.32, 25.40, 27.94, 33.02) cm], ending on p. row. Break off m. and 1st c. and cont. in 2nd c. only.
Shape armholes. Cast off 3 (3, 4, 4, 4) sts. at beg. of next 2 rows, then dec. 1 st. each end of next and foll. alt. rows until 52 (56, 60, 64, 68) sts. rem. Cont. straight until armholes measure 4½ (5, 5½, 6, 6½) ins. [11.43 (12.70, 13.97, 15.24, 16.51) cm], ending on p. row.
Shape shoulders. Cast off 7 (8, 8, 9, 9) sts. at beg. of next 2 rows, then 8 (8, 9, 9, 10) sts. at beg. of foll. 2 rows. Leave rem. 22 (24, 26, 28, 30) sts. on a holder.
FRONT. Work as given for Back until armholes measure 3 (3½, 3½, 4, 4½) ins. [7.62 (8.89, 8.89, 10.16, 11.43) cm], ending on p. row.
Shape neck. Next row. K.19 (20, 21, 22, 23), turn and cont. on these sts. only. Dec. 1 st. at neck edge of every foll. alt. rows until 15 (16, 17, 18, 19) sts. rem., then cont. straight until armhole measures same as back armhole, ending at side edge.
Shape shoulder. Cast off 7 (8, 8, 9, 9) sts. at beg. of next row. Work 1 row, then cast off rem. sts.
Return to rem. sts. Sl. centre 14 (16, 18, 20, 22)

sts. on a holder. Rejoin yarn to inner end of rem. sts. and work to correspond with other side.

SLEEVES. With No. 10 needles and m. cast on 28 (34, 34, 40, 40) sts. and work in k.1, p.1 rib for 2 (2, 2½, 3, 3) ins. [5.08 (5.08, 6.35, 7.62, 7.62) cm]. Break off m. and cont. in 2nd c. only. Change to No. 8 needles and, beg. k. row, cont. in st. st., inc. 1 st. each end of every foll. 4th row to 44 (50, 56, 62, 64) sts., then cont. straight until work measures 9 (10½, 12, 14, 16) ins. [22.86 (26.67, 30.48, 35.56, 40.64) cm] (or length required), ending on p. row.

Cast off 3 (3, 4, 4, 4) sts. at beg. of next 2 rows, then dec. 1 st. each end of next 6 (8, 10, 12, 8) rows, then each end of every foll. alt. row until 14 sts. rem. Cast off.

NECKBAND. Firstly, join right shoulder seam. R.s.f., with No. 10 needles and m. pick up and k. 15 (15, 20, 20, 20) sts. down left side of neck, k. across sts. at centre front, pick up and k. 15 (15, 20, 20, 20) sts. up right side of neck, then k. across sts. at back neck (66, 70, 84, 88, 92 sts.). Work in k.1, p.1 rib for 1 in. [2.54 cm], then cast off ribwise.

TO MAKE UP. Press work on the wrong side. Join rem. shoulder seam and neckband. Join side and sleeve seams. Set in sleeves. Press seams.

Aran Cardigan

MATERIALS: 9 (10) balls of Villawool Dinkum 8 ply; a pair of Nos. 7 and 9 needles; cable needle; 5 buttons.

MEASUREMENTS: To fit 26 (28) in. [66.04 (71.12) cm] chest. Length, 17 (18½) ins. [43.18 (46.99) cm]. Sleeve, 12 (14) ins. [30.48 (35.56) cm].

TENSION: 5 sts. to 1 inch [2.54 cm] over moss st.

ABBREVIATIONS: See page 13.

TO MAKE:

BACK. With No. 9 needles cast on 84 (88) sts. and work in k.1, p.1 rib for 8 rows, inc. 1 st. at end of last row (85, 89 sts.).

Change to No. 7 needles and cont. in patt.:

1st row. M.st. 0 (2), * m.st. 3, k.1 b., p.1, k.4, p.1, k.1 b., m.st. 3, k.1 b., p.5, c.4b., p.5, k.1 b., m.st. 3, k.1 b., p.1, k.4, p.1, k.1 b.; rep. from * once, then m.st. to end.

2nd row. M.st. 0 (2), * m.st. 3, p.1, k.1, p.4, k.1, p.1, m.st. 3, p.1, k.5, p.4, k.5, p.1, m.st. 3, p.1, k.1, p.4, k.1, p.1; rep. from * once, m.st. to end.

3rd row. M.st. 0 (2), * m.st. 3, k.1 b., p.1, c.4f., p.1, k.1 b., m.st. 3, k.1 b., p.3, cr.2b., cr.2f., p.3, k.1 b., m.st. 3, k.1 b., p.1, c.4b., p.1, k.1 b.; rep. from * once, m.st. to end.

4th row. M.st. 0 (2), * m.st. 3, p.1, k.1, p.4, k.1, p.1, m.st. 3, p.1, k.3, p.2, k.4, p.2, k.3, p.1, m.st. 3, p.1, k.1, p.4, k.1, p.1; rep. from * once, m.st. to end.

5th row. M.st. 0 (2), * m.st. 3, k.1 b., p.1, k.4, p.1, k.1 b., m.st. 3, k.1 b., p.1, cr.2b., p.4, cr.2f., p.1, k.1 b., m.st. 3, k.1 b., p.1, k.4, p.1, k.1 b.; rep. from * once, m.st. to end.

6th row. M.st. 0 (2), * m.st. 3, p.1, k.1, p.4, k.1, p.1, m.st. 3, p.1, k.1, p.2, k.8, p.2, k.1, p.1, m.st. 3, p.1, k.1, p.4, k.1, p.1; rep. from * once, m.st. to end.

7th row. M.st. 0 (2), * m.st. 3, k.1 b., p.1, c.4f., p.1, k.1 b., m.st. 3, k.1 b., p.1, k.2, p.8, k.2, p.1, k.1 b., m.st. 3, k.1 b., p.1, c.4b., p.1, k.1 b.; rep. from * once, m.st. to end.

8th row. As 6th row.

9th row. M.st. 0 (2), * m.st. 3, k.1 b., p.1, k.4, p.1, k.1 b., m.st. 3, k.1 b., p.1, cr.2f., p.4, cr.2b., p.1, k.1 b., m.st. 3, k.1 b., p.1, k.4, p.1, k.1 b.; rep. from * once, m.st. to end.

10th row. As 4th row.

11th row. M.st. 0 (2), * m.st. 3, k.1 b., p.1, c.4f., p.1, k.1 b., m.st. 3, k.1 b., p.3, cr.2f., cr.2b., p.3, k.1 b., m.st. 3, k.1 b., p.1, c.4b., p.1, k.1 b.; rep. from * once, m.st. to end.

12th row. As 2nd row.

Rep. above 12 rows until work measures 10 (11) ins. [25.40 (27.94) cm], ending on wrong side.

Shape armholes. Cont. in patt. and cast off 5 sts. at beg. of next 2 rows, then dec. 1 st. each end of every row until 67 (both sizes) sts. rem. Cont. straight until armholes measure 6½ (7) ins. [16.51 (17.78) cm], ending on wrong side.

Shape shoulders. Cast off 8 sts. at beg. of next 4 rows, then 4 sts. at beg. of foll. 2 rows. Cast off rem. sts.

LEFT FRONT. With No. 9 needles cast on 44 (46) sts. and work in k.1, p.1 rib for 8 rows. Change to No. 7 needles and cont. in patt.:

His and Hers jackets are knitted in traditional Aran stitches with k.1, p.1 rib edging.

1st row. M.st. 3 (5), k.1 b., p.1, k.4, p.1, k.1 b., m.st. 3, k.1 b., p.5, c.4b., p.5, k.1 b., m.st. 3, k.1 b., p.1, k.4, p.1, k.1 b., m.st. 3.

2nd row. M.st. 3, p.1, k.1, p.4, k.1, p.1, m.st. 3, p.1, k.5, p.4, k.5, p.1, m.st. 3, p.1, k.1, p.4, k.1, p.1, m.st. to end.

3rd row. M.st. 3 (5), k.1 b., p.1, c.4f., p.1, k.1 b., m.st. 3, k.1 b., p.3, cr.2b., cr.2f., p.3, k.1 b., m.st. 3, k.1 b., p.1, c.4b., p.1, k.1 b., m.st. 3.

4th row. M.st. 3, p.1, k.1, p.4, k.1, p.1, m.st. 3, p.1, k.3, p.2, k.4, p.2, k.3, p.1, m.st. 3, p.1, k.1, p.4, k.1, p.1, m.st. to end.

5th row. M.st. 3 (5), k.1 b., p.1, k.4, p.1, k.1 b., m.st. 3, k.1 b., p.1, cr.2b., p.4, cr.2f., p.1, k.1 b., m.st. 3, k.1 b., p.1, k.4, p.1, k.1 b., m.st. 3.

6th row. M.st. 3, p.1, k.1, p.4, k.1, p.1, m.st. 3, p.1, k.1, p.2, k.8, p.2, k.1, p.1, m.st. 3, p.1, k.1, p.4, k.1, p.1, m.st. to end.

7th row. M.st. 3 (5), k.1 b., p.1, c.4f., p.1, k.1 b., m.st. 3, k.1 b., p.1, k.2, p.8, k.2, p.1, k.1 b., m.st. 3, k.1 b., p.1, c.4b., p.1, k.1 b., m.st. 3.

8th row. As 6th row.

9th row. M.st. 3 (5), k.1 b., p.1, k.4, p.1, k.1 b., m.st. 3, k.1 b., p.1, cr.2f., p.4, cr.2b., p.1, k.1 b., m.st. 3, k.1 b., p.1, k.4, p.1, k.1 b., m.st. 3.

10th row. As 4th row.

11th row. M.st. 3 (5), k.1 b., p.1, c.4f., p.1, k.1 b., m.st. 3, k.1 b., p.3, cr.2f., cr.2b., p.3, k.1 b., m.st. 3, k.1 b., p.1, c.4b., p.1, k.1 b., m.st. 3.

12th row. As 2nd row.

Rep. above 12 rows until work measures 9½ (10½) ins. [24.13 (26.67) cm], ending at side edge. (End at front edge when working Right Front.)

Shape V. Next row. Patt. to last 6 sts., k.2 tog. t.b.l., k.1 b., m.st. 3. Rep. this dec. on every foll. alt. row 9 times altog., then on every foll. 4th row 4 times altog. At the same time, when work measures same as Back to armhole shaping, end at side edge.

Shape armhole. Cast off 5 sts. at beg. of next row, then dec. 1 st. at same edge of every row 4 (6) times altog.

Cont. until armhole measures same as Back armhole, ending at side edge. (22 sts.).

Shape shoulder. Cast off 8 sts. at beg. of next and foll. alt. row.

Work 1 row, then cast off rem. sts.

RIGHT FRONT. Work as given for Left Front, shaping V neck: m.st. 3, k.1 b., k.2 tog.

SLEEVES. With No. 9 needles cast on 34 sts. and work in k.1, p.1 rib for 2 ins. [5.08 cm].

Next (inc.) row. Rib 3, (inc., rib 2) 9 times, inc., rib to end. (44 sts.).

Change to No. 7 needles and work in 12-row patt. as given for size 26 in. chest for Left Front, inc. 1 st. each end of every 6th row to 60 (64) sts., keeping the inc. sts. in moss st. Cont. straight until work measures 12 (14) ins. [30.48 (35.56) cm], ending on wrong side. Cast off 5 sts. at beg. of next 2 rows, then dec. 1 st. at beg. of next 18 (20) rows, then dec. 1 st. each end of every foll. row until 20 sts. rem. Cast off.

TO MAKE UP. Join shoulder, side and sleeve seams. Set in sleeves. Press seams.

FRONT BAND (worked in one piece). With No. 9 needles cast on 10 sts. and work in k.1, p.1 rib for ½ in. [1.27 cm].

Next (buttonhole) row. Rib 4, cast off 3, rib to end.

Next row. Rib and cast on 3 sts. over those cast off in previous row.

Cont. in rib, making 4 more buttonholes as above at 2 (2¼) in. [5.08 (5.71) cm] intervals, then cont. straight until band fits around entire front edge. Cast off ribwise.

TO FINISH OFF. Placing buttonhole section at left side for boy's cardigan and right side for girl's cardigan, attach band to garment. Sew on buttons.

Ribbed Sweater

MATERIALS: 9 (10) balls of Villawool Cascade Nylon 8 ply Crepe; in main colour (m) and 1 ball of contrast colour (c); a pair of Nos. 8 and 10 needles; a set of 4 double-pointed No. 9 needles.

MEASUREMENTS: To fit 24 (26) in. [60.96 (66.04) cm] chest. Length, 14¾ (15) ins. [37.46 (38.10) cm]. Sleeve, 11 (12) ins. [27.94 (30.48) cm].

TENSION: 6 sts. to 1 inch [2.54 cm] over rib patt.

ABBREVIATIONS: See page 13.

TO MAKE:

BACK. With No. 10 needles and m. cast on 80 (86) sts. and work in k.2, p.2 rib for 2 ins. [5.08 cm]. Change to No. 8 needles.

1st row. P.2, (k.4, p.2) to end.

2nd row. K.2, (p.4, k.2) to end.

Rep. above 2 rows until work measures 10 ins. [25.40 cm], ending on 2nd row.

Shape armholes. Cast off 4 sts. at beg. of next 2 rows, then dec. 1 st. each end of foll. 2 (3) rows then, for 2nd size only, each end of foll. 2 alt. rows. (68 sts.). Cont. straight until armholes measure 4¾ (5) ins. [12.06 (12.70) cm], ending on 2nd row.

Sweater is knitted in a wide rib and features contrast striped bands on sleeves and polo neck.

Shape shoulders. Cast off 7 sts. at beg. of next 4 rows, then 8 sts. at beg. of foll. 2 rows. Leave rem. 24 sts. on holder.

FRONT. Work as given for Back until armholes measure 3½ (3¾) ins. [8.89 (9.52) cm].

Shape neck. Next row. Patt. 28, turn and cont. on these sts. only.

Dec. 1 st. at neck edge of foll. 4 rows, then on foll. 2 alt. rows. (22 sts.). Cont. until armhole measures same as Back armhole, ending at side edge.

Shape shoulder. Cast off 7 sts. at beg. of next row and foll. alt. row. Work 1 row, then cast off rem. sts.

Return to rem. sts. and sl. centre 12 sts. on holder. Rejoin yarn to inner end of rem. sts. and work to correspond with other side.

SLEEVES. With No. 10 needles and m., cast on 56 sts. and work in k.2, p.2 rib for 2 ins. [5.08 cm]. Change to No. 8 needles.

1st row. K.3, (p.2, k.4) to last 5 sts., p.2, k.3.

2nd row. P.3, (k.2, p.4) to last 5 sts., k.2, p.3.

Rep. above 2 rows and inc. 1 st. each end of foll. 4th row and on every foll. 6th row to 66 sts., keeping inc. sts. in patt.

For 2nd size only cont. to dec. each end of every foll. 4th row to 74 sts. Work 1 row.

Join in c. and work in stripe sequence:

1st row (right side). With c., k.

2nd, 3rd and 4th rows. Patt. in c.

5th row. With m., k.

6th, 7th and 8th rows. Patt. in m.

Rep. above 8 rows once, then rep. first 4 rows again. Break off c. and cont. with m. only.

Cont. in patt. until work measures 11 (12) ins. [27.94 (30.48) cm], ending on 2nd row.

Cast off 4 sts. at beg. of next 2 rows, then dec. 1 st. each end of next row and every foll. alt. row until 50 sts. rem. Cast off 2 sts. at beg. of next 4 rows, then 4 sts. at beg. of foll. 4 rows.

Cast off rem. sts.

POLO COLLAR. Firstly, join shoulder seams. R.s.f. and with set of No. 9 needles and m. patt. across 24 sts. of back neck, pick up and k. 24 sts. down left front neck, patt. across centre 12 sts., pick up and k. 24 sts. up right side of neck. (84 sts.). Cont. in k.4, p.2 patt. for 2 ins. [5.08 cm]. Now reverse patt. for turnover (i.e., p.4, k.2) and cont. for 1½ ins. [3.81 cm]. Join in c. and p. 1 round, then patt. 2 rounds. With m., p.1 round, then patt. 2 rounds. With c., p.1 round, then patt. 2 rounds. Break off c. and cont. with m. only. P.1 round. Beg. p.2, work in k.2, p.2 rib for 4 rounds, then cast off ribwise.

TO MAKE UP. Join side and sleeve seams. Set in sleeves.

Mix and Match Wardrobe

See photograph on page 19.

PINAFORE DRESS

MATERIALS: 7 (8) balls of Villawool Boucle Double Knitting in main colour (m) and 1 (1) ball of contrast colour (c); a pair of Nos. 8 and 10 needles; a set of 4 double-pointed No. 9 needles.

MEASUREMENTS: To fit 24 (26) in. [60.96 (66.04) cm] chest. Length, 18½ (20½) ins. [46.99 (52.07) cm].

TENSION: 6 sts. to 1 inch [2.54 cm].

ABBREVIATIONS: See page 13.

TO MAKE:

BACK. With No. 8 needles and m. cast on 99 (105) sts. and k. 10 rows. Beg. k. row, work 6 rows in st. st. Join in c. and work in stripe sequence: 4 rows c., 6 rows m., 2 rows c., 6 rows m. and 2 rows c. Break off c. and cont. with m. only and cont. until work measures 4½ (6½) ins. [11.43 (16.51) cm], ending p. row. Dec. 1 st. each end of next row and every foll. 6th row until 89 (95) sts. rem., then each end of every foll. 4th row until 69 (75) sts. rem. Cont. straight until work measures 13½ (15) ins. [34.29 (38.10) cm], ending on p. row.

Shape armholes. Cast off 4 sts. at beg. of next 2 rows, then 2 sts. at beg. of foll. 2 rows. Dec. 1 st. each end of next row and every foll. alt. row until 47 (53) sts. rem. Cont. straight until armholes measure 4½ (5) ins. [11.43 (12.70) cm], ending on p. row.

Shape neck. Next row. K.13 (16), turn and cont. on these sts. only. Dec. 1 st. at neck edge of every foll. row until 10 (12) sts. rem., then cont. straight until armhole measures 5 (5½) ins. [12.70 (13.97) cm], ending at side edge.

Shape shoulder. Cast off 5 (6) sts. at beg. of next row and foll. alt. row. Fasten off.

Return to rem. sts. Sl. centre 21 sts. on a holder. Rejoin yarn to inner end of rem. sts. and cont. to correspond with other side.

FRONT. Work as given for Back until armholes measure 1½ (2) ins. [3.81 (5.08) cm], ending on p. row.

Shape neck. Next row. K.17 (20), turn and cont. on these sts. only. Dec. 1 st. at neck edge of next

row and every foll. alt. row until 10 (12) sts. rem. Cont. straight until armhole measures same as Back armhole, ending at side edge.
Shape shoulder. Work as given for Back shoulder. Return to rem. sts. Sl. centre 13 sts. on a holder. Rejoin yarn to inner end of rem. sts. and cont. to correspond with other side.

NECKBAND. Firstly, join shoulder seams. R.s.f., with set of No. 9 needles and m., pick up and k. 23 sts. down left side of neck, k. across 13 centre sts., pick up and k. 23 sts. up right side of neck and 7 sts. down left back neck, k. across centre 21 sts., then pick up and k. 7 sts. up right back neck. (94, 94 sts.). Work in rounds of k.1, p.1 for 4 rows, then cast off ribwise.

ARMBANDS. Firstly, join side seams. R.s.f., with set of No. 9 needles and m., pick up and k. 76 (80) sts. evenly around armhole. Work in rounds of k.1, p.1 for 4 rows, then cast off ribwise.

TO FINISH OFF. Press work on the wrong side. Press seams.

JACKET

MATERIALS: 10 (11) balls of Villawool Boucle Double Knitting; a pair of Nos. 8 and 10 needles; 5 (6) buttons.
MEASUREMENTS: To fit 24 (26) in. [60.96 (66.04) cm] chest. Length, 14 (16) ins. [35.56 (40.64) cm]. Sleeve, 10½ (12) ins. [26.67 (30.48) cm].
TENSION: 6 sts. to 1 inch [2.54 cm].
ABBREVIATIONS: See page 13.

TO MAKE:
BACK. With No. 10 needles cast on 78 (84) sts. and work in k.1, p.1 rib for 2 ins. [5.08 cm]. Change to No. 8 needles and cont. in st. st. until work measures 8½ (10) ins. [21.59 (25.40) cm], ending on p. row.
Shape raglan. Cast off 6 sts. at beg. of next 2 rows, then dec. 1 st. each end of next row and every foll. alt. row until 24 (26) sts. rem. Cast off.

LEFT FRONT. With No. 10 needles cast on 36 (42) sts. and work in k.1, p.1 rib for 2 ins. [5.08 cm]. Change to No. 8 needles and cont. in st. st. until work measures same as Back to beg. of armhole shaping, ending at side edge.
Shape raglan and V neck. Cast off 6 sts. at beg. of next row, then dec. 1 st. at side edge on alt. rows to correspond with Back, at the same time, dec. 1 st. at front edge of next row and every foll. 3rd row until 11 (7) sts. rem., then dec. at raglan edge only until 2 sts. rem. K.2 tog. and fasten off.

RIGHT FRONT. Work as given for Left Front.

SLEEVES. With No. 10 needles cast on 36 sts. and work in k.1, p.1 rib for 2 ins. [5.08 cm]. Change to No. 8 needles and st. st., inc. 1 st. each end of every foll. 4th row to 60 (64) sts., then cont. straight until work measures 10½ (12) ins. [26.67 (30.48) cm] (or length required), ending on p. row.
Cast off 6 sts. at beg. of next 2 rows, then dec. 1 st. each end of next row and every foll. alt. row until 6 sts. rem. Cast off.

TO MAKE UP. Press work on the wrong side. Join raglan, side and sleeve seams. Press seams.
FRONT BAND (worked in one piece). With No. 10 needles cast on 10 sts. and work in k.1, p.1 rib for ¾ in. [1.90 cm].
Next (buttonhole) row. Rib 3, cast off 2 sts., rib to end.
Next row. In rib, casting on 2 sts. over those cast off in previous row.
Cont. in rib making 2 (3) more buttonholes at 3½ (2¾) in. [8.89 (6.98) cm] intervals, then cont. straight until band fits around entire front edge, slightly stretched. Cast off ribwise.
Attach band to garment, placing buttonhole section to Right Front for a girl or Left Front for a boy.
POCKET (2). With No. 8 needles cast on 24 sts. and work in st. st. for 3½ ins. [8.89 cm], then work 4 rows in k.1, p.1 rib. Cast off ribwise. Press pocket.
TO FINISH OFF. Attach a pocket to either side of fronts as pictured. Sew buttons to front band and pockets.

TROUSERS

MATERIALS: 10 (11) balls of Villawool Boucle Double Knitting; a pair of Nos. 8 and 10 needles; a waist length of 1 in. [2.54 cm] wide elastic.
MEASUREMENTS: To fit 25/26 (27/28) in. [63.50/66.04 (68.58/71.12) cm] hips. Length, 25 (26) ins. [63.50 (66.04) cm].
TENSION: 6 sts. to 1 inch [2.54 cm].
ABBREVIATIONS: See page 13.

TO MAKE:
WORKED IN FOUR SECTIONS
MAKE TWO PIECES. With No. 8 needles cast on 52 (54) sts. and work in k.1, p.1 rib for 4 rows. Cont. in st. st., dec. 1 st. each end of next and every foll. 14th row until 42 (44) sts. rem. Cont. straight until work measures 8 (8½) ins. [20.32 (21.59) cm], ending on p. row.
Inc. 1 st. each end of next row and every foll. 8th row to 54 (56) sts. Cont. straight until work measures 16 (16½) ins. [40.64 (41.91) cm], ending on p. row.
Shape centre front. Next row. K. to last 2 sts., k.2 tog.
Rep. above dec. at same edge on every alt. row

until 36 (38) sts. rem., then cont. straight until work measures 24 (25) ins. [60.96 (63.50) cm], ending on p. row.

Change to No. 10 needles and work in k.1, p.1 rib for 10 rows, then cast off ribwise.

Make another two pieces in same way, reversing shapings at centre front.

TO MAKE UP. Press work on the wrong side. Join side and inside leg seams. Join front and back seams. Press seams. Encase elastic to inside waist ribbing with a herringbone stitch.

SKIRT

MATERIALS: 6 (7) balls of Villawool Boucle Double Knitting; a pair of Nos. 8 and 10 needles; a waist length of 1 in. [2.54 cm] wide elastic.

MEASUREMENTS: Length 10 (11½) ins. [25.40 (29.21) cm] (or length required). Waist is adjustable with elastic.

TENSION: 6 sts. to 1 inch [2.54 cm].

ABBREVIATIONS: See page 13.

TO MAKE:

BACK AND FRONT ALIKE. With No. 8 needles cast on 86 (94) sts. and work in k.1, p.1 rib for 4 rows. Cont. in st. st. until work measures 2 ins. [5.08 cm], ending on p. row (adjust length at this point for more or less as required before beg. shaping).

Next (dec.) row. K.22 (24), sl.1, k.1, p.s.s.o., k. to last 24 (26) sts., k.2 tog., k. to end.

Work 7 rows.

Rep. above 8 rows until 70 (76) sts. rem., then cont. in st. st. until work measures 9¾ (10¼) ins. [24.76 (26.03) cm], ending on p. row.

Change to No. 10 needles and work 10 rows in k.1, p.1 rib, then cast off ribwise.

TO MAKE UP. Press work on the wrong side. Join side seams. Press seams. Encase elastic to inside waist ribbing with a herringbone stitch.

5
Knitting for Teenagers

His and Hers Aran Sweaters

MATERIALS: 16 (17, 18, 19, 20) balls of Villawool Dinkum 8 ply; a pair of Nos. 7 and 9 needles; 2 cable needles.

MEASUREMENTS: To fit 32 (34, 36, 38, 40) in. [81.28 (86.36, 91.44, 96.52, 101.60) cm] bust/chest. Length, 22 (23, 24, 24½, 25½) ins. [55.88 (58.42, 60.96, 62.23, 64.77) cm]. Sleeve, 17 (18, 18, 19, 19) ins. [43.18 (45.72, 45.72, 48.26, 48.26) cm] (or length required).

TENSION: 6 sts. to 1 inch [2.54 cm] over patt.

ABBREVIATIONS: See page 13.

TO MAKE:

BACK. With No. 9 needles cast on 110 (114, 118, 122, 126) sts. and work in k.1 b., p.1 rib for 2½ (2½, 2½, 3, 3) ins. [6.35 (6.35, 6.35, 7.62, 7.62) cm]. Change to No. 7 needles and Aran patt.:

1st row. (K.1, p.1) 0 (1, 2, 3, 4) times, * k.1, (p.1, c.4f.) twice, p.1, k.1 **, p.6, sl. next st. on cable needle and keep at back, sl. next 2 sts. on another cable needle and keep at front, k.2 sts., p.1 from first cable needle, p.1 st., then k.2 from second cable needle, p.6; rep. from * to ** once ***, p.22; rep. from * to *** once, (p.1, k.1) 0 (1, 2, 3, 4) times.

2nd row. (P.1, k.1) 0 (1, 2, 3, 4) times, * p.1, k.1, p.4, k.1, p.4, k.1, p.1 **, k.6, p.2, k.2, p.2, k.6; rep. from * to ** once *** k.1, (p.3 tog., (k.1, p.1, k.1) into next st.) 5 times, k.1; rep. from * to *** once, (k.1, p.1) 0 (1, 2, 3, 4) times.

3rd row. (K.1, p.1) 0 (1, 2, 3, 4) times, * k.1, p.1, k.4, p.1, k.4, p.1, k.1 **, p.5, cr. 2 over 1 b., p.2, cr. 2 over 1 f., p.5; rep. from * to ** once ***, p.22; rep. from * to *** once, (p.1, k.1) 0 (1, 2, 3, 4) times.

4th row. (P.1, k.1) 0 (1, 2, 3, 4) times, * p.1, k.1, p.4, k.1, p.4, k.1, p.1 **, k.5, p.2, k.4, p.2, k.5; rep. from * to ** once ***, k.1, ((k.1, p.1, k.1) into next st., p.3 tog.) 5 times, k.1; rep. from * to *** once, (k.1, p.1) 0 (1, 2, 3, 4) times.

5th row. (K.1, p.1) 0 (1, 2, 3, 4) times, * k.1, p.1, k.4, p.1, k.4, p.1, k.1 **, p.4, cr. 2 over 1 b., p.4, cr. 2 over 1 f., p.4; rep. from * to ** once ***, p.22; rep. from * to *** once, (p.1, k.1) 0 (1, 2, 3, 4) times.

6th row. (P.1, k.1) 0 (1, 2, 3, 4) times, * p.1, k.1, p.4, k.1, p.4, k.1, p.1 **, k.4, p.2, k.6, p.2, k.4; rep. from * to ** once ***, k.1, (p.3 tog., (k.1, p.1, k.1) into next st.) 5 times, k.1; rep. from * to *** once, (k.1, p.1) 0 (1, 2, 3, 4) times.

7th row. (K.1, p.1) 0 (1, 2, 3, 4) times, * k.1, (p.1, c.4f.) twice, p.1, k.1 **, p.3, cr. 2 over 1 b.,

p.6, cr. 2 over 1 f., p.3; rep. from * to ** once ***, p.22; rep. from * to *** once, (p.1, k.1) 0 (1, 2, 3, 4) times.

8th row. (P.1, k.1) 0 (1, 2, 3, 4) times, * p.1, k.1, p.4, k.1, p.4, k.1, p.1 **, k.3, p.2, k.8, p.2, k.3; rep. from * to ** once ***, k.1, ((k.1, p.1, k.1) into next st., p.3 tog.) 5 times, k.1; rep. from * to *** once, (k.1, p.1) 0 (1, 2, 3, 4) times.

9th row. (K.1, p.1) 0 (1, 2, 3, 4) times, * k.1, p.1, k.4, p.1, k.4, p.1, k.1 **, p.2, cross 2 over 1 b., p.8, cross 2 over 1 f., p.2; rep. from * to ** once ***, p.22; rep. from * to *** once, (p.1, k.1) 0 (1, 2, 3, 4) times.

10th row. (P.1, k.1) 0 (1, 2, 3, 4) times, * p.1, k.1, p.4, k.1, p.4, k.1, p.1 **, k.2, p.2, k.10, p.2, k.2; rep. from * to ** once ***, k.1, (p.3 tog., (k.1, p.1, k.1) into next st.) 5 times, k.1; rep. from * to *** once, (k.1, p.1) 0 (1, 2, 3, 4) times.

11th row. (K.1, p.1) 0 (1, 2, 3, 4) times, * k.1, p.1, k.4, p.1, k.4, p.1, k.1 **, p.1, cross 2 over 1 b., p.10, cross 2 over 1 f., p.1; rep. from * to ** once ***, p.22; rep. from * to *** once, (p.1, k.1) 0 (1, 2, 3, 4) times.

12th row. (P.1, k.1) 0 (1, 2, 3, 4) times, * p.1, k.1, p.4, k.1, p.4, k.1, p.1 **, k.1, p.2, k.12, p.2, k.1; rep. from * to ** once ***, k.1, ((k.1, p.1, k.1) into next st., p.3 tog.) 5 times, k.1; rep. from * to *** once, (k.1, p.1) 0 (1, 2, 3, 4) times.

13th row. (K.1, p.1) 0 (1, 2, 3, 4) times, * k.1, (p.1, c.4f.) twice, p.1, k.1 **, p.1, cross 2 over 1 f., p.10, cross 2 over 1 b., p.1; rep. from * to ** once ***, p.22; rep. from * to *** once, (p.1, k.1) 0 (1, 2, 3, 4) times.

14th row. As 10th row.

15th row. (K.1, p.1) 0 (1, 2, 3, 4) times, * k.1, p.1, k.4, p.1, k.4, p.1, k.1 **, p.2, cross 2 over 1 f., p.8, cross 2 over 1 b., p.2; rep. from * to ** once ***, p.22; rep. from * to *** once, (p.1, k.1) 0 (1, 2, 3, 4) times.

16th row. As 8th row.

17th row. (K.1, p.1) 0 (1, 2, 3, 4) times, * k.1, p.1, k.4, p.1, k.4, p.1, k.1 **, p.3, cross 2 over 1 f., p.6, cross 2 over 1 b., p.3; rep. from * to ** once ***, p.22; rep. from * to *** once, (p.1, k.1) 0 (1, 2, 3, 4) times.

18th row. As 6th row.

19th row. (K.1, p.1) 0 (1, 2, 3, 4) times, * k.1, (p.1, c.4f.) twice, p.1, k.1 **, p.4, cross 2 over 1 f., p.4, cross 2 over 1 b., p.4; rep. from * to ** once ***, p.22; rep. from * to *** once, (p.1, k.1) 0 (1, 2, 3, 4) times.

20th row. As 4th row.

21st row. (K.1, p.1) 0 (1, 2, 3, 4) times, * k.1, p.1, k.4, p.1, k.4, p.1, k.1 **, p.5, cross 2 over 1 f., p.2, cross 2 over 1 b., p.5; rep. from * to ** once ***, p.22; rep. from * to *** once, (p.1, k.1) 0 (1, 2, 3, 4) times.

22nd row. As 2nd row.

His and Hers sweaters are knitted in traditional Aran patterning with twisted k.1, p.1 rib edgings.

23rd row. (K.1, p.1) 0 (1, 2, 3, 4) times, * k.1, p.1, k.4, p.1, k.4, p.1, k.1 **, p.6, cross 2 over 1 f., cross 2 over 1 b., p.6; rep. from * to ** once ***, p.22; rep. from * to *** once, (p.1, k.1) 0 (1, 2, 3, 4) times.

24th row. (P.1, k.1) 0 (1, 2, 3, 4) times, * p.1, k.1, p.4, k.1, p.4, k.1, p.1 **, k.7, p.4, k.7; rep. from * to ** once ***, k.1, ((k.1, p.1, k.1) into next st., p.3 tog.) 5 times, k.1; rep. from * to *** once, (k.1, p.1) 0 (1, 2, 3, 4) times.

Rep. above 24 rows until work measures 15 (16, 16½, 16½, 17) ins. [38.10 (40.64, 41.91, 41.91, 43.18) cm], ending on wrong side.

Shape armholes. Cont. in patt. and cast off 3 (3, 4, 5, 6) sts. at beg. of next 2 rows, then dec. 1 st. each end of next row and every foll. alt. row until 96 (98, 100, 102, 104) sts. rem. Cont. straight until armholes measure 7 (7, 7½, 8, 8½) ins. [17.78 (17.78, 19.05, 20.32, 21.59) cm], ending on wrong side.

Shape shoulders. Cast off 5 sts. at beg. of next 8 rows, then 5 (6, 6, 7, 7) sts. at beg. of foll. 2 rows. Leave rem. sts. on a holder.

FRONT. Work as given for Back until armholes measure 5 (5, 5½, 6, 6½) ins. [12.70 (12.70, 13.97, 15.24, 16.51) cm], ending on wrong side.

Shape neck. Next row. Patt. 38 (39, 39, 40, 40) sts., turn and cont. on these sts. only. Cast off 2 sts. at neck edge on next row and foll. alt. row, then dec. 1 st. at same edge of every foll. row until 25 (26, 26, 27, 27) sts. rem. Cont. straight until armhole measures same as back armhole, ending at side edge.

Shape shoulder. Cast off 5 sts. at beg. of next and foll. 3 alt. rows. Work 1 row, then cast off rem. sts. Return to rem. sts. and sl. centre 20 (20, 22, 22, 24) sts. on a holder. Rejoin yarn to inner end and work to correspond with other side.

SLEEVES. With No. 9 needles cast on 52 (52, 52, 56, 56) sts. and work in k. 1 b., p.1 rib for 3 ins. [7.62 cm]. Change to No. 7 needles and Aran patt.:

1st row. (K.1, p.1) 2 (2, 2, 3, 3) times, work from * to *** of patt. once, (p.1, k.1) 2 (2, 2, 3, 3) times.

2nd row. (P.1, k.1) 2 (2, 2, 3, 3) times, work from * to *** of patt. once, (k.1, p.1) 2 (2, 2, 3, 3) times.

Cont. thus, omitting blackberry patt. and working cable and diamond centre patt., inc. 1 st. each end of next row and every foll. 6th row to 74 (76, 80, 82, 84) sts. and taking the extra sts. into the rib at each end. Cont. straight until work measures 17 (18, 18, 19, 19) ins. [43.18 (45.72, 45.72, 48.26, 48.26) cm] (or length required), ending on wrong side.

Cast off 3 (3, 4, 5, 6) sts. at beg. of next 2 rows, then dec. 1 st. each end of next 12 (10, 10, 8, 6) rows, then dec. 1 st. each end of every foll. alt. row until 48 sts. rem. Cast off 3 sts. at beg. of next 2 rows, then 4 sts. at beg. of foll. 2 rows. Cast off rem. sts.

NECKBAND. Firstly, join right shoulder seam. R.s.f. and with No. 9 needles, pick up and k. 22 sts. down left side of neck, k. across 20 (20, 22, 22, 24) sts. at centre front, pick up and k. 22 sts. up right side of neck and, finally, k. across 46 (46, 48, 48, 50) sts. at back neck (110, 110, 114, 114, 118 sts.). Work in k.1 b., p.1 rib for 1½ ins. [3.81 cm], then cast off ribwise.

TO MAKE UP. Join rem. shoulder seam and neckband. Join side and sleeve seams. Set in sleeves. Press seams.

Crew Neck Sweater

MATERIALS: 26 (27, 28, 29) balls of Villawool Nylo Tweed; a pair of Nos. 7 and 9 needles.

MEASUREMENTS: To fit 34 (36, 38, 40) in. [86.36 (91.44, 96.52, 101.60) cm] chest. Length, 24 (24½, 25, 25½) ins. [60.96 (62.23, 63.50, 64.77) cm]. Sleeve, 17 (18, 18, 19) ins. [43.18 (45.72, 45.72, 48.26) cm] (or length required).

TENSION: 5 sts. to 1 inch [2.54 cm].

ABBREVIATIONS: See page 13.

TO MAKE:

BACK. With No. 9 needles cast on 94 (98, 102, 106) sts. and work in patt. as follows:

1st row. (K.2, p.2) to last 2 sts., k.2.

2nd row. P.

Rep. above 2 rows until work measures 4 ins. [10.16 cm]. Change to No. 7 needles and cont. in patt. until work measures 16 (16, 16, 17) ins. [40.64 (40.64, 40.64, 43.18) cm], ending on wrong side.

Shape armholes. Cast off 6 sts. at beg. of next 2 rows, then dec. 1 st. each end of every foll. row until 70 (74, 78, 82) sts. rem.

Cont. straight until armholes measure 8 (8½, 9, 9½) ins. [20.32 (21.59, 22.86, 24.13) cm], ending on wrong side.

Shape shoulders. Cast off 6 sts. at beg. of next 6 rows, then 4 (5, 6, 7) sts. at beg. of foll. 2 rows. Leave rem. 26 (28, 30, 32) sts. on a holder.

FRONT. Work as given for Back until armholes measure 6 (6½, 7, 7½) ins. [15.24 (16.51, 17.78 19.05) cm].

Teenager's tweed sweater is knitted in a 2-row pattern, features long sleeves and turnover neckband.

Shape neck. Next row. Patt. 27 (28, 29, 30) sts., turn and cont. on these sts. only. Dec. 1 st. at neck edge of next row and every foll. alt. row until 22 (23, 24, 25) sts. rem. Cont. straight until armhole measures same as back armhole, ending at side edge.

Shape shoulder. Cast off 6 sts. at beg. of next row and foll. 2 alt rows. Work 1 row, then cast off rem. sts.

Return to rem. sts. Place centre 16 (18, 20, 22) sts. on a holder. Rejoin yarn to inner end of rem. sts. and work to correspond with other side.

SLEEVES. With No. 9 needles cast on 42 (42, 46, 46) sts. and work in patt. as given for Back for 2 ins. [5.08 cm]. Change to No. 7 needles and cont. in patt., inc. 1 st. each end of next row and every foll. 8th row to 66 (70, 74, 78) sts. Cont. straight until work measures 17 (18, 18, 19) ins. [43.18 (45.72, 45.72, 48.26) cm] (or length required).

Cast off 6 sts. at beg. of next 2 rows, then dec. 1 st. at beg. of every foll. row until 28 sts. rem. Cast off 2 sts. at beg. of next 6 rows, then cast off rem. sts.

NECKBAND. Firstly, join right shoulder seam. R.s.f., with No. 9 needles pick up and k. 18 sts. down left front neck, k. across centre 16 (18, 20, 22) sts., pick up and k. 18 sts. up right side of neck and, finally, k. across sts. at back neck (78, 82, 86, 90 sts.). Work in k.2, p.2 rib for 3 ins. [7.62 cm], then cast off ribwise.

TO MAKE UP. Join rem. shoulder seam and neckband end. Join side and sleeve seams. Set in sleeves. Lightly press seams.

Poncho

See photograph on page 2.

MATERIALS: 13 balls of Villawool Superknit 5 ply Crepe in main colour and 5 balls of contrast colour for the fringe; a pair of Nos. 9 and 11 needles; a No. 3.00 crochet hook; an 8 in. [20.32 cm] zip.

MEASUREMENTS: To fit 32-36 in. [81.28-91.44 cm] bust. Length, 29 ins. [73.66 cm] including fringe.

TENSION: 13½ sts. to 2 inches [5.08 cm].

ABBREVIATIONS: See page 13.

TO MAKE:

FRONT. With No. 9 needles cast on 293 sts. and work in st. st. for 2 rows.

1st (dec.) row. K.144, k.2 tog. t.b.l., k.1, k.2 tog., k. to end.

Next row. P.

Next row. K.143, k.2 tog. t.b.l., k.1, k.2 tog., k. to end.

Cont. to dec. as above on every foll. alt. row until 237 sts. rem., ending on p. row. Cont. to dec. as set, at the same time, dec. 1 st. each end of next row and every foll. 6th row 18 times altog., then on every foll. alt. row 5 times altog. (87 sts.)

Shape shoulder and neck. Next row. Cast off 5 sts., work 22 sts., turn and cont. on these sts. only. Work 1 row. Cast off 5 sts. at beg. of next row and foll. 2 alt. rows. Work 1 row, then cast off rem. sts.

Return to rem. sts. Rejoin yarn to inner end and cast off centre 33 sts., then cont. on rem. sts. to correspond with other side.

BACK. Work as given for Front until 149 sts. rem., ending on p. row.

Divide for zip opening. Cont. to dec. at outside edge as set—

Next row. Work to the 2 sts. before centre st., k.2 tog. t.b.l., turn and cont. on these sts. only. Leave rem. sts. on a spare needle. Cont. shaping until 43 sts. rem., ending on k. row.

Shape neck and shoulder. Cast off 16 sts. at beg. of next row.

Cast off 5 sts. at beg. of next row and foll. 3 alt. rows. Work 1 row, then cast off rem. sts.

Return to rem. sts. Rejoin yarn to inner end and cast off centre sts., then k.2 tog., work to end. Cont. to correspond with other side.

COLLAR. With No. 9 needles cast on 98 sts. and work in st. st. for 4 ins. [10.16 cm], then cast off.

TO MAKE UP. Press work on the wrong side. Join side and shoulder seams. Using a small backstitch join one edge of collar to neck, then fold collar in half on to outside of neck and sl. st. into position, joining side edges tog. Fold approx. ½ in. [1.27 cm] st. st. at lower edge to inside and hem down. Press seams and hem. Sew in zip. With No. 3.00 hook and r.s.f., work a row of d.c. around hemline.

FRINGE. With contrast colour cut five 9 in. [22.86 cm] lengths of yarn for each tassel and proceed as follows: With wrong side to the edge to be fringed facing you, insert a crochet hook as near as possible to the edge, fold strands in half to form a loop, put loop on hook, pull through edge of work, place hook behind all strands of yarn and draw through loop. Cont. along d.c. edge as pictured. Finally, trim ends of fringing to neaten.

Right: *Long-line jacket is knitted in stocking stitch with picot edgings, features short, set-in sleeves (see page 100 for instructions).*

Below: *Striped mini top is knitted in stocking stitch with k.1, p.1 rib edgings. Pants are knitted in stocking stitch with rib waistband and garter stitch leg edgings (see page 101 for instructions).*

Above: *Long-line waistcoat is knitted in an 8-row lacy pattern and features stocking stitch front, armhole and lower edge hems (see page 114 for instructions).*

Left: *Body of sweater is knitted in k.2, p.2 rib with contrast front band inset and neckband knitted in garter stitch (see page 106 for instructions).*

Right: *Small clutch purse is knitted entirely in garter stitch. Evening bag is knitted in a simple moss stitch variation (see page 147 for instructions).*

Below: *Bed socks are knitted entirely in garter stitch (see page 144 for instructions).*

His and Hers Sweaters

See photograph left.

MATERIALS: 16 (18, 20) balls of Villawool Super Slalom; a pair of Nos. 5 and 7 needles; a set of double-pointed No. 7 needles; cable needle.

MEASUREMENTS: To fit 32 (34, 36) in. [81.28 (86.36, 91.44) cm] bust/chest. Length, 24½ (25, 26) ins. [62.23 (63.50, 66.04) cm]. Sleeve, 17 (18, 18) ins. [43.18 (45.72, 45.72) cm].

TENSION: 13 sts. to 2½ inches [6.35 cm].

ABBREVIATIONS: See page 13.

GIRL'S SWEATER

BACK. With No. 7 needles cast on 92 (96, 104) sts. and work in k.1, p.1 rib for 2 ins. [5.08 cm], inc. 1 st. at end of last row for 3rd size only (92, 96, 105 sts.). Change to No. 5 needles and patt.:

1st row. K.3 (5, 3), * p.1, k.6, p.1, k.5; rep. from * ending last patt. with k.3 (5, 3).

2nd row. P.3 (5, 3), * k.1, p.6, k.1, p.5; rep. from * ending last rep. with p.3 (5, 3).

3rd row. K.3 (5, 3), * p.1., sl. next 3 sts. on to cable needle and keep at back of work, k.3, k.3 sts. from cable needle, p.1, k.5; rep. from * ending last rep. with k.3 (5, 3).

4th row. As 2nd row.

5th row. As 1st row.

6th row. As 2nd row.

7th row. As 1st row.

8th row. P.3 (5, 3), * k.1, p.2, k.2, p.2, k.1, p.5; rep. from * ending last rep. with p.3 (5, 3).

9th row. K.3 (5, 3), * p.1, k.2, p.2, k.2, p.1, k.5; rep. from * ending last rep. with k.3 (5, 3).

10th row. As 8th row.

11th row. As 1st row.

12th row. As 2nd row.

Cont. in 12-row patt., dec. 1 st. each end of row when work measures 5 ins. [12.70 cm]. Rep. dec. row at 3 in. [7.62 cm] intervals twice more. Work 6 rows. Inc. 1 st. each end of next row and every foll. 6th row to 92 (96, 105) sts. Cont. straight until work measures 17½ (17½, 18) ins. [44.45 (44.45, 45.72) cm], ending on wrong side.

Shape armholes. Cont. in patt. and cast off 4 sts. at beg. of next 2 rows, then dec. 1 st. each end of every foll. row until 68 (72, 81) sts. rem. Cont. straight until armholes measure 7 (7½, 8) ins. [17.78 (19.05, 20.32) cm], ending on wrong side.

Shape shoulders. Cast off 7 sts. at beg. of next 4 rows, then 6 (7, 10) sts. at beg. of foll. 2 rows. Leave rem. 28 (30, 33) sts. on a holder.

FRONT. Work as given for Back until armholes measure 5½ ins. [13.97 cm] (all sizes), ending on wrong side.

Shape neck. Next row. Patt. 26 (27, 31) sts., turn and cont. on these sts. only. Dec. 1 st. at neck edge of every row until 20 (21, 24) sts. rem. Cont. straight until armhole measures same as Back armhole, ending at side edge.

Shape shoulder. Cast off 7 sts. at beg. of next row and foll. alt. row, then 6 (7, 10) sts. at beg. of foll. alt. row.

Return to rem. sts. Leave centre 16 (18, 19) sts. on a holder.

Rejoin yarn to inner end of rem. sts. and work to correspond with other side.

SLEEVES: With No. 7 needles cast on 40 (44, 52) sts. and work in k.1, p.2 rib for 3 ins. [7.62 cm], inc. 1 st. at end of last row for 3rd size only (40, 44, 53 sts.). Change to No. 5 needles. Work in patt. as given for Back, inc. 1 st. each end of every foll. 6th row to 56 (60, 73) and working the extra sts. into st. st. as they occur. Cont. straight until work measures 17 (18, 18) ins. [43.18 (45.72, 45.72) cm (or length required), ending on wrong side.

Cont. in patt. and cast off 4 sts. at beg. of next 2 rows, then dec. 1 st. each end of every row until 16 (16, 23) sts. rem.

Cast off.

BOY'S SWEATER

BACK. Work as given for Back of Girl's Sweater until 12th patt. row has been worked. Now cont. straight in 12-row patt. until work measures 17½ (17½, 18) ins. [44.45 (44.45, 45.72) cm], ending on wrong side. Cont. as given for Girl's Sweater to end.

FRONT. Work as given for Back until armholes measure 5½ ins. [13.97 cm] (all sizes), ending on wrong side. Cont. as given for Girl's Sweater to end.

SLEEVES. As given for Girl's Sweater.

TO MAKE UP BOTH VERSIONS. Press work on the wrong side. Join shoulder, side and sleeve seams. Set in sleeves.

Polo collar. R.s.f., using set of No. 7 needles, pick up and k. 15 (18, 21) sts. down left front neck, k. across 16 (18, 19) sts. on holder at centre front, pick up and k. 15 (18, 21) sts. up right front neck, then k. across 28 (30, 33) sts. on holder at back neck (74, 84, 94 sts.). Work in rounds of k.1, p.1 rib for 4½ (5, 5) ins. [11.43 (12.70, 12.70) cm], then cast off ribwise.

His and Hers sweaters are worked in a 12-row cable pattern and feature k.1, p.1 rib polo collar and edgings. Her version is shaped into the waist.

Long-line, Short-sleeve Jacket

See photograph on page 95.

MATERIALS: 15 (16, 17, 18) balls of Villawool Superknit 4 ply Crepe; a pair of Nos. 10 and 12 needles; 12 buttons.

MEASUREMENTS: To fit 32 (34, 36, 38) in. [81.28 (86.36, 91.44, 96.52) cm] bust. Length, 28 (28, 28½, 29) ins. [71.12 (71.12, 72.39, 73.66) cm]. Sleeve, 3½ ins. [8.89 cm] (all sizes).

TENSION: 15 sts. to 2 inches [5.08 cm].

ABBREVIATIONS: See page 13.

TO MAKE:

BACK. With No. 12 needles cast on 143 (151, 159, 167) sts. and beg. k. row, work 4 rows in st. st.

Next (picot) row. K.1, (y.fwd., k.2 tog.) to end.

Change to No. 10 needles and, beg. p. row, work 17 rows in st. st. Dec. 1 st. each end of next row and every foll. 16th row until 119 (127, 135, 143) sts. rem. Cont. straight until work measures 21 ins. [53.34 cm] from picot row, ending on p. row.

Shape armholes. Cast off 4 sts. at beg. of next 2 rows, then 2 sts. at beg. of foll. 2 rows.

Next row. K.1, k.2 tog., k. to last 3 sts., sl.1, k.1, p.s.s.o., k.1.

Next row. P.

Rep. above 2 rows until 93 (99, 105, 111) sts. rem., then cont. straight until armholes measure 7 (7, 7½, 8) ins. [17.78 (17.78, 19.05, 20.32) cm], ending on p. row.

Shape shoulders. Cast off 5 (6, 6, 7) sts. at beg. of next 8 rows, then 7 (5, 7, 5) sts. at beg. of next 2 rows (39, 41, 43, 45 sts.).

Change to No. 12 needles and work 4 rows in st. st. Rep. picot row then, beg. p. row, work 3 rows in st. st. Cast off.

RIGHT FRONT. With No. 12 needles cast on 73 (77, 81, 85) sts.

Next row. K.

Next row. P. to last st., inc.

Rep. above 2 rows once, then rep. picot row as given for Back.

Change to No. 10 needles.

Next row. P. to last 2 sts., p.2 tog.

Next row. K.

Rep. above 2 rows once, then work 13 rows in st. st.

Next (buttonhole) row. K.2, y.fwd., k.2 tog., k. to last 2 sts., k.2 tog.

Work 15 rows straight.

Rep. last 16 rows until 62 (66, 70, 74) sts. rem., then work one more buttonhole on foll. 16th row as set (12 buttonholes altog.).

Cont. straight until work measures 6 rows less than Back to armholes, ending at front edge.

Shape V Front. Next row. K.1, k.2 tog., k. to end.

Work 2 rows.

Next row. P. to last 3 sts., p.2 tog., p.1.

Work 2 rows.

Next row. K.1, k.2 tog., k. to end.

Shape armhole. Cast off 4 sts. at beg. of next row.

Next row. K.

Next row. Cast off 2 sts., p. to last 3 sts., p.2 tog., p.1.

Next row. K. to last 3 sts., sl.1, k.1, p.s.s.o., k.1.

Next row. P.

Next row. K.1, k.2 tog., k. to last 3 sts., sl.1, k.1, p.s.s.o., k.1.

Cont. to dec. at armhole on every alt. row 5 (6, 7, 8) times more, at the same time, cont. to dec. at front edge on every 3rd row as set until 27 (29, 31, 33) sts. rem. Cont. straight until armhole measures same as Back armhole, ending at side edge.

Shape shoulder. Cast off 5 (6, 6, 7) sts. at beg. of next row and foll. 3 alt. rows, then 7 (5, 7, 5) sts. at beg. of foll. alt. row.

LEFT FRONT. Work as given for Right Front, reversing shapings.

SLEEVES. With No. 12 needles cast on 77 (79, 83, 87) sts. and work first five rows as given for Back. Change to No. 10 needles and, beg. p. row, cont. in st. st., inc. 1 st. each end of 2nd and every foll. 4th rows to 89 (93, 97, 101) sts. Cont. straight until work measures 3½ ins. [8.89 cm] from picot row, ending on p. row.

Cast off 4 sts. at beg. of next 2 rows.

Next row. K.1, k.2 tog., k. to last 3 sts., sl.1, k.1, p.s.s.o., k.1.

Next row. P.

Rep. last 2 rows until 55 (57, 59, 61) sts. rem. Cast off 2 sts. at beg. of next 6 rows; 3 sts. at beg. of next 6 rows, then 4 sts. at beg. of next 4 rows. Cast off rem. sts.

RIGHT FRONT BORDER. With No. 12 needles and r.s.f., pick up and k. 207 (207, 211, 215) sts. along Right Front.

1st row. P. to last st., inc.

2nd row. K.

3rd row. As 1st row.

4th row. K.1, (y.fwd., k.2 tog.) to end.

5th row. P. to last 2 sts., p.2 tog.

6th row. K.

7th row. As 5th row.

Cast off.

LEFT FRONT BORDER. Work as given for Right Front Border, working shaping at opposite end.

TO MAKE UP. Press work on the wrong side. Join shoulder, side and sleeve seams. Set in sleeves. Turn hems to inside at picot row and sl. st. into position, mitring corners at lower front edges. Press seams. Sew on buttons.

Pants and Striped Mini Top

See photograph on page 95.

MATERIALS:

Pants—6 (7, 8) balls of Villawool Cascade Nylon 5 ply Crepe in main colour (m.); a pair of Nos. 9 and 11 needles; a waist length of 1 in. [2.54 cm] wide elastic.

Mini top—5 (6, 7) balls of Villawool Cascade Nylon 5 ply Crepe in main colour (m.) and 2 balls of contrast colour (c.); a pair of Nos. 9 and 11 needles.

MEASUREMENTS: Top to fit 32 (34, 36) in. [81.28 (86.36, 91.44) cm] bust. Length, 13½ (13¾, 14) ins. [34.29 (34.92, 35.56) cm]. Sleeve, 3 (3¼, 3½) ins. [7.62 (8.25, 8.88) cm]. Pants to fit 34 (36, 38) in. [86.36 (91.44, 96.52) cm] hips.

TENSION: 13½ sts. to 2 inches [5.08 cm].

ABBREVIATIONS: See page 13.

TO MAKE:

TOP

BACK. With No. 11 needles and m. cast on 96 (102, 110) sts. and work in k.1, p.1 rib for 22 rows.

Next (inc.) row. K.7 (13, 16), (inc., k.5) 14 (14, 12) times, k. to end. (110, 116, 122 sts.).

Change to No. 9 needles and, beg. p. row, work in st. st. stripe sequence: Join in c.

Work 2 rows c., 2 rows m., 2 rows c., 6 rows m. Cont. until work measures 7¼ ins. [18.41 cm], ending on p. row.

Shape armholes. Cast off 5 sts. at beg. of next 2 rows, then dec. 1 st. each end of foll. 8 rows, then dec. 1 st. each end of foll. alt. rows until 74 (80, 86) sts. rem. Cont. straight until armholes measure 6¼ (6½, 6¾) ins. [15.87 (16.50, 17.13) cm, ending on p. row.

Shape shoulders. Cast off 6 (7, 8) sts. at beg. of next 4 rows, then 7 sts. at beg. of foll. 2 rows. Leave rem. 36 (38, 40) sts. on a holder.

FRONT. Work as given for Back until armholes

measure 4¾ (5, 5¼) ins. [12.06 (12.70, 13.33) cm], ending on p. row.

Shape neck. Next row. K.29 (31, 33), turn and cont. on these sts. only. Dec. 1 st. at neck edge of every foll. row until 19 (21, 23) sts. rem., then cont. straight until armhole measures same as Back armhole, ending at side edge.

Shape shoulder. Cast off 6 (7, 8) sts. at beg. of next row and foll. alt. row. Work 1 row, then cast off rem. sts.

Return to rem. sts. Sl. centre 16 (18, 20) sts. on a holder. Rejoin yarn to inner end of rem. sts. and work to correspond with other side.

SLEEVES. With No. 11 needles and m. cast on 64 (66, 68) sts. and work in k.1, p.1 rib for 10 rows.

Next (inc.) row. K.14 (15, 16), (inc., k.4) 10 times, k. to end. (74, 76, 78 sts.).

Change to No. 9 needles and, beg. p. row, work in st. st. for 5 rows, inc. 1 st. each end of 4th row. Now work in stripe sequence as given for Back, at the same time, inc. 1 st. each end of every foll. 6th row to 80 (84, 88) sts. Cont. until work measures 3 (3¼, 3½) ins. [7.62 (8.25, 8.88) cm], ending on p. row.

Cast off 5 sts. at beg. of next 2 rows, then dec. 1 st. each end of every alt. row until 22 sts. rem. Cast off 3 sts. at beg. of next 4 rows, then cast off rem. sts.

NECKBAND. Firstly, join right shoulder seam. R.s.f. with m. and No. 11 needles, pick up and k. 25 sts. down left side of neck, k. across front 16 (18, 20) sts., pick up and k. 25 sts. up right side of neck and, finally, k. across 36 (38, 40) sts. at back neck. (102, 106, 110 sts.). Work in k.1, p.1 rib for 8 rows, then cast off ribwise.

TO MAKE UP. Join right shoulder seam and neckband, side and sleeve seams. Set in sleeves. Lightly press seams.

PANTS

WORKED IN FOUR SECTIONS

LEFT FRONT LEG. With No. 11 needles and m. cast on 74 (77, 80) sts. and k. 10 rows. Change to No. 9 needles and, beg. p. row, work 11 rows in st. st.

Shape crutch. Dec. 1 st. at beg. of next row and at same edge of foll. 5 rows. Work 2 rows, then dec. 1 st. at same edge on next row and every foll. 3rd row until 64 (67, 70) sts. rem. Work 12 rows, then dec. 1 st. at same edge of next row and foll. 16th row. Work 2 rows, then dec. 1 st. each end of next row and 2 foll. 10th rows (56, 59, 62 sts.). ** Work 3 rows, then change to No. 11 needles and work 10 rows in k.1, p.1 rib. Cast off ribwise.

RIGHT FRONT LEG. Work as given for Left Front Leg, reversing shapings.

RIGHT BACK LEG. Work as given for Left Front Leg to **. Work 2 rows.

Shape back. 1st and 2nd rows. K.42, turn, sl.1, p. to end.

3rd and 4th rows. K.32, turn, sl.1, p. to end.

5th and 6th rows. K.22, turn, sl.1, p. to end.

K. 1 row across all sts. Change to No. 11 needles and work 10 rows in k.1, p.1 rib. Cast off ribwise.

LEFT BACK LEG. Work as given for Left Front Leg to **, reversing all shapings. Work 1 row, then shape back and finish as given for Right Back Leg, reading k. for p. and p. for k.

TO MAKE UP. Join centre front and centre back seams, then side seams. Join leg seams. Lightly press seams. Encase elastic to wrong side of waist ribbing with a herringbone stitch.

Patio Skirt

MATERIALS: 16 (17, 18, 19) balls of Villawood Purple Label Ban-Lon; a pair of Nos. 7 and 9 needles; a waist length of 1 in. wide elastic.

MEASUREMENTS: To fit 32 (34, 36, 38) in. [81.28 (86.36, 91.44, 96.52) cm] hips. Length, 40½ins. [102.87 cm] (or length required). Waist is adjustable with elastic.

TENSION: 6 sts. to 1 inch [2.54 cm] over garter st.

ABBREVIATIONS: See page 13.

TO MAKE:

BACK AND FRONT ALIKE. With No. 7 needles cast on 170 (170, 180, 180) sts. and work in patt.:

1st to 4th rows. K.

5th row. K.1, (k., winding yarn twice round needle) to last st., k.1.

6th row. K.1, (k., letting extra loop drop) to last st., k.1.

7th row. As 5th row.

8th row. As 6th row.

Rep. above 8 rows until work measures 20 ins. [50.80 cm] (work more or less as required at this point before beg. shaping), ending on 8th patt. row.

1st (dec.) row. K.2 tog., k.8 (8, 13, 13), (k.2 tog., k.13) 10 times, k.8 (8, 13, 13), k.2 tog. (158, 158, 168, 168 sts.).

Cont. in patt. until work measures 24 ins. [60.96 cm], ending on 8th row.

2nd (dec.) row. K.2 tog., k.14 (14, 10, 10), (k.2 tog., k.12) 10 (10, 11, 11) times, k.2 tog. (146, 146, 155, 155 sts.).

Cont. in patt. until work measures 28 ins. [71.12 cm], ending on 8th row.

3rd (dec.) row. K.2 tog., k.12 (12, 8, 8), (k.2 tog., k.11) 10 (10, 11, 11) times, k.2 tog. (134, 134, 142, 142 sts.).

Cont. in patt. until work measures 32 ins. [81.28 cm], ending on 8th row.

4th (dec.) row. K.2 tog., k.10 (10, 6, 6), (k.2 tog., k.10) 10 (10, 11, 11) times, k.2 tog. (122, 122, 129, 129 sts.).

Cont. in patt. until work measures 36 ins. [91.44 cm], ending on 8th row.

5th (dec.) row. K.2 tog., k.8 (8, 4, 4), (k.2 tog., k.9) 10 (10, 11, 11) times, k.2 tog. (110, 110, 116, 116 sts.).

Cont. in patt. until work measures 39 ins. [99.06 cm], ending on 8th row.

6th (dec.) row. K.10 (16, 16, 22), (k.2 tog., k.1) 30 (26, 28, 24) times, k. to end. (80, 84, 88, 92 sts.). Change to No. 9 needles and work in k.1, p.1 rib for 1½ ins. [3.81 cm].

Cast off ribwise.

TO MAKE UP. Join side seams. Encase elastic to inside waist ribbing with a herringbone stitch.

Ban-Lon skirt is knitted in an 8-row pattern with k.1, p.1 rib waistband.

6
Knitting for Women

Trouser Suit

See photograph on page 115.

CLASSIC CARDIGAN

MATERIALS: 20 (21, 22, 23, 24, 25) balls of Villawool Boucle Double Knitting; a pair of Nos. 8 and 10 needles; 11 (11, 11, 11, 12, 12) buttons.
MEASUREMENTS: To fit 32 (34, 36, 38, 40, 42) in. [81.28 (86.36, 91.44, 96.52, 101.60, 106.68) cm] bust. Length, 25 (25, 25½, 26, 26, 26¼) ins. [63.50 (63.50, 64.77, 66.04, 66.04, 66.67) cm]. Sleeve, 17 ins. [43.18 cm] (or length required).
TENSION: 6 sts. to 1 inch [2.54 cm].
ABBREVIATIONS: See page 13.

TO MAKE:
BACK. With No. 10 needles cast on 102 (108, 114, 120, 126, 132) sts. and work 10 rows in k.1, p.1 rib. Change to No. 8 needles and st. st. and cont. until work measures 18 ins. [45.72 cm], ending on p. row.
Shape armholes. Cast off 3 (4, 4, 5, 5, 6) sts. at beg. of next 2 rows, then dec. 1 st. each end of next row and foll. alt. rows until 80 (82, 84, 86, 88, 90) sts. rem. Cont. straight until armholes measure 7 (7, 7½, 8, 8, 8¼) ins. [17.78 (17.78, 19.05, 20.32, 20.32, 20.95) cm], ending on p. row.
Shape shoulders. Cast off 7 sts. at beg. of next 6 rows, then cast off rem. sts.
LEFT FRONT. With No. 10 needles cast on 49 (52, 55, 58, 61, 64) sts. and work 10 rows in k.1, p.1 rib. Change to No. 8 needles and st. st. and cont. until work measures same as Back to armhole shaping, ending at side edge.
Shape armhole. Cast off 3 (4, 4, 5, 5, 6) sts. at beg. of next row, then dec. 1 st. at side edge on alt. rows until 38 (39, 40, 41, 42, 43) sts. rem., then cont. straight until armhole measures 5 (5, 5½, 6, 6, 6¼) ins. [12.70 (12.70, 13.97, 15.24, 15.24, 15.87) cm], ending at front edge.
Shape neck. Cast off 7 (8, 9, 10, 11, 12) sts. at beg. of next row, then dec. 1 st. at neck edge of every foll. row until 21 sts. rem.
Cont. straight until armhole measures same as Back armhole, ending at side edge.
Shape shoulder. Cast off 7 sts. at beg. of next row and foll. 2 alt. rows.
RIGHT FRONT. Work as given for Left Front.
SLEEVES. With No. 10 needles cast on 44 (44, 48, 52, 52, 56) sts. and work in k.1, p.1 rib for 2½ ins. [6.35 cm]. Change to No. 8 needles and cont. in st. st., inc. 1 st. each end of every foll. 6th row to 72 (72, 78, 84, 84, 86) sts., then

cont. straight until work measures 17 ins. [43.18 cm] (or length required), ending on p. row.
Cast off 3 (4, 4, 5, 5, 6) sts. at beg. of next 2 rows, then dec. 1 st. at beg. of every row until 36 sts. rem. Cast off 2 sts. at beg. of next 8 rows, then cast off rem. sts.
NECKBAND. Firstly, join shoulder seams. R.s.f. and with No. 10 needles pick up and k. 25 sts. up right side of neck, then 38 (40, 42, 44, 46, 48) sts. across back neck and 25 sts. down left side of neck. (88, 90, 92, 94, 96, 98 sts.). Work 8 rows in k.1, p.1 rib, then cast off ribwise.
LEFT FRONT BAND. With No. 10 needles cast on 12 sts. and work in k.1, p.1 rib until band fits front edge to neck edge, then cast off ribwise. Mark positions for 11 (11, 11, 11, 12, 12) buttonholes on this band; the first ¼ in. [.63 cm] from beg. and the last in neckband, evenly spacing the others in between.
RIGHT FRONT BAND. Work as given for Left Front Band, making buttonholes to correspond with markers as follows:
Buttonhole row. Rib 4, cast off 4 sts., rib 4.
Next row. Rib and cast on 4 sts. over those cast off in previous row.
TO MAKE UP. Press work on the wrong side. Join side and sleeve seams. Set in sleeves. Attach front bands to their respective fronts. Sew on buttons. Press seams.

TROUSERS

MATERIALS: 26 (27, 28, 29, 30, 31) balls of Villawool Boucle Double Knitting; a pair of Nos. 9, 10 and 11 needles; a waist length of 1 in. [2.54 cm] wide elastic.
MEASUREMENTS: To fit 34 (36, 38, 40, 42, 44) in. [86.36 (91.44, 96.52, 101.60, 106.68, 111.76) cm] hips. Length, 41 ins. [104.14 cm] (or length required). Waist is adjustable with elastic.
TENSION: 6 sts. to 1 inch [2.54 cm].
ABBREVIATIONS: See page 13.

TO MAKE:
FIRST LEG. With No. 10 needles cast on 142 (148, 154, 160, 166, 172) sts. and k. 13 rows. Change to No. 9 needles and st. st., dec. 1 st. each end of 15th row and every foll. 14th row until 124 (130, 136, 142, 148, 154) sts. rem., then each end of every foll. 20th row until 114 (120, 126, 132, 138, 144) sts. rem. Cont. straight until work measures 31 ins. [78.74 cm] (or length required), ending on p. row. (End on k. row here when working second leg.)
Shape crutch. Next row. Cast off 2 sts., work to last 2 sts., dec. Place a marker at cast off end for front. Dec. 1 st. each end of next row and every foll. alt. row until 99 (105, 111, 117, 123, 129) sts. rem. Work 1 row, then dec. 1 st. at front edge

of every foll. 4th rows, at the same time, dec. 1 st. at back edge of foll. 7th rows until 90 (96, 102, 108, 114, 120) sts. rem. Cont. straight until work measures 6¾ ins. [17.14 cm] from crutch beg., ending on k. row. (End on p. row when working second leg.)

Shape back. 1st row. P.67 (73, 79, 85, 91, 97), turn.

2nd and alt. rows. K. (p. when working second leg).

3rd row. P. 56 (62, 68, 74, 80, 86), turn.

5th row. P. 45 (51, 57, 63, 69, 75), turn.

Cont. thus, working 11 sts. less on alt. rows until the row 'p.12 (18, 24, 30, 36, 42)' has been worked.

Next row. Work to end.

Work 2 rows without shaping, then leave sts. on holder.

SECOND LEG. Work as given for First Leg.

WAISTBAND. Firstly, join front from crutch to waist. R.s.f. and with No. 11 needles work across both sets of sts. Work in k.1, p.1 rib for 1½ ins. [3.81 cm], then cast off ribwise.

TO MAKE UP. Press work on the wrong side. Join leg seams, then back seams. Press seams. Encase elastic to inside waistband with a herringbone st.

Ribbed Sweater with Contrast Trim

See photograph on page 96.

MATERIALS: 11 (12, 13, 14) balls of Villawool Cascade Nylon 4 ply Crepe in main colour (m.) and 1 (1, 1, 1) ball of contrast colour (c.); a pair of Nos. 10 and 12 needles; 4 buttons; a press stud.

MEASUREMENTS: To fit 32 (34, 36, 38) in. [81.28 (86.36, 91.44, 96.52) cm] bust. Length, 21½ (22, 22, 22½) ins. [54.61 (55.88, 55.88, 57.15) cm]. Sleeve, 6½ ins. [16.51 cm].

TENSION: 7¾ sts. to 1 inch [2.54 cm] over rib.

ABBREVIATIONS: See page 13.

NOTE: Cast off in rib patt.

TO MAKE:

BACK. With No. 10 needles and m. cast on 132 (140, 148, 156) sts. and work in rib patt. as follows:

1st row. K.3, (p.2, k.2) to last st., k.1.

2nd row. K.1, (p.2, k.2) to last 3 sts., p.2, k.1.

Rep. above 2 rows until work measures 3 (3, 2½, 2½) ins. [7.62 (7.62, 6.35, 6.35) cm]. Cont. in rib patt. and dec. 1 st. each end of next row and every foll. 6th row until 124 (132, 140, 148) sts. rem. Cont. straight until work measures 8 (8, 7½, 7½) ins. [20.32 (20.32, 19.05, 19.05) cm], then inc. 1 st. each end of next row and every foll. 8th row to 132 (140, 148, 156) sts. Cont. straight until work measures 15 (15, 14½, 14½) ins. [38.10 (38.10, 36.83, 36.83) cm].

Shape armholes. Cont. in rib patt. and cast off 8 sts. at beg. of next 2 rows, then dec. 1 st. each end of every foll. row until 96 (104, 104, 108) sts. rem. Cont. straight until armholes measure 6½ (7, 7½, 8) ins. [16.51 (17.78, 19.05, 20.32) cm].

Shape shoulders. Cast off 11 (12, 12, 13) sts. at beg. of next 4 rows, then 10 (12, 12, 12) sts. at beg. of foll. 2 rows. Leave rem. 32 sts. on a holder.

FRONT. Work as given for Back until increasing is completed and work measures 11 (11, 10½, 10½) ins. [27.94 (27.94, 26.67, 26.67) cm], ending on wrong side of work 132 (140, 148, 156 sts.).

Divide for Front Opening. Next row. Patt. 60 (64, 68, 72) sts., turn and cont. on these sts. only. Cont. straight until work measures same as Back to beg. of armhole shaping, ending at side edge.

Shape armhole. Cast off 8 sts. at beg. of next row, then dec. 1 st. at same edge of every foll. row until 42 (46, 46, 48) sts. rem., then cont. straight until armhole measures 4½ (5, 5½, 6) ins. [11.43 (12.70, 13.97, 15.24) cm], ending at side edge.

Shape neck. Dec. 1 st. at neck edge of every foll. row until 32 (36, 36, 38) sts. rem., then cont. straight until armhole measures same as back armhole, ending at side edge.

Shape shoulder. Cast off 11 (12, 12, 13) sts. at beg. of next and foll. alt. row. Work 1 row, then cast off rem. sts.

Return to sts. on needle. Rejoin yarn to inner end and cast off centre 12 sts., then cont. on rem. sts. to correspond with other side.

SLEEVES. With No. 12 needles and m., cast on 88 (92, 92, 96) sts. and work in 2-row rib patt. as given for Back for 2 ins. [5.08 cm]. Change to No. 10 needles and cont. in patt., inc. 1 st. each end of next row and every foll. 7th row to 100 (104, 104, 108) sts., then cont. straight until work measures 6½ ins. [16.51 cm].

Cast off 8 sts. at beg. of next 2 rows, then dec. 1 st. at beg. of every row until 56 (56, 62, 62) sts. rem. Cast off 2 sts. at beg. of every row until 28 (28, 28, 30) sts. rem., then cast off.

LEFT FRONT BORDER. With No. 12 needles and c., cast on 14 sts. and work in garter st. until border fits front cast-off sts. at centre front to beg. of neck edge shaping. Leave sts. on a holder.

Mark positions for 4 buttonholes on this border—the first at ½ in. [1.27 cm] from beg. and the 4th to go in neckband, evenly spacing the others in between.

RIGHT FRONT BORDER. Work as given for Left Front Border, making 3 buttonholes to correspond with markers thus:

Buttonhole row. K. 6, cast off 3 sts., k. to end.

Next row. K. and cast on 3 sts. over those cast off in previous row.

TO MAKE UP. Join shoulder, side and sleeve seams. Attach borders to their respective fronts as pictured.

NECKBAND. R.s.f., with No. 12 needles and c., k. across 14 sts. on holder, pick up and k. 19 sts. up right side of neck, k. across sts. on back holder, pick up and k. 19 sts. down left side of neck and, finally, k. across 14 sts. on holder (98, 98, 98, 98 sts). K. 5 rows.

Next (buttonhole) row. K.6, cast off 3 sts., k. to end.

Next row. K. and cast on 3 sts. over those cast off in previous row. K. 5 rows, then cast off.

TO FINISH OFF. Set in sleeves. Lightly press seams. Sew on buttons.

Long-line Sweater with Saddle Shoulder and Polo Neck

See photograph on page 110.

MATERIALS: 27 (27, 28, 28) balls of Villawool Superknit DC8; a pair of Nos. 8 and 10 needles; a set of 4 double-pointed No. 10 needles.

MEASUREMENTS: To fit 32 (34, 36, 38) in. [81.28 (86.36, 91.44, 96.52) cm] bust. Length, 27 (27½, 28, 28½) ins. [68.58 (69.85, 71.12, 72.39) cm]. Sleeve, 17 ins. [43.18 cm] (or length required).

TENSION: 6 sts. to 1 inch [2.54 cm] over patt.

ABBREVIATIONS: See page 13.

TO MAKE:

BACK. With No. 10 needles cast on 120 (127, 134, 141) sts. and work in k.1, p.1 rib for 1 in. [2.54 cm]. Change to No. 8 needles.

1st row. (Right side) K.3, (p.2, k.5) to last 5 sts., p.2, k.3.

2nd row. P.3, (k.2, p.5) to last 5 sts., k.2, p.3.

Rep. above 2 rows until work measures 9 ins. [22.86 cm], ending on wrong side. Now work in patt.:

1st row. K.1, tw.2f., (p.2, tw.2b., k.1, tw.2f.) to last 5 sts., p.2, tw.2b., k.1.

2nd row. P.3, (k.2, p.5) to last 5 sts., k.2, p.3.

3rd row. K.1, tw.2b., (p.2, tw.2f., k.1, tw.2b.) to last 5 sts., p.2, tw.2f., k.1.

4th row. As 2nd row.

Rep. last 4 rows until work measures 14 ins. [35.56 cm], ending on 3rd row.

Next (dec.) row. P.3, (k.2, p.1, p.2 tog., p.2) to last 5 sts., k.2, p.3. (104, 110, 116, 122 sts.).

Next row. K.3, (p.2, k.4) to last 5 sts., p.2, k.3.

Next row. P.3, (k.2, p.4) to last 5 sts., k.2, p.3. Rep. above 2 rows until work measures 20 ins. [50.80 cm], ending on wrong side.

Shape armholes. Cast off 5 sts. at beg. of next 2 rows, then dec. 1 st. each end of next row and every foll. alt. row until 84 (88, 92, 96) sts. rem. Cont. straight until armholes measure 5¾ (6¼, 6¾, 7¼) ins. [14.60 (15.87, 17.14, 18.41) cm], ending on wrong side.

Shape shoulders. Cast off 7 sts. at beg. of next 6 rows, then 6 (7, 8, 9) sts. at beg. of foll. 2 rows. Work 1¼ ins. [3.17 cm] on rem. 30 (32, 34, 36) sts., ending on wrong side. Leave sts. on holder.

FRONT. Work as given for Back until armholes measure 4¼ (4½, 4¾, 5) ins. [10.79 (11.43, 12.06, 12.70) cm], ending on wrong side.

Shape neck. Next row. Work 34 (35, 36, 37) sts., turn and cont. on these sts. only. Dec. 1 st. at neck edge of every foll. row until 27 (28, 29, 30) sts. rem. Cont. straight until armhole measures same as Back armhole, ending at side edge.

Shape shoulder. Cast off 7 sts. at beg. of next row and foll. 2 alt. rows. Work 1 row, then cast off rem. sts.

Return to rem. sts. Sl. centre 16 (18, 20, 22) sts. on a holder.

Rejoin yarn to inner end of rem. sts. and work to correspond with other side.

SLEEVES. With No. 10 needles cast on 52 (54, 56, 58) sts. and work in k.1, p.1 rib for 2 ins. [5.08 cm]. Change to No. 8 needles and cont. in st. st., inc. 1 st. each end of every foll. 7th row to 78 (82, 86, 90) sts. Cont. straight until work measures 17 ins. [43.18 cm] (or length required), ending on p. row.

Cast off 5 sts. at beg. of next 2 rows, then dec. 1 st. each end of next row and every foll. alt. row until 38 (42, 42, 46) sts. rem., then each end of every row until 24 sts. rem. Cast off 4 sts. at beg. of next 2 rows. Work 4½ (4½, 4¾, 4¾) ins.

[11.43 (11.43, 12.06, 12.06) cm] on rem. 16 sts., ending on p. row. Cast off.

TO MAKE UP. Press work lightly on the wrong side. Join side and sleeve seams. Set in sleeves, then stitch saddle extensions into position (the 1¼ ins. [3.17 cm] at Back to be stitched ½ way across cast-off sts. of saddle). Press seams.

POLO COLLAR. R.s.f. and with set of No. 10 needles, pick up and k. 24 (26, 28, 30) sts. down left side of neck, k. across 16 (18, 20, 22) sts. on Front holder, pick up and k. 24 (26, 28, 30) sts. up right side of neck and, finally, k. across 30 (32, 34, 36) sts. on Back holder (94, 102, 110, 118 sts.). Work in k.1, p.1 rib for 5 ins. [12.70 cm], then cast off ribwise.

BELT. With No. 10 needles cast on 11 sts. and work in k.1, p.1 rib for 50 ins. [127.00 cm]. Cast off ribwise.

Long-line Jacket

MATERIALS: 33 (34, 35, 36) balls of Villawool Superknit 12 ply Crepe; a pair of Nos. 5 and 7 needles; 8 buttons.
MEASUREMENTS: To fit 32 (34, 36, 38) in. [81.28 (86.36, 91.44, 96.52) cm] bust. Length, 32½ (33, 33¼, 33½) ins. [82.55 (83.82, 84.45, 85.09) cm]. Sleeve, 16½ ins. [41.91 cm] (or length required).
TENSION: 9 sts. to 2 inches [5.08 cm].
ABBREVIATIONS: See page 13.

TO MAKE:
BACK. With No. 5 needles cast on 94, (98, 102, 106) sts. and work 12 rows in k.1, p.1 rib, inc. 1 st. at end of last row. (95, 99, 103, 107 sts.) Beg. k. row, work 34 rows in st. st. Cont. in st. st. and dec. 1 st. each end of next row and every foll. 16th row until 85 (89, 93, 97) sts. rem. Cont. straight until work measures 25 ins. [63.50 cm], ending on p. row.
Shape armholes. Cast off 3 (4, 5, 6) sts. at beg. of next 2 rows, then 2 sts. (all sizes) at beg. of

Long-line jacket or car coat is knitted in a bulky 12-ply yarn in stocking stitch with k.1, p.1 rib edgings, and features set-in pockets.

foll. 2 rows. Dec. 1 st. each end of alt. rows until 65 (67, 69, 71) sts. rem. Cont. straight until armholes measure 7½ (8, 8¼, 8½) ins. [19.05 (20.32, 20.95, 21.59) cm], ending on p. row.
Shape shoulders and neck. Cast off 4 (5, 4, 5) sts. at beg. of next 2 rows. **Next row.** Cast off 4 (4, 5, 5) sts., k.11 (11, 12, 12), cast off centre 27 sts., k. to end. Cont. on these last sts. only. Cast off 4 (4, 5, 5) sts. at beg. of next and foll. alt. row, at the same time, dec. 1 st. at neck edge of next 3 rows. Work 1 row, then cast off rem. sts. Rejoin yarn to inner end of rem. sts. and work to correspond with other side.

POCKET LININGS (2). With No. 5 needles cast on 29 sts. and, beg. k. row, work 34 rows in st. st. Leave aside.

RIGHT FRONT. With No. 5 needles cast on 56 (58, 60, 62) sts. and work 12 rows in k.1, p.1 rib, inc. 1 st. at side edge of last row (57, 59, 61, 63 sts.).
Next row. Rib 13, k. to end.
Next row. P. to last 13 sts., rib 13.
Rep. above 2 rows until work measures 2 ins. [5.08 cm], ending at front edge.
Next (buttonhole) row. Rib 6, cast off 2 sts., rib 5, k. to end.
Next row. P. to last 13 sts., rib to end, casting on 2 sts. over those cast off in previous row.
Cont. straight until 34 rows have been worked.
Next (pocket) row. Work 23 sts., sl. next 29 sts. on to holder, k. across sts. of one pocket lining, k. to end.
Cont. making a buttonhole as before at 4 in. [10.16 cm] intervals, at the same time, dec. 1 st. at side edge on next row and every foll. 16th row until 52 (54, 56, 58) sts. rem. Cont. straight until work measures same as Back to armholes, ending at side edge.
Shape armhole. Cont. to make buttonholes as set and cast off 3 (4, 5, 6) sts. at beg. of next row, then 2 sts. (all sizes) at beg. of foll. alt. row. Dec. 1 st. at beg. of every alt. row until 42 (43, 44, 45) sts. rem. Cont. straight until armhole measures 5½ (6, 6¼, 6½) ins. [13.97 (15.24, 15.87, 16.51) cm], ending at front edge.
Shape neck. Next row. Work 15 sts. and sl. these sts. on a holder, k. to end. Dec. 1 st. at neck edge of next 11 rows, then cont. straight until work measures same as Back to shoulder shaping, ending at side edge.
Shape shoulder. Cast off 4 (5, 4, 5) sts. at beg. of next row, 4 (4, 5, 5) sts. at beg. of foll. 2 alt. rows. Work 1 row, then cast off rem. sts.

LEFT FRONT. Work as given for Right Front, reversing position of front band and pocket opening row and omitting buttonholes.

SLEEVES. With No. 7 needles cast on 34 (34, 36, 36) sts. and work in k.1, p.1 rib for 8 rows. Change to No. 5 needles and cont. in rib, inc. 1 st. each end of every 6th row to 42 (44, 46, 48)

sts. Now cont. in st. st., inc. each end of every 6th row to 64 (66, 68, 70) sts.

Cont. straight until work measures 16½ ins. [41.91 cm] (or length required), ending on p. row. Cast off 3 (4, 5, 6) sts. at beg. of next 2 rows, then 2 sts. at beg. of foll. 2 rows. Dec. 1 st. at beg. of every row until 26 sts. rem.

Cast off 2 sts. at beg. of next 6 rows. Cast off.

NECKBAND. Firstly, join shoulder seams. R.s.f. and with No. 7 needles, work across 15 sts. of right front holder, pick up and k. 20 sts. up right front neck and 38 sts. around back neck, pick up and k. 20 sts. down left front neck and, finally, work across sts. of left front holder. (108 sts.). Work 7 rows in k.1, p.1 rib, making final button-hole in neckband. Cast off ribwise.

TO MAKE UP. Press work on the wrong side. Join side and sleeve seams. Set in sleeves. Stitch pocket linings into position. Sew on buttons. Press seams.

POCKET TOPS. With No. 5 needles work 11 rows in k.1, p.1 rib on rem. sts. Cast off ribwise. Stitch sides to garment.

Evening Top

See photograph on page 116.

MATERIALS: 17 (18, 19, 20) balls of Villawool Superknit 5 ply Crepe; a pair of Nos. 9 and 11 needles; medium crochet hook; 5 in. [12.70 cm] zip; 4 small buttons.

MEASUREMENTS: To fit 30 (32, 34, 36) in. [76.20 (81.28, 86.36, 91.44) cm] bust. Length, 23 (23½, 24, 24½) ins. [58.42 (59.69, 60.96, 62.23) cm]. Sleeve, 18 ins. [45.72 cm].

TENSION: 13½ sts. to 2 inches [5.08 cm].

ABBREVIATIONS: See page 13.

TO MAKE:

BACK. With No. 11 needles cast on 112 (118, 124, 130) sts. and k. 7 rows. Change to No. 9 needles and, beg. k. row, work in st. st. for 14 rows. Dec. 1 st. each end of next row and every foll. 14th row until 102 (108, 114, 120) sts. rem., then inc. 1 st. each end of every foll. 10th row to 110 (116, 122, 128) sts. Cont. straight until work measures 16 (16½, 16½, 17) ins. [40.64 (41.91, 41.91, 43.18) cm], ending on p. row.

Long-line sweater is made in a combination of wide rib, stocking stitch and k.1, p.1 rib...features a saddle shoulder, polo neck and an optional ribbed tie belt (see page 107 for instructions).

Shape armholes. Cast off 5 sts. at beg. of next 2 rows, then dec. 1 st. each end of every foll. row until 82 (86, 90, 94) sts. rem. Cont. straight until armholes measure 4 (4, 4½, 4½) ins. [10.16 (10.16, 11.43, 11.43) cm], ending on a p. row.

Divide for back opening. Next row. K. 41 (43, 45, 47) sts., turn and cont. on these sts. only. Cont. until armhole measures 7 (7, 7½, 7½) ins. [17.78 (17.78, 19.05, 19.05) cm], ending at side edge.

Shape shoulder. Cast off 6 sts. at beg. of next row and foll. 2 alt. rows, then 6 (7, 8, 9) sts. at beg. of foll. alt. row. Cast off rem. 17 (18, 19, 20) sts.

Return to rem. sts. Rejoin yarn to inner end of rem. sts. and work to correspond with other side.

FRONT. Work as given for Back until armholes measure 5 (5, 5½, 5½) ins. [12.70 (12.70, 13.97, 13.97) cm], ending on p. row.

Shape neck. Next row. K. 34 (35, 36, 37) sts., turn and cont. on these sts. only. Dec. 1 st. at neck edge of every foll. row until 24 (25, 26, 27) sts. rem. Cont. straight until armhole measures same as Back armhole, ending at side edge.

Shape shoulder. Cast off 6 sts. at beg. of next row and foll. 2 alt. rows. Work 1 row, then cast off rem. sts.

Return to rem. sts. Rejoin yarn to inner end, cast off centre 14 (16, 18, 20) sts., then cont. to correspond with other side.

SLEEVES. With No. 9 needles cast on 56 (56, 58, 58) sts. and, beg. k. row, work in st. st. for 16 rows. Leave aside. Work another piece in same way and on 17th row work across first set of sts. (112, 112, 116, 116 sts.). Cont. in st. st., dec. 1 st. each end of every foll. 6th row until 80 (80, 84, 84) sts. rem. Cont. straight until work measures 18 ins. [45.72 cm], ending on p. row.

Cast off 5 sts. at beg. of next 2 rows. Dec. 1 st. at beg. of next 12 (12, 16, 16) rows, then dec. 1 st. each end of every foll. row until 22 sts. rem. Cast off.

Cuffs (2). With No. 11 needles cast on 39 (39, 43, 43) sts. and work in garter st. for 2 ins. [5.08 cm]. Cast off.

TO MAKE UP. Press work on the wrong side. Join shoulder, side and sleeve seams. Set in sleeves. Oversew cuffs to sleeves, gathering sleeve edge to fit. With crochet hook work 2 rows of d.c. down side edges of cuffs and sleeve opening to neaten, forming 2 button loops on one side of each cuff in 2nd row.

NECKBAND. R.s.f. and with No. 11 needles pick up and k. 99 (103, 111, 115) sts. evenly around neck edge, then work in garter st. for 7 rows.

Next (dec.) row. (K.8, k.2 tog.) 9 (9, 10, 10) times, k. to end. K. 1 row, then cast off.

TO FINISH OFF. Insert zip to back opening. Sew buttons to each cuff. Press seams.

Sleeveless Chevron Patterned Dress

MATERIALS: 19 (20, 20, 21, 21) balls of Villa-wool Purple Label Ban-Lon; a pair of Nos. 6 and 8 needles; 4 buttons; crochet hook.

MEASUREMENTS: To fit 32 (34, 36, 38, 40) in. [81.28 (86.36, 91.44, 96.52, 101.60) cm] bust. Length, 40 (40, 40½, 40½, 41) ins. [101.60 (101.60, 102.87, 102.87, 104.14) cm] (or length required).

TENSION: 6 sts. to 1 inch [2.54 cm].

ABBREVIATIONS: See page 13.

NOTE: When measuring work always measure from edge of scallop.

TO MAKE:

BACK. With No. 6 needles cast on 170 (184, 198, 212, 226) sts. and p. 1 row, then cont. in patt. as follows:

1st row. K.1, (m.1, k.5, sl.1, k.1, p.s.s.o., k.2 tog., k.5, m.1) to last st., k.1.

2nd row. P.

Rep. above 2 rows until work measures 7 ins. [17.78 cm], ending on 1st row (adjust length for more or less as required at this point before beg. shaping).

1st (dec.) row. P.1, (p.3, p.2 tog., p.4, p.2 tog., p.3) to last st., p.1. (146, 158, 170, 182, 194 sts.). Cont. in patt.:

1st row. K.1, (m.1, k.4, sl.1, k.1, p.s.s.o., k.2 tog., k.4, m.1) to last st., k.1.

2nd row. P.

Rep. above 2 rows until work measures 14 ins. [35.56 cm], ending on 1st row.

2nd (dec.) row. P.1, (p.2, p.2 tog., p.4, p.2 tog., p.2) to last st., p.1. (122, 132, 142, 152, 162 sts.). Cont. in patt.:

1st row. K.1, (m.1, k.3, sl.1, k.1, p.s.s.o., k.2 tog., k.3, m.1) to last st., k.1.

2nd row. P.

Rep. above 2 rows until work measures 22 ins. [55.88 cm], ending on 1st row.

3rd (dec.) row. P.1, (p.1, p.2 tog., p.4, p.2 tog., p.1) to last st., p.1. (98, 106, 114, 122, 130 sts.). Cont. in patt.:

1st row. K.1, (m.1, k.2, sl.1, k.1, p.s.s.o., k.2 tog., k.2, m.1) to last st., k.1.

2nd row. P.

Rep. above 2 rows until work measures 25 ins.

Sleeveless dress is knitted in a Chevron pattern with garter stitch neck and sleeve edges

[63.50 cm]. Cont. in patt. and inc. 1 st. each end of next row and every foll. 4th row to 114 (122, 130, 138, 146) sts., including the extra sts. into the patt. where possible. Cont. straight until work measures 33½ ins. [85.09 cm], ending on wrong side.

Shape armholes. Cont. in patt. and cast off 7 sts. at beg. of next 2 rows **. Dec. 1 st. each end of every row until 72 (76, 80, 84, 88) sts. rem., then cont. straight until armholes measure 6½ (6½, 7, 7, 7½) ins. [16.51 (16.51, 17.78, 17.78, 19.05) cm], ending on wrong side.

Shape shoulders. Cast off 5 (6, 7, 6, 7) sts. at beg. of next 2 rows, then 6 (6, 6, 7, 7) sts. at beg. of next 4 rows. Leave rem. 38 (40, 42, 44, 46) sts. on a holder.

FRONT. Work as given for Back to **.

Divide for front opening. Next row. K.2 tog., patt. 45 (49, 53, 57, 61) sts., turn, and cont. on these sts. only. Dec. 1 st. at armhole edge of every foll. row until 33 (35, 37, 39, 41) sts. rem., then cont. straight until armhole measures 4½ (4½, 5, 5, 5½) ins. [11.43 (11.43, 12.70, 12.70, 13.97) cm], ending at neck edge.

Shape neck. Cast off 8 (9, 10, 11, 12) sts. at beg. of next row, then dec. 1 st. at neck edge of every foll. row until 17 (18, 19, 20, 21) sts. rem., then cont. straight until armhole measures same as back armhole, ending at side edge.

Shape shoulder. Cast off 5 (6, 7, 6, 7) sts. at beg. of next row, then 6 (6, 6, 7, 7) sts. at beg. of foll. 2 alt. rows.

Return to rem. sts. Sl. centre 6 sts. on a holder. Rejoin yarn to inner end of rem. sts. and patt. to last 2 sts., k.2 tog.

Now cont. to correspond with other side.

LEFT FRONT BORDER. With No. 8 needles cast on 6 sts. and work in garter st. until band fits along front opening, slightly stretched. Leave sts. on holder. Attach band to garment. Mark positions for 3 buttonholes on this band, remembering that the fourth buttonhole will be made in neckband.

RIGHT FRONT BORDER. Work as given for Left Front Border, making buttonholes to correspond with markers thus:

Buttonhole row. R.s.f. K.2, y.fwd., k.2 tog., k. to end.

NECKBAND. Firstly, join shoulder seams. R.s.f. and with No. 8 needles k. across 6 sts. of Right Front Border, pick up and k. 25 sts. up right side of neck, k. across sts. at back, pick up and k. 25 sts. down left side of neck, then k. across 6 sts. of Left Front Border (100, 102, 104, 106, 108 sts.). K. 1 row.

Next (buttonhole) row. K.2, y.fwd., k.2 tog., k. to end. K. 2 rows, then cast off.

ARMHOLE BORDERS. R.s.f. and with No. 8 needles pick up and k. 84 (84, 90, 90, 96) sts. around armhole. K. 4 rows, then cast off.

TO MAKE UP. Join side seams. Press seams. Sew on buttons. R.s.f. and with crochet hook, work a row of d.c. along lower scalloped edge.

Patterned Waistcoat

See photograph on page 96.

MATERIALS: 15 (16, 17) balls of Villawool Superknit 4 ply Crepe; a pair of Nos. 10 and 12 needles; 5 buttons.

MEASUREMENTS: To fit 34 (36, 38) in. [86.36 (91.44, 96.52) cm] bust. Length, 28 (28¼, 28½) ins. [71.12 (71.75, 72.39) cm].

TENSION: 7 sts. to 1 inch [2.54 cm].

ABBREVIATIONS: See page 13.

TO MAKE:

BACK. With No. 12 needles cast on 135 (141, 147) sts. and, beg. k. row, work 11 rows in st. st. K. next row to form hemline. Change to No. 10 needles and cont. in patt. as follows:

1st row. K.2, (y.fwd., sl.1, k.1, p.s.s.o., k.1, k.2 tog., y.fwd., k.1) to last st., k.1.

2nd row. P.

3rd row. K.3, (y.fwd., sl.1, k.2 tog., p.s.s.o., y.fwd., k.3) to end.

4th row. P.

5th row. (K.3, p.3) to last 3 sts., k.3.

6th row. (P.3, k.3) to last 3 sts., p.3.

7th row. As 5th row.

8th row. As 6th row.

Rep. above 8 rows, dec. 1 st. each end of every foll. 12th row until 117 (123, 129) sts. rem., then cont. straight until work measures 12 ins. [30.48 cm] from hemline, ending on wrong side. Now inc. 1 st. each end of next row and every foll. 24th row to 123 (129, 135) sts., taking the extra sts. into the patt. as they occur. Cont. straight until work measures 21 ins. [53.34 cm] from hemline, ending on wrong side.

Shape armholes. Cont. in patt. and cast off 3 (4, 5) sts. at beg. of next 2 rows, then dec. 1 st. each end of every alt. row until 99 (99, 105) sts. rem., then cont. straight until armholes measure 7 (7¼, 7½) ins. [17.78 (18.41, 19.05) cm], ending on wrong side.

Shape shoulders. Cast off 6 sts. at beg. of next 8 rows, then 7 (7, 9) sts. at beg. of foll. 2 rows. Cast off rem. sts.

LEFT FRONT. With No. 12 needles cast on 63 (69, 69) sts. and, beg. k. row, work 11 rows in st. st.

Next (hemline) row. Cast on 21 sts., k. to end. (84, 90, 90 sts.).

Change to No. 10 needles and work in patt. as given for Back over 63 (69, 69) sts., keeping front border in st. st. thus:

1st row. Patt. across 63 (69, 69) sts., k.10, sl.1, k.10.

2nd row. P.21 sts., patt. to end.

Cont. as set until 20 patt. rows have been worked, then dec. 1 st. at side edge of next row and every foll. 12th row until 54 (60, 60) patt. sts. rem., then cont. straight until work measures 12 ins. [30.48 cm] from hemline. Now inc. 1 st. at side edge of next row and every foll. 24th row to 57 (63, 63) patt. sts. (21 sts. still rem. in front border), at the same time, when work measures approx. 1 in. [2.54 cm] less than Back to beg. of armhole shaping, end at side edge.

Shape front. Next row. Patt. to last 23 sts., k.2 tog., k.10, sl.1, k.10. cont. to dec. at front edge on every foll. 6th (4th, 4th) row, at the same time, when work measures same as Back to armholes, end at side edge.

Shape armhole. Cont. in patt. and cast off 3 (4, 5) sts. at beg. of next row, then dec. 1 st. at same edge of foll. 12 (11, 10) alt. rows, then cont. to dec. at front edge only as set until 52 (52, 54) sts. rem., then cont. straight until armhole measures same as back armhole, ending at side edge.

Shape shoulder. Cast off 6 sts. at beg. of next row and foll. 3 alt. rows, then 7 (7, 9) sts. at beg. of foll. alt. row. cont. on rem. 21 front border sts. until strip fits to centre back neck, then leave sts. on a holder.

Mark positions for five buttonholes on this border—the first at 2 ins. [5.08 cm] above hemline and the fifth ½ in. [1.27 cm] below beg. of shaping, evenly spacing the others in between.

RIGHT FRONT. Work as given for Left Front, reversing all shapings and making buttonholes to correspond with markers thus:

Buttonhole row. K.4, cast off 3, k.3, sl.1, k.3, cast off 3, k.4, patt. to end.

Next row. In patt., casting on 3 sts. over those cast off in previous row.

ARMHOLE FACINGS. Firstly, join shoulder seams. R.s.f. and with No. 12 needles pick up and k. 126 (130, 134) sts. evenly around entire armhole edge. Work 8 rows in st. st., then cast off.

TO MAKE UP. Press work on the wrong side. Join side seams. Graft neck border sts. tog. and attach band to neck edge of garment, then fold border in half at sl. st. and hem into position. Fold armhole facings and lower edge hem to inside and stitch into position. Neaten buttonholes. Sew on buttons. Press seams and facings.

Classic cardigan and wide-legged trousers in boucle teamed together make a fashionable trouser suit (see page 105 for instructions).

Ski-ing Jacket and Cap

See photograph on page 118.

MATERIALS:

Jacket—12 (13, 14) balls of Villawool Super Slalom in main colour (m.) and 2 balls of contrast colour (c.); a pair of Nos. 5 and 7 needles; 5 buttons; crochet hook.

Cap—2 balls of Villawool Super Slalom in main colour (m.); a set of 4 double-pointed No. 7 needles.

MEASUREMENTS: Jacket to fit 34 (36, 38) in. [86.36 (91.44, 96.52) cm] bust. Length, 24 (25, 26) ins. [60.96 (63.50, 66.04) cm]. Sleeve, 17 ins. [43.18 cm] (or length required). Cap to fit average size head.

TENSION: 9 sts. to 2 inches [5.08 cm].

ABBREVIATIONS: See page 13.

TO MAKE:

JACKET

BACK. With No. 7 needles and m. cast on 76 (80, 84) sts. and, beg. k. row, work 5 rows in st. st. K. next row to form hemline. Change to No. 5 needles and, beg. k. row, cont. in st. st., dec. 1 st. each end of 21st (23rd, 25th) row, then each end of every foll. 8th row until 68 (72, 76) sts. rem. Work 13 rows straight, then inc. 1 st. each end of next row and every foll. 6th row to 80 (84, 88) sts. Cont. straight until work measures 17 (17½, 18) ins. [43.18 (44.45, 45.72) cm] from hemline row, ending on p. row.

Shape armholes. Cast off 4 sts. at beg. of next 2 rows, then dec. 1 st. each end of next row and foll. alt. rows until 66 (70, 74) sts. rem. Cont. straight until armhole measures 7 (7½, 8) ins. [17.78 (19.05, 20.32) cm], ending on p. row.

Shape shoulders. Cast off 7 (8, 8) sts. at beg. of next 4 rows, then 8 (7, 8) sts. at beg. of foll. 2 rows. Leave rem. 22 (24, 26) sts. on a holder.

LEFT FRONT. With No. 7 needles and m. cast on 40 (43, 46) sts. and, beg. k. row, work 5 rows in st. st.

Next (hemline) row. Cast on 5 sts., k. to end. (45, 48, 51 sts.). Change to No. 5 needles.

Turquoise top is an ideal design for evening wear. Knitted in stocking stitch, top has garter stitch edgings and features 'full' sleeves which are gathered into a fitted cuff, and zip opening at back (see page 111 for instructions).

Next row. K.

Next row. K.5, p. to end.

Rep. above 2 rows 2 (3, 4) times more. Join in c. and k. 2 rows, then cont. in 2-colour block patt. as follows:

1st row. K. to last 23 sts., * k.4 c., (1 m., 1 c.) twice, 1 m.; rep. from * once, k.5 m.

2nd row. K.5 m., * p.1 m., (1 c., 1 m.) twice, 4 c.; rep. from * once, p. to end.

3rd row. As 1st row.

4th row. As 2nd row.

5th row. K. to last 18 sts., (1 c., 1 m., 1 c., 6 m.) twice.

6th row. K.5 m., (p.1 m., 1 c.) twice, 6 m., 1 c., 1 m., 1 c., p. to end.

7th row. As 5th row.

8th row. As 6th row.

Rep. above 8 rows, dec. 1 st. at side edge of 21st (23rd, 25th) row, then at same edge of every foll. 8th row until 41 (44, 47) sts. rem. Work 13 rows straight, then inc. at same edge of next row and every foll. 6th row to 47 (50, 53) sts. Cont. straight until work measures same as Back to beg. of armhole shaping, ending at side edge. *Note:* When next contrast 2-colour block has been worked cont. with single block patt. only as pictured.

Shape armhole. Cast off 4 sts. at beg. of next row, then dec. 1 st. at same edge of next row and foll. alt. rows until 39 (42, 45) sts. rem. Cont. straight until armhole measures 5 (5½, 6) ins. [12.70 (13.97, 15.24) cm], ending at front edge.

Shape neck. Next row. K.5 and leave these sts. on a holder, cast off next 4 (4, 5) sts., patt. to end. Dec. 1 st. at neck edge on every row until 21 (23, 24) sts. rem. and armhole measures same as back armhole, ending at side edge.

Shape shoulder. Cast off 7 (8, 8) sts. at beg. of next row and foll. alt. row. Work 1 row, then cast off rem. sts.

Mark positions for five buttonholes along front edge of Left Front—the first at 3½ ins. [8.89 cm] from hemline and the last at neck edge, evenly spacing the others in between.

RIGHT FRONT. With No. 7 needles and m. cast on 40 (43, 46) sts. and, beg. p. row, work 5 rows in st. st.

Next row. Cast on 10 sts., k. to end. (50, 53, 56 sts.).

Next (hemline) row. K.

Change to No. 5 needles and, beg. k. row, work 6 (8, 10) rows in st. st. Join in c. and k. 2 rows, then cont. in patt.:

1st row. K.11 m., (1 c., 1 m.) twice, 4 c., (1 m., 1 c.) twice, 1 m., 4 c., with m. k. to end.

2nd to 4th rows. Work as set.

5th row. K.11 m., 1 c., 1 m., 1 c., 6 m., 1 c., 1 m., 1 c., with m. k. to end.

6th to 8th rows. Work as set.

Rep. above 8 rows, making double buttonholes to correspond with markers throughout as follows:

Buttonhole row. K.2, cast off 2, k.3, cast off 2, k.2, patt. to end.

Next row. In patt., casting on 2 sts. over those cast off in previous row.

At the same time, dec. 1 st. at side edge of 21st (23rd, 25th) row, then at same edge of every foll. 8th row until 46 (49, 52) sts. rem. Work 13 rows straight, then inc. at same edge of next row and every foll. 6th row to 52 (55, 58) sts. Cont. straight until work measures same as Back to beg. of armhole shaping, ending at side edge and cont. with single block patt. only where applicable to correspond with other side.

Shape armhole. Cast off 4 sts. at beg. of next row, then dec. 1 st. at same edge of next row and foll. alt. rows until 44 (47, 50) sts. rem. Cont. straight until armhole measures 5 (5½, 6) ins. [12.70 (13.97, 15.24) cm], ending at front edge.

Shape neck. Next row. K.11 and leave these sts. on a holder, cast off next 3 (3, 4) sts., patt. to end. Dec. 1 st. at neck edge of every row until 22 (23, 24) sts. rem. and armhole measures same as back armhole, ending at side edge.

Shape shoulder. As given for Left Front.

SLEEVES. With No. 7 needles and m. cast on 40 (42, 44) sts. and work in k.1, p.1 rib for 12 rows. Change to No. 5 needles and st. st., inc. 1 st. each end of every foll. 8th row to 50 (52, 54) sts. Cont. straight until work measures 17 ins. [43.18 cm] (or length required), ending on p. row. Cast off 4 sts. at beg. of next 2 rows, then dec. 1 st. at beg. of every foll. row until 22 sts. rem. Cast off 2 sts. at beg. of next 4 rows, then cast off rem. sts.

NECKBAND. Firstly, join shoulder seams. R.s.f. and with No. 7 needles sl. 11 sts. from holder on to needle, joining yarn at end of these sts.

Pick up and k. 23 sts. along neck edge, k. across 22 (24, 26) sts. at back, pick up and k. 23 sts. along left neck edge, then k.5 from holder. (84, 86, 88 sts.). Cont. to keep 5 sts. at Left Front edge in garter st. and 6 sts. at Right Front edge in garter st., work 8 rows in k.1, p.1 rib, then cast off ribwise.

TO MAKE UP. Press work on the wrong side. Join side and sleeve seams. Set in sleeves. Press seams. Turn lower edge hem to inside at hemline and stitch into position. Turn Right Front border to inside so that the double buttonholes meet. Stitch border down, then neaten buttonholes. Press hems. Sew on buttons.

FRINGE. With c. cut six 9 in. [22.86 cm] lengths of yarn for each tassel and proceed as follows: With the wrong side of the edge to be fringed facing you, insert a crochet hook as near as possible to the edge (along hemline), fold strands in half to form a loop, put loop on hook, pull through edge of work, place hook behind all strands of yarn and draw through loop. Cont. along edge at 3 st. intervals until completion. Finally, trim ends of fringing to neaten.

CAP

TO MAKE. With set of No. 7 needles cast on 84 sts., evenly spreading these sts. on 3 of the needles.

K. 5 rounds.

Next (hemline) round. P.

K. 33 rounds.

1st (dec.) round. (K.12, k.2 tog.) all round.

K. 5 rounds.

2nd (dec.) round. (K.11, k.2 tog.) all round.

K. 4 rounds.

3rd (dec.) round. (K.10, k.2 tog.) all round.

K. 3 rounds.

4th (dec.) round. (K.9, k.2 tog.) all round.

K. 2 rounds.

5th (dec.) round. (K.8, k.2 tog.) all round.

K. 1 round.

Dec. 6 times in next round and on every foll. round until 12 sts. rem.

Next round. (K.2 tog.) all round.

Break yarn; draw through all sts. and fasten off.

TO MAKE UP. Press work on the wrong side. Turn hem to inside at hemline and stitch into position. Press hem.

Long line ski jacket is knitted in stocking stitch with contrast block patterning . . . fringing at lower edge is optional. Matching pull-on cap is knitted in stocking stitch in main colour (see page 117 for instructions).

Ribbed Polo Neck Sweater

MATERIALS: 16 (17, 18, 19) balls of Villawool Cascade Nylon 4 ply Crepe; a pair of Nos. 10 and 12 needles; set of 4 double-pointed No. 12 needles.
MEASUREMENTS: To fit 32 (34, 36, 38) in. [81.28 (86.36, 91.44, 96.52) cm] bust. Length, 22½ (22½, 23, 23) ins. [57.15 (57.15, 58.42, 58.42) cm]. Sleeve, 17½ ins. [44.45 cm] (or length required).
TENSION: 8 sts. to 1 inch [2.54 cm].
ABBREVIATIONS: See page 13.

TO MAKE:

BACK. With No. 12 needles cast on 136 (144, 152, 160) sts. and work in patt.:
1st row. K.3, (p.2, k.2) to last st., k.1.
2nd row. K.1, (p.2, k.2) to last 3 sts., p.2, k.1.
Rep. above 2 rows 12 times more.
Change to No. 10 needles and cont. in 2-row patt. until work measures 15½ ins. [39.37 cm], ending on wrong side.
Shape armholes. Cast off 4 sts. at beg. of next 2 rows, then dec. 1 st. each end of every foll. row until 112 (116, 120, 124) sts. rem.
Cont. until armholes measure 7 (7, 7½, 7½) ins. [17.78 (17.78, 19.05, 19.05) cm], ending on wrong side.
Shape shoulders. Cast off 12 (12, 13, 14) sts. at beg. of next 2 rows, then 11 (12, 12, 12) sts. at beg. of next 4 rows. Leave rem. 44 (44, 46, 48) sts. on a holder.
FRONT. Work as given for Back until armholes measure 5 ins. [12.70 cm], ending on wrong side.
Shape neck. Next row. Patt. 46 (48, 49, 51) sts., turn and cont. on these sts. only. Dec. 1 st. at neck edge on next 9 (9, 9, 10) rows, then on every foll. alt. row until 34 (36, 37, 38) sts. rem.
Cont. until armhole measures same as back armhole, ending at side edge.
Shape shoulder. Cast off 12 (12, 13, 14) at beg. of next row, then 11 (12, 12, 12) sts. at beg. of foll. 2 alt. rows.
Return to rem. sts. Place centre 20 (20, 22, 22) sts. on a holder.
Rejoin yarn to inner end of rem. sts. and work to correspond with other side.
SLEEVES. With No. 12 needles cast on 56 (60, 60, 64) sts. and work 30 rows in 2-row rib patt., as given for Back. Change to No. 10 needles and cont. in rib patt., inc. 1 st. each end of next row and every foll. 4th row to 96 (100, 104, 104) sts., then each end of every foll. 6th row to 108 (112, 116, 116) sts. Cont. straight until work measures 17½ ins. [44.45 cm] (or length required), ending on wrong side.
Cast off 4 sts. at beg. of next 2 rows. Dec. 1 st. each end of every alt. row until 80 (88, 88, 88) sts. rem., then on every row until 44 sts. rem.
Cast off 4 sts. at beg. of next 6 rows.
Cast off rem. sts.
POLO COLLAR. Firstly, join shoulder seams. R.s.f. and with set of No. 12 needles, pick up and k. 28 (28, 30, 32) sts. down left side of neck, patt. across sts. on centre front holder, pick up and k. 28 (28, 30, 32) sts. up right side of neck, then patt. across sts. on Back holder. (120, 120, 128, 134 sts.). Work in rounds of k.2, p.2 rib for 7 ins. [17.78 cm], then cast off ribwise.
TO MAKE UP. Join side and sleeve seams. Set in sleeves. Lightly press seams.

Dress

See photograph on page 122.

MATERIALS: Villawool Superknit 4 ply Crepe—
Short sleeve style—26 (27, 28, 29) balls.
Long sleeve style—22 (23, 24, 25) balls.
A pair of No. 10 needles; a set of 4 double-pointed No. 11 needles.
MEASUREMENTS: To fit 32 (34, 36, 38) in. [81.28 (86.36, 91.44, 96.52) cm] bust. Length, 39 (39, 39½, 39½) ins. [99.06 (99.06, 100.33, 100.33) cm]. Short sleeve, 3½ ins. [8.89 cm] (all sizes). Long sleeve, 16 (16½, 16½, 17) ins. [40.64 (41.91, 41.91, 43.18) cm] (or length required).
TENSION: 15 sts. to 2 inches [5.08 cm].
ABBREVIATIONS: See page 13.

TO MAKE:

BACK. With No. 10 needles cast on 172 (180, 188, 196) sts. and, beg. k. row, work in st. st. for 10 rows.
Next (picot) row. K.1, (y.fwd., k.2 tog.) to last st., k.1. Beg. p. row, cont. in st. st. until work measures 6 ins. [15.24 cm] from picot row, ending on p. row (adjust length for more or less as required at this point before beg. shaping).
1st (dec.) row. K.42, sl.1, k.1, p.s.s.o., k.2 tog., k. to last 46 sts., sl.1, k.1, p.s.s.o., k.2 tog., k. to end. Cont. in st. st. for 15 rows.

White polo neck sweater is knitted entirely in k.2, p.2 rib.

2nd (dec.) row. K.41, sl.1, k.1, p.s.s.o., k.2 tog., k. to last 45 sts., sl.1, k.1, p.s.s.o., k.2 tog., k. to end. Cont. in st. st. for 15 rows.

3rd (dec.) row. K.40, sl.1, k.1, p.s.s.o., k.2 tog., k. to last 44 sts., sl.1, k.1, p.s.s.o., k.2 tog., k. to end.

Cont. to dec. as set at 15-row intervals until 116 (124, 132, 140) sts. rem., then cont. straight until work measures 27 ins. [68.58 cm] from picot row, ending on p. row. Now inc. 1 st. each end of next row and every foll. 6th row to 132 (140, 148, 156) sts., then cont. straight until work measures 31½ ins. [80.01 cm] from picot row, ending on p. row.

Shape armholes. Next row. K.2, y.fwd., k.3 tog., k. to last 5 sts., sl.1, k.2 tog., p.s.s.o., y.fwd., k.2.

Next row. P.

Rep. above 2 rows until 106 (110, 114, 118) sts. rem., ending p. row.

Next row. K.2, y.fwd., k.3 tog., k.38 (40, 42, 44), (y.fwd., k.2 tog.) 10 times, k.38 (40, 42, 44), sl.1, k.2 tog., p.s.s.o., y.fwd., k.2.

Next row. P.

Rep. above 2 rows 9 times more, adjusting sts. to comply with armhole decs. **, then cont. to dec. at armhole edge only until 76 (78, 80, 82) sts. rem., ending p. row.

Shape neck. Next row. K.2, y.fwd., k.3 tog., k.16, sl.1, k.1, p.s.s.o., k.1, turn and cont. on these sts. only.

Next row. P.

Next row. K.2, y.fwd., k.3 tog., k. to last 3 sts., sl.1, k.1, p.s.s.o., k.1.

Rep. above 2 rows until 6 sts. rem., ending on p. row.

Next row. K.2, y.fwd., k.3 tog., k.1.

Next row. P.

Next row. K.1, k.3 tog., k.1.

Next row. P.

Next row. K.3 tog., then fasten off.

Return to rem. sts. Sl. centre 28 (30, 32, 34) sts. on a holder.

Rejoin yarn to inner end of rem. sts. and work to correspond with other side.

FRONT. Work as given for Back to **, then cont. to dec. at armhole edges only until 80 (82, 84, 86) sts. rem., ending on p. row.

Shape neck. Next row. K.2, y.fwd., k.3 tog., k.22, sl.1, k.1, p.s.s.o., k.1, turn and cont. on these sts. only.

Next row. P.

Next row. K.2, y.fwd., k.3 tog., k. to last 3 sts., sl.1, k.1, p.s.s.o., k.1.

Rep. above 2 rows until 6 sts. rem., ending on p. row.

Raglan dress can be made with short or long sleeves... body is knitted in stocking stitch with a keyhole pattern on centre front, back and on sleeves. Lower, neck and sleeve edges are finished with picot hems (see page 120 for instructions).

Next row. K.2, y.fwd., k.3 tog., k.1.

Next row. P.

Next row. K.1, k.3 tog., k.1.

Next row. P.

Next row. K.3 tog., then fasten off.

Return to rem. sts. Sl. centre 20 (22, 24, 26) sts. on a holder.

Rejoin yarn to inner end of rem. sts. and work to correspond with other side.

SHORT SLEEVES. With No. 10 needles cast on 74 (80, 86, 92) sts. and, beg. k. row, work in st. st. for 10 rows, then rep. picot row as given for Back. Beg. p. row, cont. in st. st., inc. 1 st. each end of 2nd row and every foll. 4th row to 86 (92, 98, 104) sts. Cont. straight until work measures 3½ ins. [8.89 cm] from picot row, ending on p. row.

Next row. K.2, y.fwd., k.3 tog., k. to last 5 sts., sl.1, k.2 tog., p.s.s.o., y.fwd., k.2.

Next row. P.

Rep. above 2 rows until 60 (62, 64, 66) sts. rem., ending on p. row.

Next row. K.2, y.fwd., k.3 tog., k.15 (16, 17, 18), (y.fwd., k.2 tog.) 10 times, k.15 (16, 17, 18), sl.1, k.2 tog., p.s.s.o., y.fwd., k.2.

Next row. P.

Rep. above 2 rows 9 times more, adjusting sts. to comply with armhole decs., then cont. to dec. at armhole edges only until 8 sts. rem., ending on p. row.

Next row. (K.2 tog., y.fwd.) 3 times, k.2 tog.

Next row. P.

Cast off.

LONG SLEEVES. With No. 10 needles cast on 56 (62, 68, 74) sts. and, beg. k. row, work in st. st. for 10 rows, then rep. picot row as given for Back. Beg. p. row, cont. in st. st., inc. 1 st. each end of 9th and every foll. 8th row to 86 (92, 98, 104) sts., then cont. straight until work measures 16 (16½, 16½, 17) ins. [40.64 (41.91, 41.91, 43.18) cm] from picot row (or length required), ending on p. row. Now cont. as given for short sleeve version to end.

NECK BORDER. Firstly, join shoulder seams. R.s.f. and with set of No. 11 needles, pick up and k. 24 sts. down left side of neck, k. across centre front sts., pick up and k. 24 sts. up right side of neck, 4 sts. across sleeve top, 18 sts. down right side of back neck, k. across sts. on holder at back, pick up and k. 18 sts. up left side of back neck then, finally, pick up and k. 4 sts. across rem. sleeve top (140, 144, 148, 152 sts.). K. 3 rounds.

Next (picot) round. (K.2 tog., y.fwd.) to end.

K. 4 rounds, then cast off.

TO MAKE UP. Press work on the wrong side. Join side and sleeve seams. Set in sleeves. Turn hems at lower, sleeve and neck edges to inside at picot row and sl. st. into position. Press seams and hems.

7
Knitting for Men

Shirt Style Sweater

See photograph on page 126.

MATERIALS: 25 (26, 27) balls of Villawool Superknit DC8; a pair of Nos. 8, 9 and 10 needles; 3 buttons.

MEASUREMENTS: To fit 38 (40, 42) in. [96.52 (101.60, 106.68) cm] chest. Length, 28½ (29½, 30½) ins. [72.39 (74.93, 77.47) cm]. Sleeve, 18 (19, 20) ins. [45.72 (48.26, 50.80) cm].

TENSION: 6 sts. to 1 inch [2.54 cm].

ABBREVIATIONS: See page 13.

TO MAKE:

BACK. With No. 9 needles cast on 120 (126, 132) sts. and, beg. k. row, work in st. st. for 10 rows, then cont. in patt.:

1st row. (K.1, p.1) to end.

2nd row. As 1st row.

3rd row. (P.1, k.1) to end.

4th row. As 3rd row.

Rep. above 4 rows until work measures 6 ins. [15.24 cm], then change to No. 8 needles and cont. in patt. until work measures 20½ (21½, 22) ins. [52.07 (54.61, 55.88) cm], ending on wrong side.

Shape armholes. Cont. in patt. and cast off 6 sts. at beg. of next 2 rows, then dec. 1 st. each end of every foll. row until 88 (92, 96) sts. rem. Cont. straight until armholes measure 8½ (8½, 9) ins. [21.59 (21.59, 22.86) cm].

Shape shoulders and neck. Next row. Cast off 8 sts., patt. 29 (30, 31) sts., turn and cont. on these sts. only. Cast off 3 sts. at neck edge at beg. of next row and foll. 2 alt. rows, at the same time, cast off at shoulder edge 8 sts. twice and 4 (5, 6) sts. once.

Return to rem. sts. Rejoin yarn to inner end of rem. sts. and cast off centre 14 (16, 18) sts., then cont. to correspond with other side.

FRONT. Work as given for Back until work measures same as Back to beg. of armhole shaping.

Shape armholes and divide for front opening. Next row. Cast off 6 sts., patt. 50 (53, 56) sts. and cont. on these sts. only. Dec. 1 st. at armhole edge on every foll. row until 40 (42, 44) sts. rem., then cont. straight until armhole measures 6 ins. [15.24 cm], ending at neck edge.

Shape neck. Dec. 1 st. at neck edge of next and every foll. row 12 (13, 14) times altog. and when armhole measures same as back armhole end at side edge.

Shape shoulder. Cast off 8 sts. at beg. of next and foll. 2 alt. rows. Work 1 row, then cast off rem. sts.

Return to rem. sts.

Rejoin yarn to inner end and cast off centre 8 sts., then cont. to correspond with other side.

SLEEVES. With No. 10 needles cast on 54 (54, 58) sts. and work in k.1, p.1 rib for 3 ins. [7.62 cm]. Change to No. 8 needles and cont. in patt. as given for Back, inc. 1 st. each end of next and every foll. 8th row to 84 (84, 88) sts. and keeping the extra sts. in patt. Cont. straight until work measures 18 (19, 20) ins. [45.72 (48.26, 50.80) cm] (or length required).

Cast off 6 sts. at beg. of next 2 rows, then dec. 1 st. at beg. of foll. 22 rows, then each end of every row until 24 sts. rem. Cast off.

RIGHT FRONT BORDER. With No. 10 needles cast on 12 sts. and work in k.1, p.1 rib for 6 ins. [15.24 cm], then cast off ribwise.

Mark positions for 2 buttonholes on this border—the first at 2 ins. [5.08 cm] from the beginning and the second 2 ins. [5.08 cm] above first marker.

LEFT FRONT BORDER. Work as given for Right Front Border, making buttonholes to correspond with markers:

Buttonhole row. Rib 4, cast off 4, rib to end.

Next row. Rib and cast on 4 sts. over those cast off in previous row.

TO MAKE UP. Press work on the wrong side. Join shoulder, side and sleeve seams. Set in sleeves. Press seams. Turn st. st. hem at lower edge to inside and slip st. down. Attach borders to their respective sides at front opening.

COLLAR. R.s.f. and with No. 10 needles pick up and k. approx. 108 (110, 116) sts. evenly around neck edge. Work in k.1, p.1 rib for 6 rows, making final buttonhole to correspond with border.

Next row. Cast off 5 sts., rib to last 5 sts., cast off 5 sts. Change to No. 8 needles and cont. in rib until work measures 3½ (4, 4) ins. [8.89 (10.16, 10.16) cm], ending with wrong side facing.

** **Next row.** Rib 12, turn. **Next row.** Rib to end.

Next row. Rib 8, turn. **Next row.** Rib to end.

Next row. Rib 4, turn. **Next row.** Rib to end. **

Next row. Rib across all sts.

Rep. from ** to ** once, then cast off ribwise.

TO FINISH OFF. Press hem. Sew on buttons.

Polo Sweater with Centre Patterned Panel

See photograph on page 128.

MATERIALS: 28 (29, 30, 31) balls of Villawool Superknit DC8 in main colour (m.) and 1 (1, 1, 1) ball of contrast colour (c.); a pair of Nos. 8 and 10 needles; a set of double-pointed No. 10 needles.
MEASUREMENTS: To fit 38 (40, 42, 44) in. [96.52 (101.60, 106.68, 111.76) cm] chest. Length, 24½ (26, 26, 26) ins. [62.23 (66.04, 66.04, 66.04) cm]. Sleeve, 19 (20, 20, 20) ins. [48.26 (50.80, 50.80, 50.80) cm].
TENSION: 23 sts. to 4 inches [10.16 cm].
ABBREVIATIONS: See page 13.

TO MAKE:
BACK. With No. 10 needles and m. cast on 120 (126, 132, 138) sts. and work in k.1, p.1 rib for 2½ ins. [6.35 cm], inc. 1 st. at end of last row (121, 127, 133, 139 sts.). Change to No. 8 needles and st. st. until work measures 15 (16, 16, 16) ins. [38.10 (40.64, 40.64, 40.64) cm], ending on p. row.
Shape armholes. Cast off 5 sts. at beg. of next 2 rows, then dec. 1 st. each end of every row until 93 (97, 101, 105) sts. rem.
Cont. straight until armholes measure 9½ (10, 10, 10) ins. [24.13 (25.40, 25.40, 25.40) cm], ending on p. row.
Shape shoulders. Cast off 7 sts. at beg. of next 6 rows, then 5 (6, 7, 8) sts. at beg. of foll. 2 rows. Leave rem. 41 (43, 45, 47) sts. on a holder.
FRONT. With No. 10 needles and m. cast on 124 (130, 136, 142) sts. and work in k.1, p.1 rib for 2½ ins. [6.35 cm], inc. 1 st. at end of last row (125, 131, 137, 143 sts.). Change to No. 8 needles and cont. in st. st. with centre panel as follows:
1st row. K.46 (49, 52, 55) m., (1 c., 2 m., 3 c., 2 m.) 4 times, 1 c., with m., k. to end.
2nd row. P.46 (49, 52, 55) m., (1 c., 2 m., 3 c., 2 m.) 4 times, 1 c., with m., p. to end.
3rd row. K.47 (50, 53, 56) m., (1 c., 2 m., 1 c., 2 m., 1 c., 1 m.) 4 times, with m., k. to end.
4th row. P.47 (50, 53, 56) m., (1 c., 2 m., 1 c., 2 m., 1 c., 1 m.) 4 times, with m., p. to end.

Shirt style sweater is knitted in a 4-row moss stitch variation pattern, and features hemmed lower edge with k.1, p.1 rib cuffs and collar (see page 125 for instructions).

5th row. K.48 (51, 54, 57) m., (1 c., 3 m.) 8 times, with m., k. to end.
6th row. P.48 (51, 54, 57) m., (1 c., 3 m.) 8 times, with m., p. to end.
7th row. K.49 (52, 55, 58) m., (1 c., 1 m., 1 c., 2 m., 1 c., 2 m.) 3 times, 1 c., 1 m., 1 c., with m., k. to end.
8th row. P.49 (52, 55, 58) m., (1 c., 1 m., 1 c., 2 m., 1 c., 2 m.) 3 times, 1 c., 1 m., 1 c., with m., p. to end.
9th row. K.50 (53, 56, 59) m., (1 c., 2 m., 3 c., 2 m.) 3 times, 1 c., with m., k. to end.
10th row. P.50 (53, 56, 59) m., (1 c., 2 m., 3 c., 2 m.) 3 times, 1 c., with m., p. to end.
11th row. As 7th row.
12th row. As 8th row.
13th row. As 5th row.
14th row. As 6th row.
15th row. As 3rd row.
16th row. As 4th row.
Rep. above 16 rows until work measures same as Back to armhole shaping, ending on wrong-side row
Shape armholes. Cont. in patt. and cast off 5 sts. at beg. of next 2 rows, then dec. 1 st. each end of every row until 97 (101, 105, 109) sts. rem. Cont. straight until armholes measure 7½ (7¾, 7¾, 7¾) ins. [19.05 (19.68, 19.68, 19.68) cm], ending on wrong side.
Shape neck. Next row. Patt. 38 (39, 40, 41) sts., turn and cont. on these sts. only. Dec. 1 st. at neck edge of every foll. row until 28 (29, 30, 31) sts. rem. Cont. straight until armhole measures same as Back armhole, ending at side edge.
Shape shoulder. Cast off 8 sts. at beg. of next row and foll. 2 alt. rows. Work 1 row, then cast off rem. sts.
Return to rem. sts. Rejoin yarn to inner end and cast off centre 21 (23, 25, 27) sts., then cont. on rem. sts. to correspond with other side.

SLEEVES. With No. 10 needles and m. cast on 56 (60, 60, 62) sts. and work in k.1, p.1 rib for 3½ ins. [8.89 cm]. Change to No. 8 needles and st. st., inc. 1 st. each end of every 5th row to 100 (104, 104, 104) sts. Cont. straight until work measures 19 (20, 20, 20) ins. [48.26 (50.80, 50.80, 50.80) cm], ending on p. row.
Cast off 5 sts. at beg. of next 2 rows, then dec. 1 st. at beg. of every row until 80 sts. rem. Dec. 1 st. each end of every foll. row until 24 sts. rem. Cast off.

TO MAKE UP. Press work on the wrong side. Join shoulder, side and sleeve seams.
Polo collar. R.s.f., using set of No. 10 needles and m., pick up and k. 83 (85, 87, 89) sts. evenly around front neck, then k. across sts. on holder at back neck (124, 128, 132, 136 sts.). Work in rounds of k.1, p.1 rib for 7 ins. [17.78 cm]. Cast off ribwise.
TO FINISH OFF. Set in sleeves. Press seams.

Raglan Sweater with Contrast Trim

See photograph on page 1.

MATERIALS: 20 (21, 22, 23) balls of Villawool Superknit DC8 in main colour (m.) and 2 (2, 2, 2) balls of contrast colour (c.); a pair of Nos. 8, 9 and 10 needles; a set of 4 double-pointed No. 10 needles.

MEASUREMENTS: To fit 38 (40, 42, 44) in. [96.52 (101.60, 106.68, 111.76) cm] chest. Length, 27½ (28, 28½, 29) ins. [69.85 (71.12, 72.39, 73.66) cm]. Sleeve, 18 ins. [45.72 cm] (or length required).

TENSION: 23 sts. to 4 inches [10.16 cm].

ABBREVIATIONS: See page 13.

TO MAKE:

BACK. With No. 9 needles and m. cast on 118 (124, 130, 136) sts. and work in k.1, p.1 rib for 1½ ins. [3.81 cm]. Change to No. 8 needles and cont. in st. st. until work measures 18 ins. [45.72 cm], ending on p. row.

Shape raglan. Cast off 6 sts. at beg. of next 2 rows.

Next row. K.1, sl.1, k.1, p.s.s.o., k. to last 3 sts., k.2 tog., k.1.

Next row. P.

Rep. above 2 rows until 34 (36, 38, 40) sts. rem. Leave sts. on holder.

FRONT. Work as given for Back until 54 (56, 58, 60) sts. rem. in raglan shaping, ending on p. row.

Shape neck. Next row. K.1, sl.1, k.1, p.s.s.o., k.17, turn and cont. on these sts. only.

Next row. P.

Next row. K.1, sl.1, k.1, p.s.s.o., k. to last 2 sts., k.2 tog.

Rep. above 2 rows until 3 sts. rem., ending on p. row.

Next row. K.1, sl.1, k.1, p.s.s.o.

P. 2 tog. and fasten off.

Return to sts. on needle. Sl. centre 14 (16, 18, 20) sts. on a holder. Rejoin yarn to inner end of rem. sts.

Next row. K. to last 3 sts., k.2 tog., k.1.

Next row. P.

Next row. Sl.1, k.1, p.s.s.o., k. to last 3 sts., k.2 tog., k.1.

Now cont. to correspond with other side.

SLEEVES. With No. 10 needles and m. cast on 48 (50, 52, 54) sts. and work in k.1, p.2 rib for 2½ ins. [6.35 cm], inc. 1 st. at end of last row (49, 51, 53, 55 sts.). Change to No. 8 needles. Join in c. in next row.

Next row. With m. k.20 (21, 22, 23), k. 9 c., with m., k. to end.

Next row. With m., p.20 (21, 22, 23), p. 9 c., with m., p. to end.

Cont. in st. st. with centre c. stripe, twisting colours around each other to avoid a gap, inc. 1 st. each end of 5th and every foll. 6th row to 73 (75, 77, 79) sts., then each end of every foll. 4th row to 85 (89, 93, 97) sts. Cont. straight until work measures 18 ins. [45.72 cm] (or length required), ending on p. row.

Place a marker each end of last row. Work 8 rows. Keeping centre 9 sts. in c., work as follows:

Next row. K.1, sl.1, k.1, p.s.s.o., work to last 3 sts., k.2 tog., k.1.

Next row. P.

Rep. above 2 rows until 13 sts. rem., ending on p. row. Leave sts. on holder.

NECKBAND. Firstly, join raglan seams, sewing last 8 rows of sleeve seams to cast off sts. at armholes. R.s.f., with set of No. 10 needles and c., k. across sts. at back neck and left sleeve, pick up and k. 20 (20, 21, 21) sts. down left side of neck, k. across centre front sts., pick up and k. 20 (20, 21, 21) sts. up right side of neck, then k. across sts. of right sleeve (114, 118, 124, 128 sts.). Work in rounds of k.1, p.1 rib for 3 ins. [7.62 cm], then cast off ribwise.

TO MAKE UP. Press work on the wrong side. Join side and sleeve seams. Press seams. Fold neckband in half to wrong side and sl. st. into position.

Polo neck sweater is knitted in stocking stitch with k.1, p.1 rib trim, features centre front contrast patterning (see page 127 for instructions).

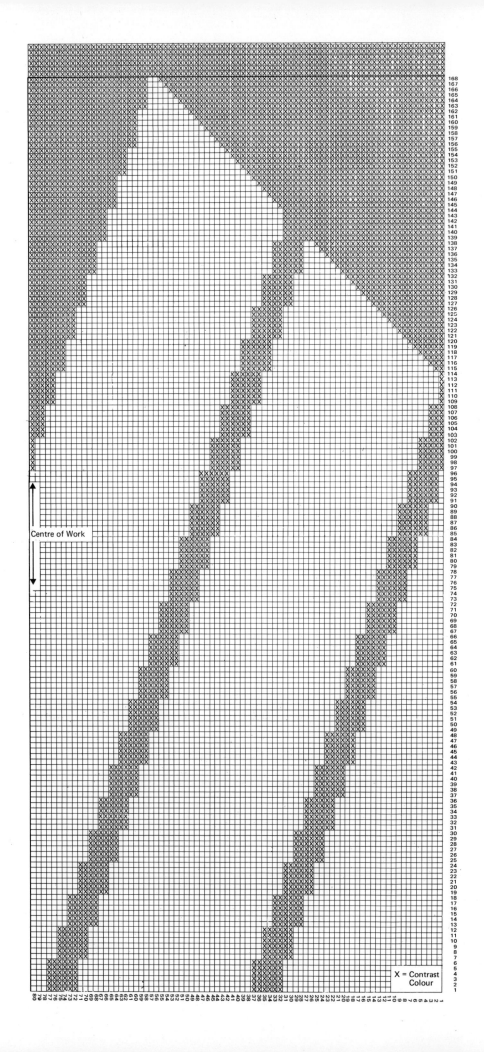

Centre of Work

X = Contrast Colour

130

Navy and Red Overpull

See photograph on page 133.

MATERIALS: 17 (17, 18) balls of Villawool Superknit 4 ply Crepe in main colour (m.) and 7 (7, 8) balls of contrast colour (c.); a pair of Nos. 11 (10, 9) needles; a pair of No. 12 needles and a set of 4 double-pointed No. 12 needles.

MEASUREMENTS: To fit 38 (40, 42) in. [96.52 (101.60, 106.68) cm] chest. Length, 26½ (27, 27) ins. [67.31 (68.58, 68.58) cm]. Sleeve, 19 ins. [48.26 cm] (or length required).

TENSION: 15 sts. to 2 inches [5.08 cm] on No. 10 needles.

ABBREVIATIONS: See page 13.

NOTE. Use separate balls of yarn instead of carrying yarn across work.

TO MAKE:

BACK. With No. 12 needles and m. cast on 160 sts. and work in k.1, p.1 rib for 3 ins. [7.62 cm]. Change to No. 11 (10, 9) needles and p. 1 row. Join in c. and beg. foll. chart in st. st., beg. k. row, and working from stitch No. 1 to stitch No. 80 and then from stitch No. 80 back to stitch No. 1. Cont. until work measures 17 ins. [43.18 cm], ending on p. row.

Shape armholes. Cast off 3 (4, 4) sts. at beg. of next 2 rows, then dec. 1 st. each end of every foll. row until 130 sts. rem.

Cont. straight until 168 rows have been worked, then break off m. and cont. with c. only. At the same time, when armholes measure 3¼ (3½, 3½) ins. [8.25 (8.89, 8.89) cm], inc. 1 st. each end of next row and every foll. 8th row to 140 sts. Cont. straight until armholes measure 9½ (10, 10) ins. [24.13 (25.40, 25.40) cm], ending on p. row.

Shape shoulders. Cast off 9 sts. at beg. of next 8 rows, then 10 sts. at beg. of foll. 2 rows. Leave rem. 48 sts. on a holder.

FRONT. Work as given for Back until 1 row before beg. of armhole shaping.

Shape V. Next row. Patt. 80 sts., turn and cont. on these sts. only. Dec. 1 st. at neck edge on next row and every foll. 3rd row until 24 decs. altog. have been worked, at the same time shaping armhole.

Shape armhole. Cont. in patt. and cast off 3 (4, 4) sts. at beg. of next row, then dec. 1 st. at same edge of foll. 12 (11, 11) rows. Cont. straight until armhole measures 3¼ (3½, 3½) ins. [8.25 (8.89, 8.89) cm], then inc. 1 st. at side edge on next row and every foll. 8th row until 5 inc. altog. have been worked. Cont. until armhole measures same as back armhole, ending at side edge (46 sts.).

Shape shoulder. Return to rem. sts. Rejoin yarn to inner end of rem. sts. and work to correspond with other side.

SLEEVES. With No. 12 needles and m. cast on 72 sts. and work in k.1, p.1 rib for 3 ins. [7.62 cm]. Change to No. 11 (10, 9) needles and st. st., inc. 1 st. each end of every foll. 6th row to 110 sts. Cont. straight until work measures 19 ins. [48.26 cm] (or length required), ending on p. row.

Cast off 3 (4, 4) sts. at beg. of next 2 rows, then dec. 1 st. at beg. of next 24 rows. Dec. 1 st. each end of next 20 rows, then cast off 3 sts. at beg. of next 4 rows. Cast off rem. sts.

NECKBAND. Firstly, join shoulder seams. R.s.f., with set of No. 12 needles and c. pick up and k. 106 sts. down left side of neck, 1 st. from centre front, pick up and k. 105 sts. up right side of neck and, finally, k. across 48 sts. at back neck. (260 sts.). Break off c. and join in m. and work in rounds of k.1, p.1, dec. 1 st. either side of centre V st. on every round thus: k.2 tog., t.b.l., k.1, k.2 tog. When 12 rows have been worked, cast off ribwise.

TO MAKE UP. Press work on the wrong side. Join side and sleeve seams. Set in sleeves. Press seams.

Casual Jacket

See photograph on page 135.

MATERIALS: 43 (44, 45, 46) balls of Villawool Nylo Tweed; a pair of Nos. 8 and 10 needles; 16 buttons.

MEASUREMENTS: To fit 38 (40, 42, 44) in. [96.52 (101.60, 106.68, 111.76) cm] chest. Length, 27¾ (28, 28¼, 28½) ins. [70.48 (71.12, 71.75, 72.39) cm]. Sleeve, 19 (19, 20, 20) ins. [48.26 (48.26, 50.80, 50.80) cm] (or length required).

TENSION: 5 sts. to 1 inch [2.54 cm].

ABBREVIATIONS: See page 13.

TO MAKE:

BACK. With No. 8 needles cast on 103 (109, 113, 117) sts.

Next (m.st.) row. K.1, (p.1, k.1) to end.

Rep. above row until work measures 18 ins. [45.72 cm].

Shape armholes. Cont. in m.st. and cast off 3 (3, 3, 4) sts. at beg. of next 2 rows, then dec. 1 st. each end of next row and every foll. alt. row until 85 (91, 95, 101) sts. rem. Cont. straight until armholes measure 9¾ (10, 10¼, 10½) ins. [24.76 (25.40, 26.03, 26.67) cm].

Shape shoulder. Cast off 5 sts. at beg. of next 8 rows, then 6 (8, 8, 10) sts. at beg. of next 2 rows. Cast off rem. 33 (35, 39, 41) sts.

RIGHT FRONT. With No. 8 needles cast on 61 (63, 65, 67) sts. and work in m.st. as given for Back until work measures same as Back to armhole shaping, ending at side edge.

Shape armhole. Cast off 3 (3, 3, 4) sts. at beg. of next row, then dec. 1 st. at same edge of alt. rows until 52 (54, 56, 59) sts. rem. Cont. straight until armhole measures 7¼ (7½, 7¾, 8) ins. [18.41 (19.05, 19.68, 20.32) cm], ending at front edge.

Shape neck. Cast off 8 sts. at beg. of next row, then dec. 1 st. at neck edge of every foll. row until 26 (28, 28, 30) sts. rem., then cont. straight until armhole measures same as Back armhole, ending at side edge.

Shape shoulder. Cast off 5 sts. at beg. of next row and foll. 3 alt. rows. Work 1 row, then cast off rem. sts.

Mark positions for six buttonholes along front edge of Right Front—the first at 2½ ins. [6.35 cm] from hemline and the last at neck edge, evenly spacing the others in between.

LEFT FRONT. Work as given for Right Front, making buttonholes to correspond with markers as follows:

Buttonhole row. M.st. 4, cast off 3 sts., m.st. to end.

Next row. In m.st., casting on 3 sts. over those cast off in previous row.

SLEEVES. With No. 8 needles cast on 55 (57, 57, 59) sts. and work in m.st. for 3 ins. [7.62 cm]. Inc. 1 st. each end of next row and every foll. 12th (12th, 11th, 10th) row to 71 (73, 75, 79) sts., then cont. straight until sleeve measures 19 (19, 20, 20) ins. [48.26 (48.26, 50.80, 50.80) cm] (or length required).

Cast off 3 (3, 3, 4) sts. at beg. of next 2 rows, then dec. 1 st. at beg. of next 18 rows, then each end of every foll. row until 17 sts. rem. Cast off.

COLLAR. With No. 10 needles cast on 111 (113, 117, 119) sts. and work in m.st. for 4½ ins. [11.43 cm]. Change to No. 8 needles and work 2 rows, then cast off loosely.

POCKET (MAKE 4). With No. 8 needles cast on 27 sts. and work in m.st. for 5½ ins. [13.97 cm], then cast off.

TO MAKE UP. Join shoulder, side and sleeve seams. Set in sleeves. Lightly press seams. Sew cast off edge of collar to neck edge, leaving approx. 8 cast-off sts. free at outer edges. Sew pockets to fronts as pictured. Sew buttons to Right Front, pockets and sleeve edges as pictured. Neaten buttonholes.

Short-sleeve Skivvy

See photographs on right and on page 134.

MATERIALS: 14 (14, 15) balls of Villawool Superknit 4 ply Crepe; a pair of Nos. 10 and 12 needles; a set of 4 double-pointed No. 12 needles.

MEASUREMENTS: To fit 38 (40, 42) in. [96.52 (101.60, 106.68) cm] chest. Length, 25¾ (26, 26) ins. [65.40 (66.04, 66.04) cm]. Sleeve, 3½ ins. [8.89 cm].

TENSION: 15 sts. to 2 inches [5.08 cm].

ABBREVIATIONS: See page 13.

TO MAKE:

BACK. With No. 12 needles cast on 148 (154, 160) sts. and work in k.1, p.1 rib for 2 ins. [5.08 cm]. Change to No. 10 needles and st. st. and cont. until work measures 16½ ins. [41.91 cm], ending on p. row.

Shape armholes. Cast off 3 sts. at beg. of next 2 rows, then dec. 1 st. each end of every foll. row until 118 (124, 130) sts. rem. Cont. straight until armhole measures 3½ (3¾, 3¾) ins. [8.89 (9.52, 9.52) cm].

Now inc. 1 st. each end of next row and every foll. 8th row to 128 (134, 140) sts., then cont. straight until armholes measure 9¼ (9½, 9½) ins. [23.49 (24.13, 24.13) cm], ending on p. row.

Shape shoulders. Cast off 8 (11, 14) sts. at beg. of next 2 rows, then 8 sts. at beg. of foll. 8 rows. Leave rem. 48 sts. on a holder.

Two-colour sweater has patterned back and front and plain sleeves, is worn over polo neck skivvy (see page 131 for instructions).

Above: *Long-line ribbed waistcoat is knitted in a wide rib with k.2, p.2 rib edgings. Front has V shaping, and waistcoat can be worn buttoned-up or undone as shown in picture (see page 136 for instructions). Short sleeve sweater or skivvy is knitted in stocking stitch with k.1, p.1 ribbing, and features polo collar (see page 132 for instructions).*

Left: *Three-colour ribbed boucle sweater features a separate ribbed collar which is attached during make up (see page 137 for instructions).*

Right: *Loose fitting jacket is designed for casual wearing, made in moss stitch entirely with set-in sleeves and patch pockets which are optional (see page 131 for instructions).*

FRONT. Work as given for Back until armholes measure 7¼ (7½, 7½) ins. [18.41 (19.05, 19.05) cm], ending on p. row. (128, 134, 140 sts.).

Shape neck. Next row. K.52 (54, 56) sts., turn and cont. on these sts. only. Dec. 1 st. at neck edge of every foll. row until 40 (43, 46) sts. rem., then cont. straight until armhole measures same as back armhole, ending at side edge.

Shape shoulder. Cast off 8 (11, 14) sts. at beg. of next row, then 8 sts. at beg. of foll. 4 alt. rows. Return to rem. sts. Place centre 24 (26, 28) sts. on a holder. Rejoin yarn to inner end of rem. sts. and work to correspond with other side.

SLEEVES. With No. 12 needles cast on 86 (88, 90) sts. and work in k.1, p.1 rib for 6 rows. Change to No. 10 needles and st. st., inc. 1 st. each end of every foll. 3rd row to 100 (106, 106) sts. Cont. straight until work measures 3½ ins. [8.89 cm], ending on p. row.

Cast off 3 sts. at beg. of next 2 rows, then dec. 1 st. at beg. of every row until 70 (74, 74) sts. rem., then each end of every row until 30 (34, 36) sts. rem. Cast off 3 sts. at beg. of next 4 rows, then cast off rem. sts.

POLO COLLAR. Firstly, join shoulder seams. R.s.f. and with set of No. 12 needles pick up and k. 36 sts. down left side of neck, k. across 24 (26, 28) sts. on front holder, pick up and k. 36 sts. up right side of neck and, finally, k. across 48 sts. at back neck. (144, 146, 148 sts.). Work in k.1, p.1 rib rounds for 5 ins. [12.70 cm], then cast off ribwise.

TO MAKE UP. Press work on the wrong side. Join side and sleeve seams. Set in sleeves. Press seams.

Long-line Waistcoat

See photograph on page 134.

MATERIALS: 24 (25, 26, 27) balls of Villawool Superknit DC8; a pair of Nos. 9 and 10 needles; a set of 4 double-pointed No. 10 needles, 6 buttons.

MEASUREMENTS: To fit 38 (40, 42, 44) in. [96.52 (101.60, 106.68, 111.76) cm] chest. Length, 27 (28½, 30, 30) ins. [68.58 (72.39, 76.20, 76.20) cm].

TENSION: 7 sts. to 1 inch [2.54 cm].

ABBREVIATIONS: See page 13.

TO MAKE:

BACK. With No. 10 needles cast on 150 (156, 162, 168) sts. and work in rib patt.:

1st row. (P.1, k.4, p.1) to end.
2nd row. (K.1, p.4, k.1) to end.

Rep. above 2 rows until work measures 6 ins. [15.24 cm], then change to No. 9 needles and cont. in rib patt. until work measures 17 (18, 19, 19) ins. [43.18 (45.72, 48.26, 48.26) cm], ending on wrong side.

Shape armholes. Cont. in rib patt. and cast off 12 sts. at beg. of next 2 rows, then dec. 1 st. at beg. of every foll. row until 114 (120, 126, 132) sts. rem. Cont. straight until armholes measure 10 (10½, 11, 11) ins. [25.40 (26.67, 27.94, 27.94) cm], ending on wrong side.

Shape shoulders. Cast off 11 (12, 12, 13) sts. at beg. of next 4 rows, then cast off 11 (11, 13, 13) sts. at beg. of next 2 rows. Cast off rem. 48 (50, 52, 54) sts.

LEFT FRONT. With No. 10 needles cast on 78 (84, 90, 96) sts. and work in 2-row rib patt., as given for Back, until work measures 6 ins. [15.24 cm]. Change to No. 9 needles and cont. in rib patt. until work measures 15 ins. [38.10 cm], ending at side edge.

Shape front. Dec. 1 st. at end of next row and every foll. 3rd row until work measures same as Back to armhole shaping, ending at side edge.

Shape armhole. Cont. to dec. on every foll. 3rd row as set, cast off 12 sts. at beg. of next row, then dec. 1 st. at side edge on alt. rows 6 times altog. Cont. to dec. at front edge only until 33 (35, 37, 39) sts. rem., then cont. straight until work measures same as Back to shoulder shaping, ending at side edge.

Shape shoulder. Cast off 11 (12, 12, 13) sts. at beg. of next and foll. alt. row. Work 1 row, then cast off rem. sts.

RIGHT FRONT. Work as given for Left Front, reversing shapings.

ARMHOLE BANDS. Firstly, join shoulder and side seams. R.s.f., using No. 10 double-pointed needles, pick up and k. 148 (152, 156, 156) sts. evenly around armhole edge. Work 8 rows in k.2, p.2 rib, then cast off ribwise.

BUTTONHOLE BAND. R.s.f., using No. 10 double-pointed needles, beg. at centre back and pick up and k. 236 (248, 260, 260) sts. down left front edge. Work 4 rows in k.2, p.2 rib.

Next (buttonhole) row. Rib 8 (cast off 4 sts., rib 16), 6 times, rib to end.

Next row. Rib and cast on 4 sts. over those cast off in previous row. Rib 4 more rows, then cast off ribwise.

BUTTON BAND. R.s.f., using No. 10 double-pointed needles, beg. at right front lower edge and pick up and k. 236 (248, 260, 260) sts. to centre back. Work to correspond with buttonhole band, omitting buttonholes.

TO MAKE UP. Press seams. Sew on buttons. Join centre back neck seam.

Striped Boucle Sweater

See photograph on page 134.

MATERIALS: 9 (9, 10, 10) balls of Villawool Boucle Double Knitting in main colour (m.); 9 (9, 10, 10) balls of 1st contrast (1st c.) and 8 (8, 9, 9) balls of 2nd contrast (2nd c.); a pair of Nos. 8 and 10 needles.

MEASUREMENTS: To fit 38 (40, 42, 44) in. [96.52 (101.60, 106.68, 111.76) cm] chest. Length, 26 (26½, 27, 27½) ins. [66.04 (67.31, 68.58, 69.85) cm]. Sleeve, 18½ ins. [46.99 cm] (or length required).

TENSION: 6 sts. to 1 inch [2.54 cm].

ABBREVIATIONS: See page 13.

TO MAKE:

BACK. With No. 10 needles and m. cast on 120 (124, 132, 136) sts. and work in k.1, p.1 rib for 16 rows, inc. 1 st. at end of last row (121, 125, 133, 137) sts.). Change to No. 8 needles and 1st c. and work in rib patt.:

1st row. K.4, (p.1, k.3) to last st., k.1.

2nd row. K.1, (p.3, k.1) to end.

Rep. above 2 rows until 16 patt. rows have been worked, then work 16 rows in 2nd c. and 16 rows in m.

Cont. in three colour 48-row striped rib patt. until work measures 18 ins. [45.72 cm], ending on wrong side.

Shape raglan. Cont. in patt. and cast off 4 sts. at beg. of next 2 rows, then dec. 1 st. each end of next row and every foll. alt. row until 41 (41, 45, 45) sts. rem. Work 1 row, then cast off in patt.

FRONT. Work as given for Back until 61 (61, 65, 65) sts. rem. in raglan shaping, ending on right side.

Shape neck. Next row. Patt. 20 sts., turn and cont. on these sts. only. Cont. to shape raglan on alt. rows, at the same time, dec. 1 st. at neck edge of foll. 8 rows. When 2 sts. rem. in raglan shaping, k.2 tog. and fasten off.

Return to rem. sts. Rejoin yarn to inner end and cast off centre 21 (21, 25, 25) sts., then cont. on rem. sts. to correspond with other side.

SLEEVES. With No. 10 needles and m. cast on 52 (56, 60, 64) sts. and work in k.1, p.1 rib for 16 rows, inc. 1 st. at end of last row (53, 57, 61, 65 sts.). Change to No. 8 needles and 1st c. and work in striped rib patt., as given for Back, inc. 1 st. each end of every foll. 6th row to 93, (97, 101, 105) sts. Cont. straight until work measures 18½ ins. [46.99 cm] (or length required), ending on wrong side.

Cont. in patt. and cast off 4 sts. at beg. of next 2 rows, then dec. 1 st. each end of next row and every foll. alt. row until 13 sts. rem. Work 1 row, then cast off.

COLLAR. With No. 10 needles and m. cast on 124 (124, 132, 132) sts. and work in k.1, p.1 rib for 6 rows. Change to No. 8 needles and work 10 rows of rib patt., as given for Back, inc. 1 st. at end of 1st row (125, 125, 133, 133 sts.). With 1st c. work 16 rows of rib patt., then with 2nd c. work 16 rows of rib patt. Cast off in patt.

TO MAKE UP. Press work lightly on wrong side. Join raglan, side and sleeve seams. Join collar seam, then, with right side of collar to wrong side of sweater and placing seam at back, sew cast-off edge of collar evenly around neck edge. Press seams.

Classic Sweater

See photograph on page 138.

MATERIALS: VILLAWOOL SUPERKNIT 5 PLY CREPE.

V neck style—20 (21, 22, 23) balls.

Crew neck style—20 (21, 22, 23) balls.

Polo neck style—21 (22, 23, 24) balls.

A pair of Nos. 10 and 12 needles; a set of 4 double-pointed No. 12 needles.

MEASUREMENTS: To fit 38 (40, 42, 44) in. [96.52 (101.60, 106.68, 111.76) cm] chest. Length, 25½ (26½, 27, 27½) ins. [64.77 (67.31, 68.58, 69.85) cm]. Sleeve, 18 (19, 19, 20) ins. [45.72 (48.26, 48.26, 50.80) cm] (or length required).

TENSION: 7 sts. to 1 inch [2.54 cm].

ABBREVIATIONS: See page 13.

TO MAKE:

BACK (all styles). With No. 12 needles cast on 141 (149, 157, 165) sts. and work in k.1, p.1 rib for 2 ins. [5.08 cm].

Change to No. 10 needles and cont. in st. st. until work measures 17 (17½, 17½, 17½) ins. [43.18 (44.45, 44.45, 44.45) cm], ending on p. row.

Shape raglan. Cast off 8 sts. at beg. of next 2 rows **.**

Next row. K.1, sl.1, k.1, p.s.s.o., k. to last 3 sts., k.2 tog., k.1.

Next row. P.

Rep. above 2 rows until 41 (43, 45, 47) sts. rem., ending on p. row.

Leave sts. on holder.

FRONT—V NECK STYLE. Work as given for Back to **.

Shape neck. Next row. K.1, sl.1, k.1, p.s.s.o., k. 59 (63, 67, 71) sts., turn and cont. on these sts. only.

Next row. P.

Next row. K.1, sl.1, k.1, p.s.s.o., k. to last 3 sts., sl.1, k.1, p.s.s.o., k.1.

Cont. to dec. at neck edge on every 4th row 17 (18, 19, 20) times more, at the same time, dec. at raglan edge as set until 2 sts. rem., k.2 tog. and fasten off.

Return to sts. on needle. Sl. centre st. on a safety pin. Rejoin yarn to inner end of rem. sts.

Next row. K. to last 3 sts., k.2 tog., k.1.

Next row. P.

Next row. K.1, k.2 tog., k. to last 3 sts., k.2 tog., k.1. Now cont. to correspond with other side.

FRONT—CREW OR POLO NECK STYLE. Work as given for Back to **.

Next row. K.1, sl.1, k.1, p.s.s.o., k. to last 3 sts., k.2 tog., k.1.

Next row. P.

Rep. above 2 rows until 65 (67, 69, 71) sts. rem., ending p. row.

Shape neck. Next row. K.1, sl.1, k.1, p.s.s.o., k.21, turn and cont. on these sts. only.

Next row. P.

Next row. K.1, sl.1, k.1, p.s.s.o., k. to last 3 sts., sl.1, k.1, p.s.s.o., k.1.

Rep. above 2 rows 8 times more, then p. 1 row. (5 sts.)

Next row. K.1, sl.1, k.2 tog., p.s.s.o., k.1.

Next row. P.3.

Next row. K.1, sl.1, k.1, p.s.s.o.

P.2 tog. and fasten off.

Return to sts. on needle. Sl. centre 17 (19, 21, 23) sts. on a holder. Rejoin yarn to inner end of rem. sts.

Next row. K. to last 3 sts., k.2 tog., k.1.

Next row. P.

Next row. K.1, k.2 tog., k. to last 3 sts., k.2 tog., k.1. Now cont. to correspond with other side.

SLEEVES. With No. 12 needles cast on 57 (61, 63, 65) sts. and work in k.1, p.1 rib for 4 ins. [10.16 cm]. Change to No. 10 needles and cont. in st. st., inc. 1 st. each end of next row and every foll. 6th (6th, 5th, 5th) row to 93 (99, 105, 111) sts., then cont. straight until work measures 18 (19, 19, 20) ins. [45.72 (48.26, 48.26, 50.80) cm] (or length required allowing for cuff turnback), ending on p. row. Place a marker each end of last row. Work 10 rows.

Next row. K.1, sl.1, k.1, p.s.s.o., k. to last 3 sts., k.2 tog., k.1.

Next row. P.

Rep. above 2 rows until 9 sts. rem., ending on p. row. Leave sts. on holder.

V NECKBAND. Firstly, join raglan seams, sewing last 10 rows of sleeve seams to cast off sts. at armholes. R.s.f., with set of No. 12 needles, k. across sts. of right sleeve, back neck and left sleeve, knitting 2 sts. tog. at each seam, pick up and k. 82 (86, 90, 94) sts. down left side of neck, k. centre st., then pick up and k. 82 (86, 90, 94) sts. up right side of neck (220, 230, 240, 250 sts.).

Rib round. Work in k.1, p.1 rib to 2 sts. before centre front st., p.2 tog., k.1, p.2 tog., rib to end of round.

Rep. above round for 1¼ ins. [3.17 cm], then cast off ribwise.

CREW NECKBAND. Firstly, join raglan seams, sewing last 10 rows of sleeve seams to cast off sts. at armholes. R.s.f., with set of No. 12 needles, k. across sts. of right sleeve, back neck and left sleeve, knitting 2 sts. tog. at each seam, pick up and k. 26 sts. down left side of neck, k. across centre front sts., then pick up and k. 26 sts. up right side of neck (124, 128, 132, 136 sts.). Work in rounds of k.1, p.1 rib for 3 ins. [7.62 cm], then cast off ribwise.

POLO COLLAR. Work as given for Crew Neckband, working a further 5 ins. [12.70 cm] in k.1, p.1 rib, then cast off ribwise.

TO MAKE UP. Press work on the wrong side. Join side and sleeve seams. Press seams. Fold crew neckband in half to inside and sl. st. into position.

Perfectly plain, 5-ply, stocking stitch sweater has k.1, p.1 edgings, and the instructions give a choice of three necklines—V, crew or polo (see page 137 for instructions).

8
Accessories

Headscarf is knitted entirely in garter stitch (see page 142 for instructions).

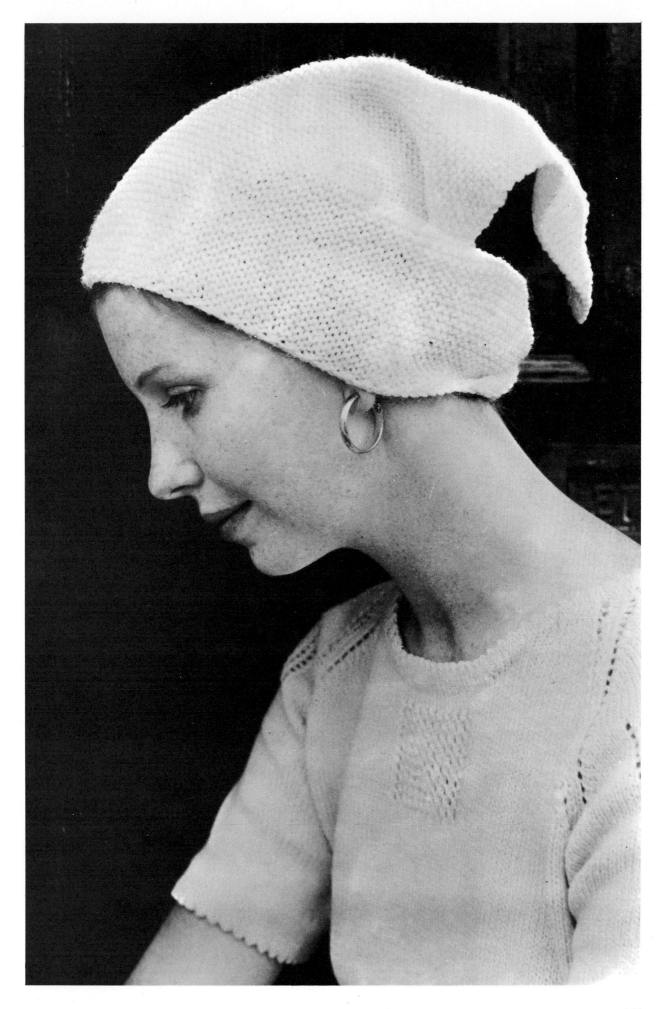

Headscarf

See photograph on page 141.

MATERIALS: 3 balls of Villawool Purple Label Ban-Lon; a pair of No. 6 needles.
MEASUREMENT: To fit average size head.
TENSION: 11 sts. to 2 inches [5.08 cm].
ABBREVIATIONS: See page 13.

TO MAKE: With No. 6 needles cast on 170 sts.
1st row. Sl.1, k. to end.
2nd row. As 1st row.
3rd row. Sl.1, sl.1, k.1, p.s.s.o., k. to last 3 sts., k.2 tog., k.1.
4th row. Sl.1, k. to end.
Rep. 3rd and 4th rows until 6 sts. rem.
Next row. Sl.1, sl.1, k.1, p.s.s.o., k.2 tog., k.1.
Next row. Sl.1, k. to end.
Next row. Sl.1, k.1, p.s.s.o., k.2 tog.
Next row. Sl.1, k.1.
Next row. K.2 tog. and fasten off.

Gloves

MATERIALS: 4 balls of Villawool Nylo Tweed; a pair of Nos. 8 and 9 needles.
MEASUREMENT: To fit 7½ in. [19.05 cm] hand, or as required.
TENSION: 6 sts. to 1 inch [2.54 cm].
ABBREVIATIONS: See page 13.

TO MAKE:
RIGHT GLOVE. With No. 9 needles cast on 44 sts. and work in rib of k.1, p.1 for 2¾ ins. [6.98 cm], ending on right side of work.
Change to No. 8 needles and, beg. with p. row, work 5 rows in st. st. **.
Thumb gusset. Next row. K.23, m.1, k.2, m.1, k.19.
Next row. P.
Rep. above 2 rows 5 times, working 2 sts. more at centre after each inc. to 56 sts. Work 6 rows straight.
Shape thumb. Next row. K.38, turn, p.14 and cast on 3 sts., turn.
Cont. on these 17 sts. for 2 ins. [5.08 cm], ending on p. row.
Shape top. Next row. K.2, (k.2 tog., k.1) to end.
Next row. P.
Next row. (K.2 tog.) to end; break yarn and thread through rem. sts.; draw up and fasten off.
Join seam to base of thumb. R.s.f., join in yarn at base of thumb, pick up and k. 3 sts., k. to end. (45 sts.). Work 7 rows.
Shape first finger. Next row. K.29, turn, p.13 and cast on 3 sts., turn.
Cont. on these 16 sts. for 2½ ins. [6.35 cm], ending on p. row.
Shape top. Next row. K.1, (k.2 tog., k.1) to end.
Next row. P.
Next row. K.1, (k.2 tog.) to end; break yarn and thread through rem. sts.; draw up and fasten off.
Join seam to base.
Shape second finger. R.s.f., join in yarn at base of first finger, pick up and k. 3 sts., k.5, turn, p.13 and cast on 3 sts., turn.
Cont. on these 16 sts. for 2¾ ins. [6.98 cm], ending on p. row, then finish as given for first finger.
Shape third finger. Work as given for second finger until 2½ ins. [6.35 cm] have been worked, then finish as given for first finger.
Shape fourth finger. R.s.f., join in yarn at base of third finger, pick up and k. 3 sts., k. to end.
Cont. on these 15 sts. for 1¾ ins. [4.44 cm], ending on p. row.
Next row. (K.2 tog., k.1) to end.
Next row. P.
Next row. (K.2 tog.) to end.
Finish as given for first finger.
TO MAKE UP. Press work on the wrong side. Join seams.
LEFT GLOVE. Work as given for Right Glove to **.
Shape thumb. Next row. K.19, m.1, k.2, m.1, k.23.
Next row. P.
Rep. above 2 rows 5 times, working 2 sts. more at centre after each inc. to 56 sts. Work 6 rows straight.
Next row. K.32, cast on 3 sts., turn and p.17, turn.
Cont. as given for Right Glove, having cast on 3 sts. at opposite ends.

Tweed gloves are knitted entirely in stocking stitch.

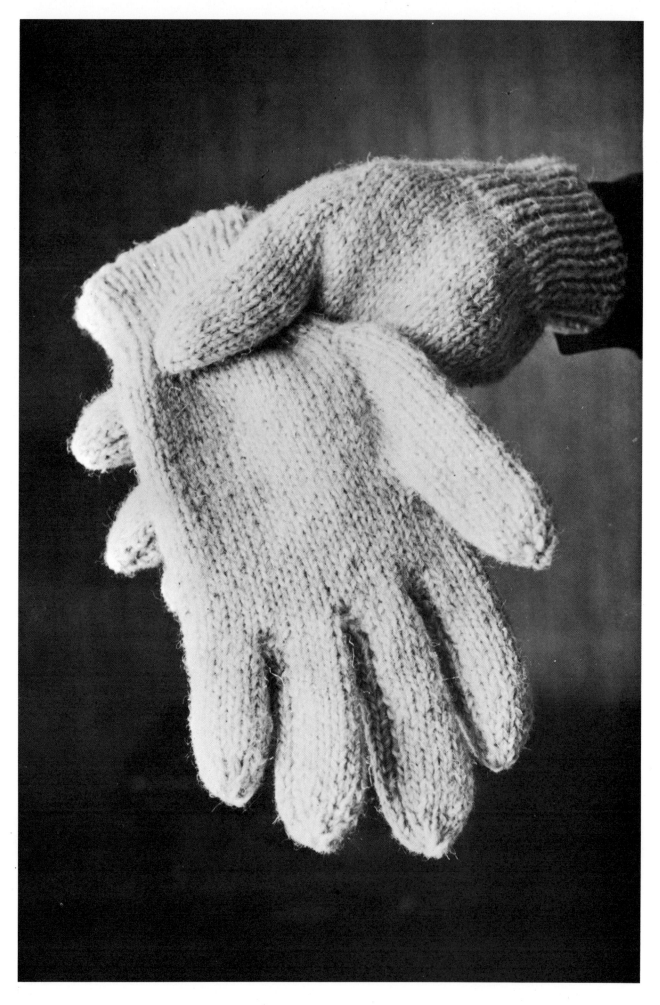

Polo Inset

MATERIALS: 2 balls of Villawool Superknit 4 ply Crepe; a pair of No. 10 needles.
MEASUREMENT: To fit average neck size.
TENSION: 9 sts. to 1 inch [2.54 cm].
ABBREVIATIONS: See page 13.

TO MAKE:
BACK. With No. 10 needles cast on 60 sts.
1st row. P.1, k.2, (p.2, k.2) to last st., p.1.
2nd row. K.1, (p.2, k.2) to last 3 sts., p.2, k.1.
Rep. above 2 rows until work measures 7½ ins. [19.05 cm], ending on 2nd row.
Cast off ribwise.
FRONT. With No. 10 needles cast on 72 sts.
1st row. P.1, k.2, (p.2, k.2) to last st., p.1.
2nd row. K.1, (p.2, k.2) to last 3 sts., p.2, k.1.
Rep. above 2 rows until work measures 13 ins. [33.02 cm], ending on 2nd row.
Cast off ribwise.
TO MAKE UP. Using a flat seam join sides for 5 ins. [12.70 cm]. Turn collar in half to outside.

Loop Stitch Ear Warmer

See photograph on page 146.

MATERIALS: 4 balls of Villawool Superknit DC8; a pair of No. 8 needles; quantity of 1½ in. [3.81 cm] wide ribbon.
MEASUREMENT: Approx. 22 x 4 ins. [55.88 x 10.16 cm].
ABBREVIATIONS: See page 13.
TO MAKE: With No. 8 needles cast on 25 sts.
1st row. P.8, * insert needle into the next stitch as if to k., wind yarn over the right hand needle and round the first finger of left hand twice, then over right hand needle again, draw all 3 loops through st., put 3 loops on to left hand needle and k. tog. with st. (1 loop st. made), k.1; rep. from * to last 9 sts., make a loop as above in next st., p.8.
2nd row. K.
Rep. above 2 rows for 11 ins. [27.94 cm], ending on 1st row, then cast off.
Make another piece in same way.
TO MAKE UP. Flat seam pieces tog. at cast-off edges. Press st. st. sections only on the wrong side. Fold st. st. sections to inside and seam tog. Cut ribbon in two and attach a length to each end.

Bed Socks

See photograph on page 97.

MATERIALS: 3 balls of Villawool Superknit 5 ply Crepe; a pair of No. 8 needles; ribbon.
MEASUREMENT: To fit average size foot.
TENSION: 6 sts. to 1 inch [2.54 cm].
ABBREVIATIONS: See page 13.

TO MAKE: With No. 8 needles cast on 96 sts. and work in g.st., inc. 1 st. each end of every foll. row to 110 sts. Cont. straight until work measures 2½ ins. [6.35 cm] from beg., then dec. 1 st. each end of every foll. row until 96 sts. rem. Cast off 23 sts. at beg. of next 2 rows. (50 sts.).
Next (ribbonhole) row. K.3, * y.fwd., k.2 tog., k.5; rep. from * ending with k.3 instead of k.5.
Cont. in g.st. for 2¼ ins. [5.71 cm] (or length required), then cast off.
TO MAKE UP. Fold work in half and join foot seam, then shaped toe edges and instep. Thread ribbon through ribbonholes and tie at front.

Polo collar inset is knitted in k.2, p.2 rib.

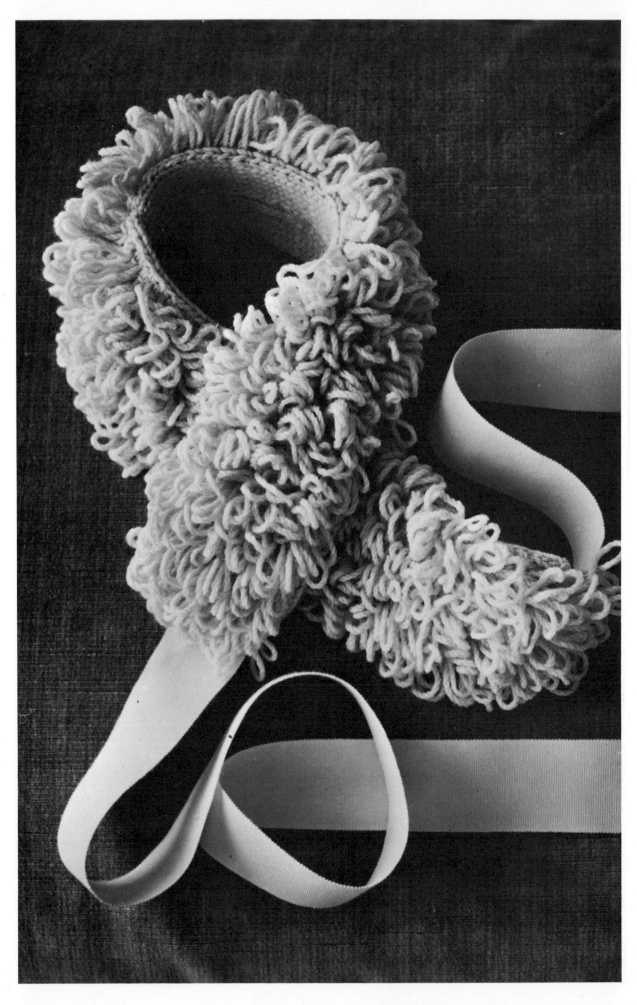

Clutch Purse

See photograph on page 97.

MATERIALS: 2 balls of Villawool Purple Label Ban-Lon; a pair of No. 8 needles; 4½-5 in. [11.43-12.70 cm] mount; lining.
MEASUREMENT: 5 x 9 ins. [12.70 x 22.86 cm].
TENSION: 6 sts. to 1 inch [2.54 cm].
ABBREVIATIONS: See page 13.
NOTE: Use yarn double throughout.

TO MAKE: With No. 8 needles cast on 32 sts. and work in garter st., inc. 1 st. each end of next and every foll. 2nd row to 56 sts. Tie a marker at centre of last row, then cont. until work measures 6 ins. [15.24 cm] from marker. Dec. 1 st. each end of the next and every foll. 2nd row until 32 sts. rem. Work 1 row, then cast off.
TO MAKE UP. Cut lining larger than knitted piece and join seams to within 1½ ins. [3.81 cm]. Fold knitted piece in half and join side edges. Run a gathering stitch along top of purse and lining; draw up to the width of mount and neatly attach.

Evening Bag

See photograph on page 97.

MATERIALS: 2 balls of Villawool Purple Label Ban-Lon; a pair of No. 8 needles; 3½-4 in. [8.89-10.16 cm] mount; lining.
MEASUREMENT: 5½ x 6 ins. [13.97 x 15.24 cm].
TENSION: 6 sts. to 1 inch [2.54 cm].
ABBREVIATIONS: See page 13.
NOTE: Use yarn double throughout.

TO MAKE: With No. 8 needles cast on 34 sts. and work in patt.:
1st, 2nd and 3rd rows. (K.1, p.1) to end.
4th, 5th and 6th rows. (P.1, k.1) to end.

Loop stitch ear warmer is made in two pieces which are joined at the centre. Ribbon ties are attached to each end (see page 144 for instructions).

Rep. above 6 rows, at the same time, inc. 1 st. each end of next 4 rows (42 sts.).
Cont. straight until work measures 11 ins. [27.94 cm], ending on 3rd or 6th row. Dec. 1 st. each end of next 4 rows, then work 6 rows straight. Cast off in patt.
TO MAKE UP. Cut lining larger than knitted piece and join seams to within 1½ ins. [3.81·cm] of top. Fold knitted piece in half and join side edges. Neatly attach bag and lining to the mount.

Socks

See photograph on page 150.

MATERIALS: 5 balls of Villawool Superknit 4 ply Crepe; a set of 4 double-pointed No. 11 needles.
MEASUREMENTS: Length, 17 ins. (43.18 cm) from beg. to end. Size, adjustable.
TENSION: 8 sts. to 1 inch [2.54 cm] over patt.
ABBREVIATIONS: See page 13.

TO MAKE: With set of No. 11 needles cast on 80 sts. (26 x 26 x 28) and work in k.1, p.1 rib for 3½ ins. [8.89 cm], then cont. in patt.:
1st round. (K.3, p.2) to end.
2nd, 3rd and 4th rounds. As 1st round.
5th round. P.1, (k.3, p.2) to last 4 sts., k.3, p.1.
6th, 7th and 8th rounds. As 5th round.
9th round. (P.2, k.3) to end.
10th, 11th and 12th rounds. As 9th round.
13th round. K.1, (p.2, k.3) to last 4 sts., p.2, k.2.
14th, 15th and 16th rounds. As 13th round.
17th round. K.2, (p.2, k.3) to last 3 sts., p.2, k.1.
18th, 19th and 20th rounds. As 17th round.
Rep. above 20 rounds until work measures 15 ins. [38.10 cm] (or length required).
Shape toe. 1st round. (K.3, k.2 tog.) to end (64 sts.).
2nd round. K.
3rd round. K.
4th round. (K.7, k.2 tog.) to last 10 sts., k.7, k.3 tog. (56 sts.).
5th and 6th rounds. As 2nd and 3rd rounds.
7th round. (K.6, k.2 tog.) to end. (49 sts.).
8th and 9th rounds. As 2nd and 3rd rounds.
10th round. (K.5, k.2 tog.) to end (42 sts.).
11th and 12th rounds. As 2nd and 3rd rounds.
13th round. (K.4, k.2 tog.) to end (35 sts.).
14th and 15th rounds. As 2nd and 3rd rounds.
16th round. (K.3, k.2 tog.) to end (28 sts.).

17th and 18th rounds. As 2nd and 3rd rounds.
19th round. (K.2, k.2 tog.) to end (21 sts.).
20th and 21st rounds. As 2nd and 3rd rounds.
22nd round. (K.1, k.2 tog.) to end (14 sts.).
23rd and 24th rounds. As 2nd and 3rd rounds.
25th round. (K.2 tog.) to end (7 sts.).
Break yarn; run thread through rem. sts.; draw up and fasten off.

Beret

MATERIALS: 2 balls of Villawool Boucle Double Knitting; a pair of Nos. 8 and 10 needles.
TENSION: 6 sts. to 1 inch [2.54 cm].
ABBREVIATIONS: See page 13.

TO MAKE: With No. 10 needles cast on 110 sts. and work in k.1, p.1 rib for 7 rows.
Next (inc.) row. Rib 5, (inc., rib 2) to last 6 sts., inc., rib to end (144 sts.).
Change to No. 8 needles and cont. in st. st. until beret is wide enough for individual measurement, approx. 3½ ins. [8.89 cm], ending on p. row.
Shape top. 1st (dec.) row. (K.4, k.2 tog.) to end.
Work 3 rows in st. st.
2nd (dec.) row. (K.3, k.2 tog.) to end.
Work 3 rows in st. st.
Cont. to dec. as above until 24 sts. rem., then work 5 rows straight.
Next row. (K.2 tog.) to end. Break yarn and thread through rem. sts; draw up and fasten off.
TO MAKE UP. Press work on the wrong side. Join back seam, then press seam.

Tie

See photograph on page 153.

MATERIALS: 2 balls of Villawool Superknit 5 ply Crepe; a pair of No. 9 needles.
MEASUREMENT: Approx. 48 ins. [121.92 cm] long.
TENSION: 13 sts. to 2 inches [5.08 cm].
ABBREVIATIONS: See page 13.

TO MAKE: With No. 9 needles cast on 19 sts.
1st row. K.3, (p.1, k.1) to last 4 sts., p.1, k.3.
2nd row. K.1, p.3, (k.1, p.1) to last 5 sts., k.1, p.3, k.1.
Rep. above 2 rows until work measures 12 ins. [30.48 cm], ending on 2nd row.
Shape tie. ** **Next row.** K.3, p.2 tog., (p.1, k.1) to last 6 sts., p.1, p.2 tog., k.3 (17 sts.).
Next row. K.1, p.3, (p.1, k.1) to last 5 sts., p.4, k.1.
Next row. K.3, p.1, (p.1, k.1) to last 5 sts., p.2, k.3.
Next row. K.1, p.3, (p.1, k.1) to last 5 sts., p.4, k.1.
Rep. last 2 rows once more.
Next row. K.3, p.2 tog., (k.1, p.1) to last 6 sts., k.1, p.2 tog., k.3 (15 sts.). **
Next row. K.1, p.3, (k.1, p.1) to last 5 sts., k.1, p.3, k.1.
Next row. K.3, (p.1, k.1) to last 4 sts., p.1, k.3.
Next row. K.1, p.3, (k.1, p.1) to last 5 sts., k.1, p.3, k.1.
Rep. last 2 rows once more.
Rep. from ** to ** once more (11 sts.).
Next row. K.1, p.3, k.1, p.1, k.1, p.3, k.1.
Next row. K.3, (p.1, k.1) to last 4 sts., p.1, k.3.
Next row. K.1, p.3, k.1, p.1, k.1, p.3, k.1.
Rep. last 2 rows until work measures 48 ins. [121.92 cm]. Cast off.
TO MAKE UP. Press work lightly on the wrong side. Turn st., st. section to inside and hem down.

Boucle beret is knitted in stocking stitch with k.1, p.1 ribbed headband.

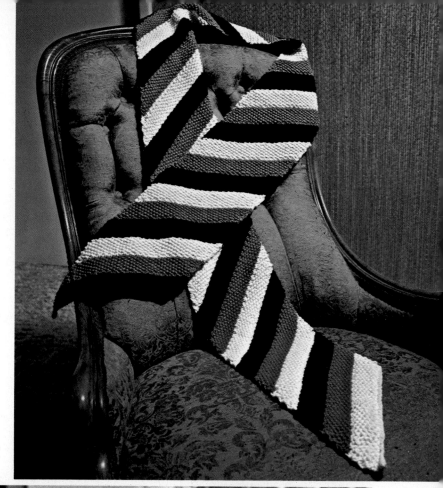

Left: *Easy-to-make socks are designed in a textured pattern to fit foot size required...there is no heel shaping (see page 147 for instructions).*

Right: *Three-colour scarf is knitted in moss stitch in a bias stripe design (see page 155 for instructions).*

Below: *Main part of dog coat is knitted in stocking stitch with a multi-colour loop stitch 'collar'. The underbody is knitted in k.1, p.1 rib for elasticity (see page 161 for instructions).*

Body of octopus is knitted in stocking stitch. The legs are made of plaited yarn. Large features are embroidered in contrasting yarn (see page 160 for instructions).

Tie is knitted in moss stitch (see page 148 for instructions).

153

Lady's Hat

MATERIALS: 5 balls of Villawool Superknit 12 ply Crepe; a pair of Nos. 6 and 9 needles.
MEASUREMENT: To fit an average size head.
TENSION: 9 sts. to 2 inches [5.08 cm] on No. 6 needles.
ABBREVIATIONS: See page 13.

TO MAKE: With No. 9 needles cast on 100 sts. Change to No. 6 needles and patt.:
***1st row.** (P.1, k.2) to last st., p.1.
2nd row. (K.1, y.fwd., k.2, pass st. formed by y.fwd. over the k.2, k.2) to end.
Rep. above 2 rows 3 times more. *
Change to No. 9 needles and k. 1 row, then p. 1 row.
Change back to No. 6 needles. **
Rep. from * to ** 3 times, then from * to * once.
Change to No. 9 needles.
Next row. K.4, (k.2 tog., sl.1, k.2 tog., p.s.s.o., k.10) 6 times, k.2 tog., sl.1, k.2 tog., p.s.s.o., k.1.
Next row. P.
Change to No. 6 needles and work from * to *, noting that 2nd row reps. end on k.1 not k.2.
Change to No. 9 needles.
Next row. K.1, (k.2 tog., k.1) to end.
Next row. P.
Next row. (K.2 tog.) to last st., k.1.
Next row. P.
Rep. above 2 rows once.
Thread yarn through rem. sts.; draw up and fasten off.
TO MAKE UP. Join seam. Make a pom pom and attach to top of hat.

Striped Scarf

See photograph on page 151.

MATERIALS: 3 balls of Villawool Superknit DC8 in main colour (m.), 3 balls of 1st contrast (1st c.) and 3 balls of 2nd contrast (2nd c.); a pair of No. 8 needles.
MEASUREMENT: Approx. 65 ins. [165.10 cm] long.
TENSION: 23 sts. to 4 inches [10.16 cm].
ABBREVIATIONS: See page 13.

TO MAKE: With No. 8 needles and m. cast on 45 sts.
***1st row.** K.
2nd row. Inc. in 1st st., (k.1, p.1) to last 2 sts., k.2 tog.
3rd row. K.1, (p.1, k.1) to end.
4th row. Inc. in 1st st., (p.1, k.1) to last 2 sts., p.2 tog.
5th row. P.1, (k.1, p.1) to end.
Rep. from 2nd to 5th rows once, then rep. 2nd, 3rd and 4th rows again *. Break off m. and join in 1st c., then rep. from * to *.
Break off 1st c. and join in 2nd c., then rep. from * to *. Cont. working in stripes as set until work measures approx. 65 ins. [165.10 cm] long, ending with a complete stripe. Cast off.

Patterned pull-on hat is knitted in 12-ply crepe and features a large pom-pom.

9
Toys and Bazaar Items

One coat hanger covering is worked in garter stitch, the other in loop stitch (see page 160 for instructions).

Hot Water Bottle Cover

MATERIALS: 5 balls of Villawool Superknit DC8; a pair of Nos. 8 and 9 needles; 2 buttons.
MEASUREMENT: 13 ins. x 10 ins. [33.02 x 25.40 cm].
TENSION: 23 sts. to 4 inches [10.16 cm].
ABBREVIATIONS: See page 13.

TO MAKE: With No. 9 needles cast on 64 sts. and k. 9 rows.
Change to No. 8 needles and work in patt.:
1st row. (K.4, p.4) to end.
2nd, 3rd and 4th rows. As 1st row.
5th row. (P.4, k.4) to end.
6th, 7th and 8th rows. As 5th row.
Cont. in 8-row patt. until work measures 12 ins. [30.48 cm], ending on a 4th or 8th row.
Change to No. 9 needles and k. 8 rows, then cast off. Make another piece in the same way.
TO MAKE UP. Press work on the wrong side. Neatly join the side and lower edges, leaving 3½ in. [8.89 cm] opening in centre of lower edge. Make 2 button loops on one side of top and sew the buttons on the other side to correspond with loops.

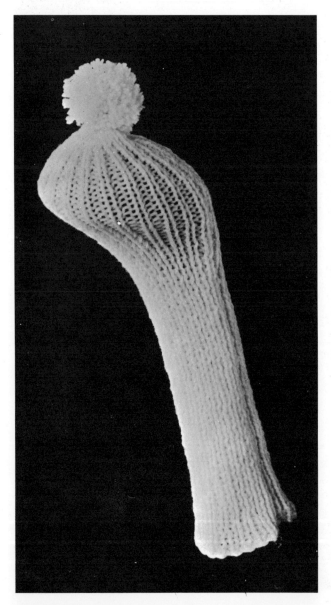

Golf Club Cover

MATERIALS: 2 balls of Villawool Superknit DC8 and a pair of No. 8 needles.
MEASUREMENT: Length, 11½ ins. [29.21 cm], excluding pom pom.
TENSION: 6 sts. to 1 inch [2.54 cm].
ABBREVIATIONS: See page 13.

TO MAKE: With No. 8 needles cast on 54 sts. and work in k.1, p.1 rib for 11½ ins. [29.21 cm]. Break yarn, leaving a 12 in. [30.48 cm] length. Thread needle to yarn and run through the sts.; draw up and fasten off.
TO MAKE UP. Join seam. Attach a pom pom to top.

Golf club cover is knitted in k.1, p.1 rib and trimmed with a pom-pom.

Hot water bottle cover is knitted in basket stitch.

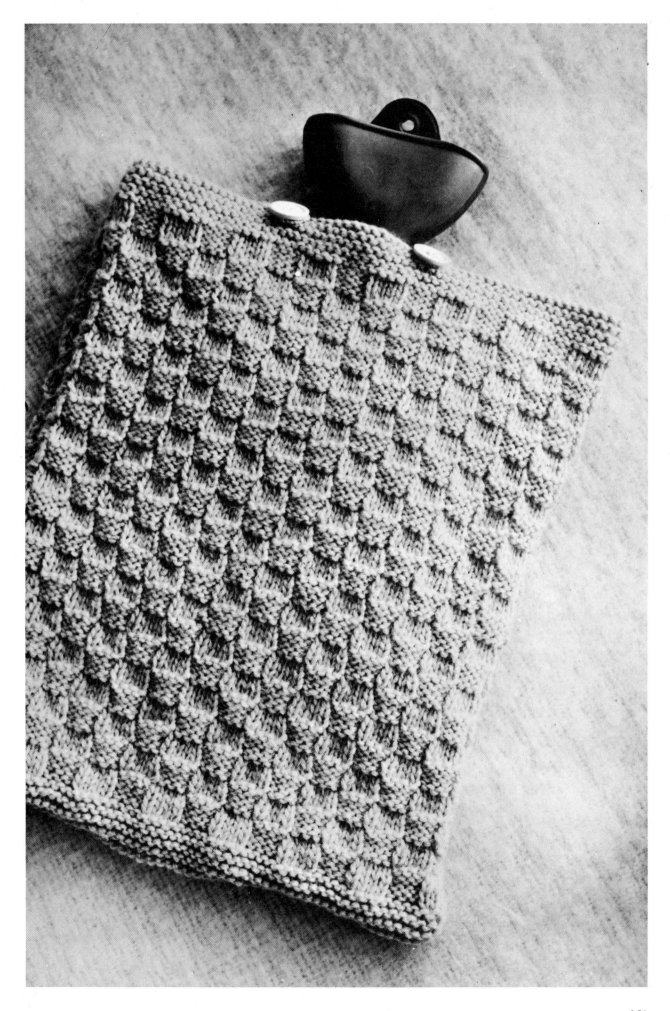

Two Coathangers

See photograph on page 157.

GARTER STITCH COAT HANGER

MATERIALS: 1 ball of Villawool Superknit DC8; a pair of No. 6 needles; coat hanger; foam rubber; ribbon.
ABBREVIATIONS: See page 13.

TO MAKE: With No. 6 needles cast on 19 sts. and work in g.st. until knitting is long enough to cover coat hanger, then cast off.
TO MAKE UP. Cover coat hanger with foam rubber and secure.
Place knitted piece over the hanger and join edges tog. Cover hook with yarn or ribbon. Trim with a ribbon bow (optional).

LOOP STITCH COAT HANGER

MATERIALS: 2 balls of Villawool Purple Label Ban-Lon; a pair of No. 8 needles; coat hanger; foam rubber; ribbon.
ABBREVIATIONS: See page 13.

TO MAKE: With No. 8 needles cast on 14 sts. and k. 1 row, then cont. in loop patt.:
1st row. K.1, * insert needle into the next st. as if to k., wind yarn over the right hand needle and round the first finger of left hand twice, then over right hand needle again, draw all 3 loops through st., put 3 loops on to left hand needle and k. tog. with st. (1 loop st. made); rep. from * to last st., k.1.
2nd row. K.
Rep. these 2 rows until work is long enough to cover coat hanger, ending on a loop st. row, then cast off.
TO MAKE UP. Cover coat hanger with foam rubber and secure. Place knitted piece over the hanger and join edges tog. Cover hook with yarn or ribbon. Trim with a ribbon bow (optional).

Toy Octopus

See photograph on page 152.

MATERIALS: 12 balls of Villawool Slalom; a pair of No. 2 needles; stuffing; small quantity of red yarn.
MEASUREMENT: Approx. 12 ins. [30.48 cm] high.
TENSION: 7 sts. to 2 ins. [5.08 cm].
ABBREVIATIONS: See page 13.

TO MAKE: Using two strands of yarn tog. cast on 5 sts. for base.
1st row. (K. and inc. in next st., p.1) to last st., k. and inc. (8 sts.).
2nd row. P.
3rd row. (K. and inc. in next st.) to end. (16 sts.). Work 3 rows.
7th row. As 3rd row (32 sts.).
Work 5 rows.
13th row. As 3rd row (64 sts.).
Work 11 rows.
25th row. As 3rd row (128 sts.).
Work 12 rows.
Next row. (K.1, p.1) to end.
Next row. (K.2 tog.) to end (64 sts.).
Work 10 rows in st. st.
Next row. (K.1, p.1) to end.
Next row. (K.2 tog.) to end (32 sts.).
Work 4 rows in st. st.
Next row. (K.1, p.1) to end.
Next row. (K.2 tog.) to end (16 sts.).
Work 2 rows in st. st., then break yarn, leaving a length.
Thread needle to yarn and run through the sts.; draw up and fasten off.
TO MAKE UP. Press work on the wrong side. Join seams tog., leaving an opening, then stuff firmly. Sew up opening.
LEGS. Cut 144 strands of yarn 66 ins. [167.64 cm] long and divide into 4 groups of 36 strands. Tie end securely about 2 ins [5.08 cm] from the end, then divide these 36 strands evenly into 3 groups of 12 strands and plait. Tie firmly 2 ins. [5.08 cm] from the end, leaving a tassel 2 ins. [5.08 cm] long. Join each of the 4 legs in centre over each other and firmly attach to base (8 legs). With red yarn embroider eyes, nose and mouth as illustrated. Make a pom pom approx. 5 ins. [12.70 cm] in diameter and attach to top.

Dog Coat

See photograph on page 151.

MATERIALS: 4 balls of Villawool Superknit DC8 and 1 ball each of four contrasting colours for collar; a pair of Nos. 8 and 9 needles.

MEASUREMENT: Length, approx. 14½ ins. [36.83 cm].

TENSION: 23 sts. to 4 inches [10.16 cm].

ABBREVIATIONS: See page 13.

TO MAKE:

MAIN PART. With No. 8 needles cast on 55 sts. and work in k.1, p.1 rib for 6 rows.

Next row. K.

Next row. K.3, p. to last 3 sts., k.3.

Rep. above 2 rows until work measures 2½ ins. [7.35 cm], ending on p. row. Cont. in st. st.. without the k.3 border each end, cast on 7 sts. at beg. of next 2 rows (69 sts.). Cont. in st. st. for 10 rows.

Next row. K.16, inc. in next st., k.34, inc. in next st., k.17. Work 13 rows.

Next row. K.16, inc. in next st., k.36, inc. in next st., k.17. Work 13 rows.

Next row. K.16, inc. in next st., k.38, inc. in next st., k.17. Work 13 rows.

Next row. Inc. in first st., k.15, inc. in next st., k.40, inc. in next st., k.15, inc. in next st., k.1 (79 sts.). Work 7 rows.

Next row. K.11, turn.

Work 20 rows on these 11 sts. Break yarn. Join yarn to sts. on left-hand needle.

Next row. K.57, turn.

Work 20 rows on these 57 sts. Break yarn. Join yarn to rem. sts. on left-hand needle and work 21 rows on these rem. sts.

Next row. P. across all sts.

Work 5 rows.

Shape shoulders. 1st row. K.21, sl.1, k.2 tog., p.s.s.o., k. to end.

2nd row. P.21, sl.1, p.2 tog. t.b.l., p.s.s.o., p. to end.

3rd row. K.20, sl.1, k.2 tog., p.s.s.o., k. to end.

4th row. P.20, sl.1, p.2 tog. t.b.l., p.s.s.o., p. to end.

5th row. K.19, sl.1, k.2 tog., p.s.s.o., k. to end.

6th row. P.19, sl.1, p.2 tog. t.b.l., p.s.s.o., p. to end.

7th row. K.18, sl.1, k.2 tog., p.s.s.o., k. to end.

8th row. P.18, sl.1, p.2 tog. t.b.l., p.s.s.o., p. to end.

9th row. K.17, sl.1, k.2 tog., p.s.s.o., k. to end.

10th row. P.17, sl.1, p.2 tog. t.b.l., p.s.s.o., p. to end. Work 9 rows.

Striped ball is knitted in a combination of knit and purl and is fitted over a rubber ball.

COLLAR. Join in 3 contrasting colours and work a loop stitch row alternating the colours: k.1, * insert needle into the next st. as if to k., wind yarn over the right hand needle and round the first finger of left hand twice, then over right hand needle again, draw all 3 loops through st., put 3 loops on to left hand needle and k. tog. with st. (1 loop st. made); rep. from * to last st., k.1.

K. 1 row in main colour.

With 4th contrasting colour work a loop stitch row.

K. 1 row in main colour.

With 3 contrasting colours work a loop stitch row.

K. 1 row in main colour, then cast off.

UNDERBODY. With No. 9 needles cast on 30 sts. and work in k.1, p.1 rib, dec. 1 st. each end of 10th row, then every foll. 8th row until 10 sts. rem. Cont. straight until ribbing measures length of main part, excluding 2½ ins. [7.35 cm] at beg. Cast off ribwise.

TO MAKE UP. Press main part on the wrong side. Attach underbody to main part, excluding the 2½ ins. [7.35 cm] at beg.

Striped Ball

MATERIALS: 1 ball of Villawool Purple Label Ban-Lon in main colour (m.) and 1 ball of contrast colour (c.); a pair of No. 8 needles; rubber ball 3 ins. [7.62 cm] in diameter; tapestry needle.

MEASUREMENT: 3 ins. [7.62 cm] in diameter.

TENSION: 6¼ sts. to 1 inch [2.54 cm].

ABBREVIATIONS: See page 13.

NOTE: Sl. all sts. purlwise.

TO MAKE: With No. 8 needles and m. cast on 18 sts.

1st row. (m.) Sl.1, k.16, sl.1.

2nd row. (m.) Sl. 2 sts., k.15, sl.1.

3rd, 4th, 5th and 6th rows. As 2nd row. Join in c.

7th row. (c.) P.18.

8th row. (c.) P.18.

9th, 10th, 11th, 12th, 13th and 14th rows. (c.) Work as given for 2nd row.

15th row. (m.) P.18.

16th row. (m.) P.18.

17th, 18th, 19th, 20th, 21st and 22nd rows. (m.) Work as given for 2nd row.

23rd row. (c.) P.18.

24th row. (c.) P.18.

Cont. as before until there are 5 m. stripes and 5 c. stripes, ending on 14th row. Cast off p.wise, leaving an end for sewing seam.

TO MAKE UP. Using a flat seam sew cast-on and cast-off sts. tog. over ball. Using a tapestry needle draw up all sl. sts. tog. at each end and fasten off.

Toy Poodle

MATERIALS: 2 balls of Villawool Slalom; a pair of No. 5 needles; 2 buttons; stuffing; small quantity of black yarn.

MEASUREMENT: Approx. 11½ ins. [29.21 cm] high.

TENSION: 9 sts. to 2 inches [5.08 cm] over st. st.

ABBREVIATIONS: See page 13.

TO MAKE:

BODY. Cast on 22 sts. and work in st. st. for 10 rows. Cont. in st. st. and dec. 1 st. each end of the foll. 5th, 11th and 15th rows. Cont. on these 16 sts. without shaping until work measures 6 ins. [15.24 cm], ending on k. row. Cast off 6 sts. at beg. of next 2 rows, then cont. on rem. 4 sts. for Tail:

Next row. P. to end and cast on 3 sts.

Next row. K.7, cast on 3 sts.

Next row. P.

Work 2 rows, then dec. 1 st. each end of next and foll. 4th row. Work 3 rows straight, then cast off.

LEGS. Cast on 7 sts. and work in st. st. for 8 rows, ending p. row.

Next row. Inc. in each st. (14 sts.).

Next row. P. to last st., inc. (15 sts.).

Cont. in moss st.:

Next row. K.1, (p.1, k.1) to end.

Rep. above row 23 times, then cast off.

Make three more pieces in the same way.

NECK AND HEAD. Cast on 19 sts. and work in moss st. for 5 rows.

Cont. in moss st. and cast on 4 sts. at beg. of next 4 rows (35 sts.).

Work 4 rows straight, then cast off 2 sts. at beg. of every row until 15 sts. rem. Work 4 rows, then cast off.

EARS. Cast on 3 sts. and work in moss st., inc. 1 st. each end of every 3rd row to 7 sts. Cont. straight until work measures 2 ins. [5.08 cm], then dec. 1 st. each end of next 2 rows. K.3 tog. and fasten off.

Make another piece in same way.

TO MAKE UP. Using a backstitch join long seam and wide end of Body and stuff. Join Tail seam and stuff. Join back seam of Body and join Tail at the same time. Sew Head seams, leaving an opening at neck. Stuff and join to top of wide end of Body piece. Join seams of legs, leaving opening at top. Stuff and close opening, then sew to sides of Body as illustrated. Cut six lengths of yarn 2 ins. [5.08 cm] long. Firmly tie yarn round lengths at centre to secure and join to ears. Make two small pom poms and attach to Head and Tail as illustrated. Embroider nose with black yarn. Sew on buttons in position for eyes.

Poodle is knitted in a combination of stocking stitch and moss stitch. Ears are trimmed with tassels and head and tail are trimmed with pom-poms.

Rabbit is knitted entirely in garter stitch (see page 164 for instructions).

Toy Rabbit

See photograph on page 163.

MATERIALS: 2 balls of Villawool Dinkum 8 ply; a pair of No. 12 needles; stuffing; small quantities of black and blue yarn for features.
MEASUREMENT: Approx. 11½ ins. [29.21 cm] high.
TENSION: 7 sts. to 1 inch [2.54 cm].
ABBREVIATIONS: See page 13.

TO MAKE:
** FIRST BACK LEG. Cast on 14 sts., * k. 7 rows.
Next row. K. and inc. 1 st. each end (16 sts.). K. 7 rows.
Next row. K. and inc. 1 st. each end. (18 sts.). K. 10 rows *. Break yarn. With same needle holding 18 sts. cast on 14 sts. for SECOND LEG and work from * to * (18 sts.). Do not break yarn.
Next row. K.18 of one section, then k.18 of other section (36 sts.). Work as follows:
1st and 2nd rows. K.
3rd row. K.2 tog., k. to last 2 sts., k.2 tog.
4th, 5th and 6th rows. K.
7th to 14th rows. As 3rd to 6th rows.
Next row. (K.2 tog., k.2) to last 2 sts., k.2 tog. (22 sts.).
Next row. As above (16 sts.).
K. 16 rows. Cast off 3 sts. at beg. of next 2 rows, then cast off 2 sts. at beg. of next 2 rows. Cast off rem. sts. **. Make another piece working from ** to **. Join these two pieces tog., leaving neck open. Stuff body and legs.
HEAD. Cast on 12 sts.
1st row. K.
2nd row. Inc., k. to end.
3rd and 4th rows. K.
5th row. As 2nd row.
6th row. K. to last st., inc.
7th row. K. and inc. 1 st. each end.
8th row. As 6th row.
9th row. As 2nd row.
10th and 11th rows. As 8th and 9th rows.
12th to 18th rows. K.
19th row. K.2 tog., k. to end.
20th row. K. to last 2 sts., k.2 tog.
21st to 30th rows. As 19th and 20th rows.
31st row. K.2 tog., k. to last 2 sts., k.2 tog.
Cast off. Work another piece in same way. Join seam, leaving neck open. Stuff head.
EARS. Cast on 3 sts. and k. 1 row.
1st row. K. and inc. 1 st. each end.

2nd, 3rd and 4th rows. K.
Rep. 1st to 4th rows to 17 sts., then k. 17 rows straight.
Next row. K.1, (k.2 tog.) to end (9 sts.).
Cast off.
Make three more pieces in same way. Join two pieces tog., leaving an opening at cast-on edges. Join other two pieces tog. in the same way. Stitch ears to the head.
TAIL. Cast on 9 sts.
1st row. K.
2nd row. K. and inc. 1 st. each end.
3rd and 4th rows. As 1st and 2nd rows.
K. 9 rows.
Next row. K.2 tog., k. to last 2 sts., k.2 tog.
Next row. K.
Rep. above 2 rows twice more, then cast off.
Make another piece in same way. Join seam, leaving a space for stuffing. Attach tail to body.
FEET. Cast on 11 sts.
1st row. K.
2nd row. K. and inc. 1 st. each end.
3rd and 4th rows. As 1st and 2nd rows.
K. 12 rows.
Next row. K.2 tog., k. to last 2 sts., k.2 tog.
Next row. K.
Rep. above 2 rows once more.
Next row. K.2 tog., k. to last 2 sts., k.2 tog.
Cast off.
Make three more pieces in the same way. Join each pair tog., leaving an opening for stuffing. Attach feet to the legs. Mark feet with big sewing stitches in black yarn.
FRONT LEGS. Cast on 24 sts.
1st row. K.
2nd row. Inc., k.10, inc. in next 2 sts., k.10, inc. (28 sts.). K. 7 rows.
Next row. K.2 tog., k.10, (k.2 tog.) twice, k.10, k.2 tog.
Next row. K.2 tog., k.8, (k.2 tog.) twice, k.8, k.2 tog.
K. 15 rows.
Next row. K. and inc. 1 st. each end.
K. 1 row.
Next row. K.2 tog., k. to last 2 sts., k.2 tog.
Rep. above row twice more. Cast off.
Make another piece in same way. Fold each piece in half lengthwise and join seams, leaving an opening at the top end for stuffing. Sew front legs to shoulders and mark feet with big sewing stitches in black yarn. Mark nose, eyes and mouth with black yarn, then fill the eyes with blue yarn.

Index